BRUMBACK LIBRARY

3 3045 03191 1114

D0926684

THE CURIOUS WORLD OF
SAMUEL PEPYS AND JOHN EVELYN

THE CURIOUS WORLD
OF
SAMUEL PEPYS
AND
JOHN EVELYN

MARGARET WILLES

YALE UNIVERSITY PRESS
NEW HAVEN AND LONDON

920
WIL

Drawings of John Evelyn's cabinet of curiosities © 2017 Nicola Morrison

Copyright © 2017 Margaret Willes

All rights reserved. This book may not be reproduced in whole or in part, in any form (beyond that copying permitted by Sections 107 and 108 of the U.S. Copyright Law and except by reviewers for the public press) without written permission from the publishers.

For information about this and other Yale University Press publications, please contact:
U.S. Office: sales.press@yale.edu   yalebooks.com
Europe Office: sales@yaleup.co.uk   yalebooks.co.uk

Set in Adobe Caslon Pro by IDSUK (DataConnection) Ltd
Printed in Great Britain by Gomer Press Ltd, Llandysul, Ceredigion

Library of Congress Cataloging-in-Publication Data

Names: Willes, Margaret, author.
Title: The curious world of Samuel Pepys and John Evelyn / Margaret Willes.
Description: New Haven, CT: Yale University Press, [2017] | Includes
    bibliographical references and index.
Identifiers: LCCN 2017010612 | ISBN 9780300221398 (alk. paper)
Subjects: LCSH: Pepys, Samuel, 1633–1703—Friends and associates. | Great
    Britain—History—Stuarts, 1603–1714—Biography. | Evelyn, John,
    1620–1706—Friends and associates. | Great Britain—Court and
    courtiers—Biography. | Cabinet officers—Great Britain—Biography. |
    Diarists—Great Britain—Biography.
Classification: LCC DA447.P4 W62 2017 | DDC 941.06092/2—dc23
LC record available at https://lccn.loc.gov/2017010612

A catalogue record for this book is available from the British Library.

10 9 8 7 6 5 4 3 2 1

To the Feline Diarists

CONTENTS

ILLUSTRATIONS

59. Gallery of the Palais de Justice, engraving by Abraham Bosse, *c.* 1638. © The Trustees of the British Museum.

60. Woodcut of a chapman from *Make Room for Christmas*, one of Pepys's 'Penny Merriments', *c.* 1680. By permission of the Pepys Library, Magdalene College, Cambridge (PL 362,22).

61. Advertisement depicting a London coffee-house, *c.* 1700. Douce adds. 138 (84), The Bodleian Libraries, the University of Oxford.

62. Early seventeenth-century set of the Cries of London. By permission of the Pepys Library, Magdalene College, Cambridge (PL 2973,422–3).

63. Page from Marcellus Laroon's *Cryes of the City of London Drawne after the Life*, 1687. By permission of the Pepys Library, Magdalene College, Cambridge (PL 2973,437).

64. First page of Pepys's diary, 1 January 1660. By permission of the Pepys Library, Magdalene College, Cambridge (PL 1836).

65. First page of Evelyn's diary, or 'Kalendarium', referring to 1620. © The British Library Board. All rights reserved (Add. Ms 78323).

INTRODUCTION
Curiouser and Curiouser

SAMUEL PEPYS IS now one of the best-known figures from Restoration England. John Evelyn is not so well known, although very familiar to historians of the period and those interested in garden history. Two centuries ago, however, the fame of both men was in danger of slipping into the twilight zone.

Then, William Upcott came calling. In 1814, the librarian and bibliophile paid a visit to Wotton, the Surrey home of the Evelyn family. Upcott had been to Wotton the previous April with William Bray, the authority on the history of Surrey, to look at reorganising and cataloguing the family library following a fire. On this second occasion, Upcott was received by Lady Evelyn, the widow of Sir Frederick, last direct descendant of John Evelyn, who asked her visitor what his hobbies might be. Upcott's answer could be described as indicating something of an obsessive: the collection of provincial copper tokens and of 'autographs, or original letters, written by men who have distinguished themselves in every walk of life'. Upcott was even to name his house in Upper Street, Islington, Autograph Cottage.

His hostess's response was to show him a pile of old papers that were being used for cutting out patterns for a dress. Upcott spotted amongst them original letters addressed to John Evelyn, by this time known principally as the author of *Sylva*, a book on forest trees first published in 1664. Lady Evelyn then declared, 'Oh, if you like papers like that, you shall have plenty, for Sylva Evelyn ... and those who succeeded him kept all their correspondence, which has furnished the kitchen with an abundance of waste paper.' Among these papers was one of the volumes of Evelyn's diary, emerging over a century after his death in 1706.[1]

Upcott is a Janus figure: a light-fingered individual who made off with manuscripts and prints from the Evelyn family collection; yet also the man who recognised the significance of the material that he was shown. With William Bray, he persuaded Lady Evelyn that the diary should be published, and shortly before her death she gave permission to make the first selection of material. While Bray made the transcripts from the manuscripts, Upcott carried out the proofreading, although he always claimed an important role for himself. The result duly appeared in 1818 as *Memoirs Illustrative of the Life and Writings of John Evelyn*.

Regency England now had a first-hand account of an 'inside man' at the Stuart court in the second half of the seventeenth century, a witness to the restoration of Charles II, the Great Plague and the Great Fire in London, the tumultuous times with a Catholic heir to the English throne, and the overthrow of James II in what is often called the Glorious Revolution. Moreover, in an interesting digression in his 1821 novel *Kenilworth*, Sir Walter Scott wrote of 'the celebrated Mr Evelyn, whose "Silva" is still the manual of British planters; and whose life, manners, and principles, as illustrated in his Memoirs, ought equally to be the manual of English gentlemen'.[2]

The publication of John Evelyn's diary reminded Richard Griffin, Lord Braybrooke, that among the books of the seventeenth-century naval administrator Samuel Pepys in Magdalene College, Cambridge, was also a diary. Braybrooke had a close connection with Magdalene: his father had been the hereditary keeper of the Pepys Library, and his younger brother was the Master of the college. This diary was in six volumes, written in Thomas Shelton's system of shorthand. Braybrooke and his brother recruited an impoverished student from St John's College, the Reverend John Smith, to transcribe the text for the unprincely sum of £200. Blissfully unaware of a copy of Shelton's *Tutor to Tachygraphy* located on a nearby shelf, Smith learned the characters of the diary by comparing Pepys's shorthand account of Charles II's escape after the Battle of Worcester with the version in longhand. Painstakingly, over three years he produced the text that formed the basis of the first edition of the diary published in two volumes in 1825.[3] Braybrooke acted as the editor, stipulating that in format and typography the printed edition should reflect Evelyn's diary.

This diary, too, provided a first-hand account of an insider at the centre of life in Restoration London, but this time a civil servant at the Navy Board, with frequent contact with the King and his brother, the Duke of York. It also gives a detailed account of Pepys's personal life and activities. His reputation had, in fact, endured better than Evelyn's for the administrative practices that he established for the navy were still in place at the time of Nelson. That reputation, however, must have been dented by the appearance of the first edition of his diary. Although it was severely bowdlerised, many Victorians came to disapprove of the character blemishes and moral turpitude to which Pepys cheerfully admitted. Even a third, fuller version of the diary, published by Henry Wheatley in the 1890s, omitted what the *Dictionary of National Biography* described as 'passages which cannot possibly be printed'. On the other hand, Evelyn appealed to the Victorians for the reasons given by Sir Walter Scott – as a man of Christian piety, gentility and integrity.

With the coming of the twentieth century, these qualities began to militate against John Evelyn. In 'Rambling Round Evelyn', an essay published in the first volume of *The Common Reader* in 1925, Virginia Woolf made plain her exasperation:

> He was, we cannot help suspecting, something of a bore, a little censorious, a little patronising, a little too sure of his own merits, and a little obtuse to those of other people. Or what is the quality, or absence of quality, that checks our sympathies? Partly, perhaps, it is due to some inconsistency which it would be harsh to call by so strong a name as hypocrisy.[4]

She felt that a remark recorded by Pepys in his diary after a morning spent with Evelyn summed up the man: 'In fine, a most excellent person he is, and must be allowed a little for a little conceitedness; but he may well be so, being a man so much above others.'[5]

Evelyn, however, had a champion in the bibliographical scholar Sir Geoffrey Keynes, who wrote a study of his writings published in 1934. In the preface to his *Study in Bibliophily*, Keynes noted with sadness that for every reader of Evelyn's diary, there were 100 or 200 who read the journal kept by Pepys. He recognised that Evelyn's record of facts and events was dry and sometimes dull compared to 'the rich human fare provided by Pepys's self-revelation. Yet Evelyn was in some ways the bigger man of the two, more versatile, less self-seeking and self-indulgent – and it is exactly for these qualities that it is so easy to like him less.' Perhaps deliberately taking the very passage from Pepys's diary that Woolf had chosen, Keynes pointed out that a few months later Pepys had written, 'The more I know him, the more I love him.'[6] Both his diary and his correspondence show how perceptive Pepys was about people. He does not explain his change of mind about Evelyn, but it seems likely that he had recognised that under the carapace of conceit and high-minded confidence was an insecure and sometimes vulnerable individual.

Keynes had been accorded rare access to Evelyn's papers. Although the family had recovered, at considerable expense, the depredations made by Upcott, they had yet to recover their confidence in researchers. But Esmond de Beer, a New Zealand scholar with a particular affinity for the seventeenth century, was able to use an existing transcript in the 1920s to begin work on a new edition of Evelyn's diary, or rather diaries, collating various versions. In 1955, six volumes of the diary were published, complete with introduction, appendices, 12,000 footnotes, a full index, and separate essays on various topics, including Evelyn's proposal for the rebuilding of London after the Great Fire of 1666.[7]

As Keynes noted, Pepys had been getting much more attention. In 1903 a club was founded in his name to honour Pepys's memory. On 26 May of that year, Henry Wheatley, the editor of the 1890s version of the diary, met up with three friends at the Garrick Club in London to celebrate the bicentenary of the diarist's death. They resolved to dine annually and 'to hold meetings at which they would hear readings from the

Diary, listen to music of his ear, and give and listen to papers on various aspects of his life'.[8] Also in 1903 the historian J.R. Tanner published the first volume of his descriptive catalogue of the naval manuscripts in the Pepys Library at Magdalene, and was to go on to produce three more volumes, as well as writing an introduction to the diary along with a biographical sketch of Pepys's life after he had stopped keeping his journal. Sir Arthur Bryant drew on Tanner's notes (rather too heavily, in the eyes of some historians, and without proper acknowledgement) for his three-volume biography of Pepys published in the 1930s.[9] Bryant has roused considerable controversy in the breasts of academic historians for various reasons, but there can be no dispute that in his day he was hugely popular, and brought Samuel Pepys to a very wide audience.

A scholarly edition of Pepys's diary in full was considered as early as the 1930s, but concerns were expressed about possible prosecution for obscenity. When, in 1960, Penguin Books were just so prosecuted for their publication of D.H. Lawrence's *Lady Chatterley's Lover*, C.S. Lewis persuaded the fellows of Magdalene that a new edition of the diary should nonetheless be unexpurgated. It took Robert Latham and the Pepys Library at Magdalene, teamed up with William Matthews in California, more than thirty years to complete work on the project; Matthews died before the last volume was issued. Just as de Beer had provided a model of scholarship with the diary of Evelyn, so Latham and Matthews paid Pepys a great tribute with a fully annotated text in nine volumes, along with an index and an invaluable *Companion* in which every aspect of his life was covered by experts in the different fields. The final volume was published in 1983 to great critical acclaim.[10]

In 1977 the library, prints and furniture belonging to John Evelyn were sold by the family. Luckily, his huge collection of papers was acquired by the British Library, enabling more work to be undertaken on him. Frances Harris, the curator at the library chiefly responsible for arranging and cataloguing his papers, wrote a wonderfully sensitive account of Evelyn's friendship with Margaret Godolphin, *Transformations of Love*. His letterbooks have recently been published in two volumes by Douglas Chambers and David Galbraith.[11] The correspondence between Evelyn and Pepys has also been edited and published by Guy de la Bédoyère, taking as his title *Particular Friends*, from the tribute that Evelyn wrote in his diary on the death of Pepys.[12]

I have long been intrigued by the fact that Evelyn and Pepys should have been friends. Legend has it that Admiral Nelson met the Duke of Wellington in the antechamber of the Colonial Office, their only recorded personal encounter. Would that they had gone on to become friends and record for posterity their battles against Napoleon, but no such luck. With Pepys and Evelyn we have the two great recorders of Restoration England and the opportunity to consider not only their friendship, but also their joint portrait of their times. In this book I have concentrated on this friendship and their mutual interests to produce a picture of Restoration England that is much more intimate than conventional histories might allow. Although I have sketched their lives, this is not a biography: that has already been done, latterly by Claire Tomalin for Pepys and Gillian Darley for Evelyn, to celebrate the 300th anniversaries of their respective deaths.[13] Both Pepys and Evelyn lived a long time, taking part in a huge range of activities, during one of the most tumultuous periods of English history, and it is no mean achievement for their biographers to have created such excellent studies of their lives.

That Pepys and Evelyn would become great friends was by no means a foregone conclusion. They came from very different backgrounds, were very different in temperament, and were brought together by chance when they worked together to relieve the suffering of sailors injured and impoverished by the Anglo-Dutch Wars. But friendship did develop, perhaps because of the underlying quality that both possessed – great curiosity. While today it tends to describe somebody who is inquisitive and nosey, and is particularly applied to cats, in the seventeenth century it meant a desire for knowledge, especially of science and the arts. It was applied to careful or elaborate workmanship, and could also describe the strange, rare and exotic. The quality of curiosity seems to have touched not only Pepys and Evelyn but, like stardust, also those who have studied their lives. De Beer, for instance, has been described as possessing great curiosity, and this could likewise be said of Latham and Matthews. And we, who read the diaries, become increasingly curious about Samuel Pepys and John Evelyn, and want to know more about them and their responses to the world they inhabited.

I have therefore chosen to organise the book like a cabinet of curiosities. John Evelyn had at least three such pieces of furniture, and also referred to the rooms where he and his wife Mary kept collections as cabinets of curiosity. We do not know whether Pepys also owned a cabinet, although I am sure he did; he certainly regarded his library as a cabinet on a grand scale. When Evelyn's furniture was sold in 1977, the Geffrye Museum in Hackney acquired the cabinet that Mary Evelyn had commissioned in 1652 from a Dutch ébéniste in Paris. It is a most exotic piece, the ebony case adorned with flowers and fruit from the Middle East, the interior decorated with marquetry made up of ivory and rare South American woods. The ebony of the exterior has darkened even further with time, so that photographs do not do justice to the intricacy of the work. Therefore I asked the artist Nicola Morrison to make drawings of the cabinet, showing not only the rich decoration, but how it can gradually be opened up.

These drawings have been used to signal the three parts of the book. The exterior of the cabinet acts as a prelude to the public careers of Evelyn and Pepys and places them in the context of the extraordinary political times in which they lived. The front with the outer doors open looks at their private lives, focusing on their families and friends. The inner sanctum of the cabinet with its drawers then marks the investigation in depth of the areas of particular interest to the two men: science and the Royal Society, the theatre and music, gardens and gardening, their fascination with the wider world, and their books and libraries. Through these 'drawers', we can appreciate much of the culture of Restoration England as exemplified by Samuel Pepys and John Evelyn.

In order to write on such a range of subjects, I have been helped by several people who have brought to bear their particular areas of expertise: Susan North and Beverly Lemire on women's exotic clothes; David Marsh, Sally Jeffery and Catherine Davis on the gardens of the period and in particular the tuberose; Dr Stephen Harris for pointing out the connection between William Dampier and Pepys and Evelyn; Giles

Mandelbrote, Alice Ford-Smith and Hilary Ely on late seventeenth-century and early eighteenth-century libraries; Hazel Forsyth on the topography of seventeenth-century London and Angelo Hornak on its post-Fire churches. I should like to thank Hannah Fleming for allowing Nicola Morrison and me access to the Evelyn cabinet in the Geffrye Museum, and to the librarians at the Pepys Library at Magdalene College, the Bodleian, the Lindley Library and the British Library for their infinite patience. Lastly, I am very grateful to my editors at Yale, Robert Baldock and Rachael Lonsdale, for asking me to write this book, and for working with me on its exciting path.

PART I

'The World Do Not Grow Old at All'

1

TWO WORLDS

J OHN EVELYN AND Samuel Pepys, the diarists forever linked as the major observers of England in the second half of the seventeenth century, also developed a close friendship. Yet they came from two very different worlds. Evelyn was born at Wotton House in Surrey on 31 October 1620. Eighty years later, in a letter to Pepys, he described his birthplace as 'an old extravagant house'.[1] Wotton was a rambling Tudor mansion of brick, with a skyline marked by tall chimneys and a surrounding moat, tucked between the Surrey Hills and the North Downs (Plate 1). As a child, Evelyn made a sketch of the house, showing the south, garden front, marking the upper 'chamber window where I was borne'.

The Evelyn family had become rich through the manufacture of gunpowder. John's grandfather, George, clearly a man of driving enterprise, secured the lucrative monopoly from Elizabeth I around the year 1565, and established mills at Long Ditton and Godstone, and probably also at Wotton where he bought an estate in 1579. By his two marriages he produced no fewer than twenty-four children, six of whom survived him. John's father Richard was the only son of the second marriage, inheriting the Wotton estate. He did not engage in the manufacture of gunpowder, preferring to become a pillar of local society, serving as sheriff of Sussex and Surrey in 1633, and supporting charitable institutions, including the grammar school and almshouses in Guildford.

John noted of his father that he was 'wonderfully prosperous in all his Undertakings, the more remarkable, as without the accession of any lucrative Office, he pass'd his whole time in the Country & in good husbandry'. He also described his father as 'a studious decliner of Honor & Titles': in 1630 Richard Evelyn even incurred a fine from Charles I when he refused to pay for a knighthood (one of the ways that the monarch sought to improve his finances).[2] John Evelyn took note of this, and continued the tradition, writing to his wife how, on being offered a knighthood, he had 'got most dextrously off' and escaped the court 'a squire as pure as ever I went'.[3]

John Evelyn's first years were spent on the Wotton estate. In a letter to Pepys in 1700 he gives some idea of the 'good husbandry' there: 'I passe the day in the fields, among the horses and oxen, sheep and cowes, bulls and sows ... We have, I thanke God, finished our hay-harvest prosperously. I am sewing [draining] of ponds, lo[o]king after my hinds, providing carriage and tackle against reaping time and sowing'.[4] But this same countryside was not only agricultural, it was also industrial. Richard Evelyn was a keen husbandman of his woods, which were substantial, maintaining them to produce charcoal, a vital ingredient of gunpowder. The nearest watercourse to Wotton was the Tillingbourne, which powered mills to manufacture gunpowder along with other commodities.

John did not spend long at Wotton, however. In 1625 there was an outbreak of the plague that was sufficiently serious for Parliament to be removed from London to Oxford. Five-year-old John was sent to stay with his maternal grandfather, John Stansfield, at Cliffe, just outside the Sussex town of Lewes. Why he did not return to Wotton when the threat of plague had passed is not clear, although Evelyn's attribution of his mother's death in 1637 to excessive grief after some of his siblings died could suggest that she was of a depressive nature.

John Stansfield's family was originally from the north of England, but he was born in Lewes some time in the 1550s. Like Evelyn's other grandfather, George, he was a man of enterprise, establishing a shipping business at Newhaven, at the mouth of the Ouse. Ships left here with a variety of cargoes: iron bound for the West Country, wheat for Marseilles, lead for Newfoundland. Stansfield also traded with London and with the northern ports of France. Ships returned with coal from South Wales, salt from the Huguenot port of La Rochelle, almonds from Malaga and stoneware from Rotterdam. Proffering some advice in the 1670s, Evelyn stoutly declared that 'It is a grave mistake to think Commerce and Merchandise a diminution to the dignity of Gentleman', and that to be a merchant 'brings us in as well as carries out many usefull things for Life. And as to other Trades, I see no reason it should the more dishonour to sell a yard of silke or Cloth than hoggs or sheepe.'[5]

John Stansfield and his second wife, Jane, had Puritan leanings – not surprising, as Lewes is known for its staunch Protestant tradition. During the reign of Mary Tudor, seventeen Protestant martyrs were burned at the stake in front of the Star Inn, and there is a memorial to them on Cliffe Hill today, with their memory evoked every year on 5 November. A vein of Puritanism ran through the rock of Anglicanism that was John Evelyn's faith.

After Stansfield's death, Jane married a barrister, William Newton, and moved to Southover House, a handsome building of Caen stone taken in 1572 from the ruins of the dissolved priory of Lewes, and here John Evelyn spent the rest of his childhood. His father wanted John to go to Eton, but his son persuaded him that he should instead attend the local free school in Southover. Remarkably, for children at this time were expected to obey their parents in all matters, John's wishes prevailed. One clue as to why this happened is John's description of Jane Newton as his 'too indulgent Grand-mother'.[6] In the event, he later regretted the decision, feeling that he got an inadequate education at the school.

In February 1637 he was admitted, along with his two brothers, George and Richard, to the Middle Temple, and three months later became a fellow-commoner at Balliol College to study the ordinary arts course. Oxford University was at this time dominated by William Laud, who became Chancellor in 1630 and, three years later, Archbishop of Canterbury. As President of St John's College, he had made it a stronghold of the Arminian faction: Jacobus Arminius was a Dutch theologian who criticised the dominant Calvinist dogma of predestination. Beneath this doctrinal debate lay a vital struggle for power, for Laud regarded it as his mission to bring a counter-reformation in the Church of

England, without a return to Rome. The principles of episcopal and priestly authority and orthodoxy, outwardly expressed in ordered ritual, were to be reasserted. This policy was doomed to failure, and Laud was impeached and executed in 1645. However, during the 1630s he was determined that the university should be converted to his point of view. For Jane Newton, with her Puritan sympathies, this was untenable, and she wrote to Evelyn when he first went up to Oxford to warn him against Laudian practice, which smacked of Catholicism.[7] Evelyn did not succumb: his adherence to the traditional form of Anglicanism remained a central tenet of his life.

Fellow-commoners, or gentlemen-commoners as they were sometimes known, were able to take their meals with the fellows and to enjoy their privileges. In some colleges this meant that they could also be exempted from the academic exercises required of students. Richard Evelyn, as a 'decliner of honours and titles', chose Balliol for his son because the college offered no such exemption. In his diary, John describes these exercises: 'I offered my first exercise in the Hall, and answerd myne Opponent: and upon the 11th following declaimed in the Chapell before the Master, Fellows & Scholars according to the Custome.'[8] Balliol had earlier had the reputation for unruliness, but the Master during Evelyn's time, Thomas Lawrence, had dealt firmly with it. Evelyn noted with grudging approval his severity 'considering that the extraordinary remissnesse of discipline had (til his coming) much detracted from the reputation of that colledg'.[9]

Evelyn passed quickly over his time at university in his diary, although he expressed the opinion that his tutor at Balliol, George Bradshaw, was negligent in his duty. He left without graduating, but this was usual for men who had no requirement of a degree for their professional advancement. His opinion, expressed with hindsight, that he had been let down in his education both at school and at university, is perhaps a symptom of his feeling of intellectual inferiority in comparison to some of the brilliant men that he was to come to know. But, to be fair to his teachers, his discursive character may well have had a part to play too.

This, then, was the gentlemanly world of the young John Evelyn. As a second son, he was not expected to take on the management of the estate at Wotton, and family inheritances enabled him to be a man of leisure. This stands in complete contrast to the world of the young Samuel Pepys. He was born on 23 February 1633 in Salisbury Court, just south of Fleet Street. A map of 1658 by Newcourt and Faithorne shows this western-most part of the City packed with houses (Plate 2). In fact, Salisbury Court was a rare piece of open land, the site of the London palace of the bishops of Salisbury. Pepys's birthplace was on the north side, right next to the door of St Bride's Church. Sloping gently down to the Thames, the court must have provided a good playground for Samuel and his friends. To the west lay the gardens of the Temple Inns of Court. To the east, the houses in crowded ranks dipped down to the Fleet, which by the seven-teenth century had become a noxious sewer.

Pepys's father, John, was a tailor serving the legal community. An inventory made for the house in 1661, when Samuel was trying to sort out his father's affairs, shows how it centred on the tailor's shop and cutting room, with a looking glass prominent among the contents. The kitchen opened onto a yard at the rear, with the stairs to the living quar-ters above at the back of the building, which was tall, narrow and timber-framed, with a jetty sticking out over the street, just like thousands of others in London.[10] Letters in John's hand show him to be not very literate, nor at ease with the pen, although he was musical – a pair of virginals in one of the upper chambers feature in the inventory.

Samuel's mother, Margaret, the daughter of a Whitechapel butcher, worked as a laundry maid before her marriage. It is highly likely that she could neither read nor write. Margaret emerges from references in her son's diary as difficult and quarrelsome, but her life must have been unimaginably hard. For nearly twenty years she was constantly preg-nant, bearing eleven children, two of whom died at birth, while five others did not survive infancy. Moreover, she suffered from 'the stone', a condition inherited by Samuel. Looking back to his childhood, he wrote that he could not remember a period without pain, and in 1658 he famously endured the operation to have a stone the size of a tennis ball removed.[11]

Echoing John Evelyn's sojourn with his grandparents in Lewes, Samuel and his brother Thomas were sent out of London from time to time, again possibly because of the recurrent threat of plague. Their mother's sister was employed as a servant in Newington Green, and a nurse was found for the two boys in the nearby hamlet of Kingsland. Now part of the London borough of Hackney, in the seventeenth century this was a rural area where Samuel played with his bow and arrows in the open fields.

He was also sent to stay with his father's relatives. The Pepys family situation was complex. While John and Margaret existed in straitened circumstances, other members of the family enjoyed a very different lifestyle. Cousin John, a neighbour in Salisbury Court, was a prosperous barrister who had served the great lawyer and legal writer Sir Edward Coke. After Coke's death, cousin John Pepys worked as agent to his son Sir Robert and his wife Lady Theophila Berkeley, who had a grand country house, Durdans, near Epsom. At some time around 1642 Samuel was taken off to Durdans and co-opted into a private production of Beaumont and Fletcher's romantic comedy, *Philaster, or Love Lies a-Bleeding*. The play was very much of its period, with love and high sentiment combined with confusion and cross-dressing. Samuel was given the leading female role of Arethusa, and looking back nearly twenty years later exclaimed, 'What a ridiculous thing it would have been for me to have acted a beautiful woman.'[12] His stay at Durdans gave him not only a taste for theatricals, which was to turn into a passion, but also a glimpse at the world of the country house, with its grand rooms, library and fine gardens, an environment much more familiar to John Evelyn.

Evelyn had been born in 1620 into a relatively peaceful world, although quarrels were soon to break out between the King, James I, and his Parliament. In December 1621, Parliament produced the 'Great Protestation' which declared: 'That the liberties, franchises, privileges, and jurisdictions of parliament are the ancient and undoubted birthright and inheritance of the subjects of England, and that the arduous and urgent affairs concerning the king, state, and defense of the realm ... are proper subjects and matter of council and debate in parliament.' James responded by tearing out the page that contained the protestation from the journal of the Commons and dissolving Parliament in

February 1622. He also arrested some of Parliament's leading men, including Sir Edward Coke, who had insisted that 'the King himself should be under no man, but under God and the law'.[13] The fuse of the conflict between Crown and Parliament had been lit. Slow-burning it may have been, but it fizzed away through the rest of James's reign and into that of his son, Charles I.

By the 1640s, the two quarrels that particularly concerned Charles's subjects were the threat to Protestantism and the fear that the King, encouraged by his Catholic French wife, Henrietta Maria, was intent on becoming an absolute ruler. Nowhere was this fear more openly expressed than in London. One writer, the Reverend Richard Baxter, later observed that 'the war was begun in our streets before the King or the Parliament had any armies'.[14] In May 1641, two of the King's most hated servants, Archbishop Laud and the Earl of Strafford, were taken to the Tower. City mobs agitated for the latter's execution, accompanying the Members of Parliament who went to Charles to urge him to sign the Bill of Attainder that sent Strafford to his death. This execution was a far more popular event than the wedding two weeks earlier of the King's nine-year-old daughter Mary and William, Prince of Orange, aged twelve. The following January, Charles attempted to arrest five members in the Commons chamber but found that, as he put it, 'the birds had flown'. Pursuing them into the City, he was mobbed by huge numbers shouting for privilege of Parliament. A week later he left London with his family, never to return until his trial and execution in Whitehall.

The formal marking of the outbreak of the English Civil War took place at Nottingham on 22 August 1642 when the King raised his standard. The following November, with his nephew, Prince Rupert of the Rhine, he gave battle at Brentford, to the west of London. John Evelyn had intended to take part but, according to his diary, he arrived too late, retiring instead to the family home at Wotton. Although the Royalists won the battle, the King failed to push his advantage and march on the capital. Instead, in a grave misjudgement, Rupert allowed his troops to sack Brentford, increasing alarm in the City, where fortifications had already been thrown up when news had arrived of the battle of Edgehill. In December Evelyn visited London and viewed these

fortifications, describing them as the 'so much celebrated line of commu-
nication', although he was careful not to let on that he had gone to fight
on the King's side at Brentford.[15]

In the spring of 1643, still alarmed at the prospect of a Royalist attack,
Parliament ordered the digging of trenches and further building of
ramparts and forts to close all the main roads into London. More than
20,000 people came out to work on the defences, with men, women and
children provided with baskets and spades by sailors and officers of the
trained bands of militia. Samuel Pepys may have taken part in this exercise, and he certainly would have witnessed it. But it was now time for
him to gain some education, and another branch of the family took this
in hand. His great-aunt Paulina had made a very good marriage to Sir
Sidney Montague, producing a son, Edward, who lived at Hinchingbrooke
House in Huntingdonshire. Samuel's uncle, Robert, who acted as Edward
Montague's agent, lived nearby at Brampton. Robert, serving in the local
militia as Captain Pepys, had no children and, taking to Samuel, decided
to make him his heir. He ensured that Samuel attended the free grammar
school in Huntingdon. The free element was available to the sons of citizens of the town, but Edward Montague had been a pupil at the school
and, as the local landowner, may have got Samuel a place, or paid for him.

Huntingdon School enjoyed a reputation for rigorous education
with excellent results, sending many pupils, including Oliver Cromwell,
to Cambridge. Latin dominated the curriculum, with the aim of getting
the boys to think and write in the language as easily as in English. Pepys
responded well, and Claire Tomalin makes the interesting point that his
skill in reading Latin may have helped to leave his English uncluttered
for his diary, a language of life as opposed to elaborate constructions of
the classroom.[16] While attending Huntingdon School, Pepys probably
lived at Brampton with his uncle, but also got to know the Montague
household at Hinchingbrooke. Although Edward Montague was away,
rising rapidly up the ranks of the Parliamentary army, his young wife
Jemima was in residence, welcoming the ten-year-old boy. This was to
be a relationship that became very important in Samuel's life.

By 1646 Pepys was back in London and a pupil at St Paul's School,
one of the finest in the country. Here he again received a rigorous

education of the kind that John Evelyn felt he lacked. The description of the school makes it sound both ancient and modern. The boys studied six days a week, with a free afternoon on Thursdays. The entire school, 150 pupils, sat in one room, with an inscription on the high windows that ran *Aut Doce, Aut Disce, Aut Discede* ('Either teach, or study, or leave'). At one end sat the high master, at the other the surmaster. Boys were assigned to classes by achievement, not age. Greek was started in the sixth form, Hebrew in the eighth. Regular oral examinations and the reading out of compositions in Latin turned pupils into effective speakers, a skill that Pepys was later to find invaluable. The boys were drawn from widely different levels of society, from scions of gentry families to boys like Samuel with working-class parents. St Paul's was the most strongly Puritan of all the London schools, and its headmaster at the time, John Langley, had a particular animus against Archbishop Laud, testifying against him in the trial that led to his execution in 1645.

The school was located in St Paul's Churchyard, the largest open space in London, equivalent to about twenty-two modern football pitches. This area had long staged the life of the capital, with public activities ranging from acrobatic shows and open-air sermons to people doing penance, and heretical books – and on occasion heretics themselves – being burnt. The Victorian writer Thomas Carlyle called Paul's Cross in the Churchyard the 'Times Newspaper of the Middle Ages', and it continued in this role into the seventeenth century. In the 1640s part of the old, battered Gothic cathedral had been turned into a shopping precinct, and sometimes provided stabling for army horses. In the summer of 1647 and again in November 1648 the New Model Army appeared in the City. The early Parliamentarian troops were poorly organised and equipped, but through the 'New Model Ordinance', Oliver Cromwell and Thomas Fairfax had created a truly professional fighting force. The sight of these troops, 18,000 strong, marching through the London streets with Cromwell at the head, must have been intensely exciting for schoolboys like Pepys.

The year before Samuel's arrival at St Paul's, the King had been decisively defeated at the Battle of Naseby on 14 June 1645, the turning point of the Civil War. The following year Charles surrendered himself to the Scots, only to be turned over to Parliament in January 1647. Every effort to come to a peaceful solution failed, often because of the obdurate and untrustworthy character of the King and, as the months passed, splits began to appear between Parliament and the New Model Army. Eventually, in December 1648, a group of republican army officers went to the House of Commons, arrested 45 members and sent away another 186 whom they considered unlikely to support their plans to get rid of the King: this intervention is known as 'Pride's Purge' after one of the leading figures, Colonel Thomas Pride. The scene was now set for Charles I to be put on trial, and the drama moved westwards, to the great hall at Westminster. The final act took place on the smallest of stages: the execution of Charles on a scaffold outside the banqueting house of Whitehall Palace, on 30 January 1649. The boys of Westminster School were locked inside for the day to prevent them attending. It is not known what action St Paul's School took, but whatever their decision, Samuel Pepys was a witness at the execution. One of his friends remembered that he 'was a great roundhead' as a boy, and he revealed, somewhat nervously, in his diary in 1660 how he returned to school and told his friends that if he had to preach a sermon on the King, it would be 'The memory of the wicked shall rot'.[17]

The twenty-eight-year-old John Evelyn's response stands in complete contrast. In his diary he wrote, 'The Villanie of the Rebells proceeding now so far as to Trie, Condemne. & Murder our excellent King, the 30 of this Moneth, struck me with such horror that I kept the day of his Martyrdom a fast, & would not be present, at that execrable wickednesse'.[18] Evelyn has clearly here amended his account at a later time, as was his wont, but it conveys vividly the shock felt by many, even those opposed to Charles I, at the contrived death of an anointed sovereign. On the day of the execution, Evelyn remained at his house in Deptford, receiving an account of the proceedings from his older brother George:

> They have this day between twelve & one of the clock executed the king: it was done upon a Scaffold erected on purpose over against the banqueting house in White Hall ... The execution was disguised; his head was strucke off at one blow & after wards held up to

the people & the usual words uttered behold the head of a traytor. Sir I am sorry to be the sad messenger of this day's tragedy; it is now past & we must submit.[19]

John Evelyn had spent the 1640s travelling in Europe. His father died in 1640, and an inheritance passed down to him from his maternal grandfather enabled him to be master of his own destiny. Evelyn decided to go to the Low Countries – Holland and the Spanish Netherlands – departing in July 1641. His choice was probably coloured by the fact that the Earl of Arundel was also planning to visit the Spanish Netherlands. Although Evelyn had got his way about his schooling, his father had not encouraged the boy's penchant for art, pointing out to him that 'painting & such like things will doe you noo good hereafter'.[20] Thomas Howard, 2nd Earl of Arundel, had been the leading English art collector in the first part of the seventeenth century, the patron of many artists, including Rubens and Van Dyck, and the architect Inigo Jones. Evelyn considered him his mentor, and was delighted by the Earl's encouragement to develop his artistic tastes and skills.

The scholar Esmond de Beer, who has produced the definitive edition of Evelyn's diary, found that many of the entries relating to his travels depended on existing or later topographical accounts. But the notes about Holland are different, demonstrating the impact that an enlightened nation built on merchant enterprise had upon Evelyn. Amsterdam, which he reached in mid-August, particularly impressed him. Of the part known as Emperors Street he wrote: '[it] is an ample & long streete, appearing like a Citty in a Forest, the Lime-trees, planted just before each house, and just at the margent of that goodly Aquæduct, so curiously wharfed with *Klincard* Brick, which likewise paves the streetes, than which nothing could be more usefull & neate'. The land here had been taken from the sea, 'supported by millions of Piles, with vast Expense, & fitted for the most busy Concourse of Trafiquers, & people of Commerce, beyond any place or Mart in the world'. As Amsterdam was the headquarters of the Dutch East India Company, he purchased 'Indian, and other Exotic natural Curiositys'. He was able to indulge his love of books, visiting the bookshop of Blaeu, the celebrated mapmakers, and the printing house of Hondius, where he watched the pages coming off the presses.[21]

Although Inigo Jones had designed the banqueting house at Whitehall in the Italian Renaissance style, it remained one of just a few classical buildings in England, so Evelyn was struck by the many examples he saw during his journeys. In Amsterdam again he noted how the city gates were 'composed of very magnificent pieces of Architecture; some of the antien & best manner'.[22] In Delft he admired the city hall with its 'very stately Portico supported with choice Columns of Black-Marble'.[23]

At Leiden, Evelyn matriculated at the university. Leiden University reflected the politics of the sixteenth century and the struggle of the Dutch against the Spanish. William the Silent, the Prince of Orange, resolved that a place of learning should be available to educate a new generation of leaders for the developing Dutch nation, and Leiden was chosen as a reward for its bravery in resisting a Habsburg siege in 1572, when it stood in the path of Philip of Spain's conquest of the provinces of Holland and Zeeland; dykes were cut, flooding the land around the town, and when a storm swelled the waters still further, the Spanish fled and the Dutch Sea Beggars were able to relieve the city, saving the Dutch Republic. It was felt that if Leiden University was to live up to the highest ideals of medical education, then students should attend not only the classroom, the disputation hall and the library, but also the anatomical theatre, the chemistry laboratory and the botanical garden, which was laid out by the celebrated botanist, Carolus Clusius. An engraving made in 1610 shows the beds arranged according to particular families of plants, and a gallery for protecting delicate plants over winter (Plate 3). Here also were kept curiosities of natural history, which Evelyn lists in his diary.

In Antwerp, in the Spanish Netherlands, Evelyn met up with the Earl of Arundel before returning to England where the Civil War had begun. In November 1642 he actually took up arms to fight at the Battle of Brentford (p. 9), but this marked the end of his military career. He rather vaguely noted in his diary that he could do no more for the King, though this may mask disillusion about Charles's strategic competence: Evelyn certainly felt that Prince Rupert had acted rashly and foolishly. Instead, he made arrangements to travel again in Europe, this time to Italy and France, and for several years.

It took nearly a year for Evelyn to make the journey from England to Rome, arriving there on the evening of 4 November 1644. In a letter to a friend twenty years later he recalled that for an annual outlay of £300 he was able in Rome to pay for 'my severall Masters, Mathematics, Musique, Languages, etc, besides a Servant or two, and the amassing of no inconsiderable Collection too of Pictures, Medaills, and other trifles'.[24] A few days earlier, while in Florence, he had made one of his most extravagant purchases: a cabinet of curiosities, following advice from Francis Bacon that a philosopher, in addition to a garden and a library, should have a cabinet in which to assemble 'whatsoever the hand of man by exquisite art or engine hath made rare in stuff, form or motion, whatsoever singularity chance and the shuffle of things hath produced, whatsoever Nature hath wrought in things that want life and may be kept'.[25] This particular piece had eighteen mosaic panels showing birds and flowers, made up from coloured stones, with a larger, central panel depicting an architectural perspective of arches, commissioned from the craftsman Domenico Benotti. From another craftsman, Vincentio Brocchi, he bought plaster statuettes that were then bronzed, along with ormolu enrichments, and a gilt bronze door decorated with the figure of Orpheus. A third craftsman was then commissioned to make up the various pieces into one piece of furniture, possibly when Evelyn was still in Florence, or when he arrived in Rome. This very lavish piece is now in the Victoria and Albert Museum (Plate 4).[26]

One of his memorable visits in Rome was to Father Athanasius Kircher at the Jesuit Church of the Gesù, where he was given a tour of the dispensary, laboratory and gardens. In his diary he described how Kircher 'with Dutch [German] patience shew'd us his perpetual motions, Catoptrics, Magnetical experiments, Modells, and a thousand other crotchets & devises'.[27] Kircher, Professor of Mathematics at the Collegio Romano, was an exceptional polymath, the author of around forty major works in such diverse fields as comparative religion, geology, medicine and the theory of music. As Evelyn noted, Kircher was interested in mechanical inventions, including automata and a magnetic clock. He was one of the first people to observe microbes through a microscope, and proposed that the plague was caused by an infectious micro-organism. Little wonder that he has been described as 'Master of a Hundred Arts'.

Evelyn took the opportunity while in Rome to visit some of the gardens outside the city, including the Villa Medici, the Villa Aldobrandi at Frascati and the Villa d'Este at Tivoli, admiring the sophisticated constructions of cascades, grottoes and automata. At the papal garden on the Quirinale he 'observ'd the glorious hedges of myrtle above a mans height; others of Laurell, Oranges, nay of Ivy and Juniper'.[28] Visits like these were to provide important sources of inspiration for his gardening future, as shown in Chapter 7.

Moving northwards through Italy, Evelyn spent time in Padua, where he studied human physiology with Johann Vesling, Professor of Anatomy. In the university's anatomy theatre he viewed dissections from one of the galleries that spiral up the building. From Vesling's assistant, Giovanni Leoni, who was about to leave for Poland, Evelyn bought a set of anatomical tables. These extraordinary boards had mounted on them the arteries, veins and nervous systems, dried relics from dissections. A fourth board, showing the liver, gastric nerves and 'other vesseles', was made specially for him by Leoni. Evelyn dispatched them via Venice to England, noting how they were 'the first of that kind [that] had ben ever seene in our Country, & for ought I know, in the World'. After many adventures they arrived in London in April 1649.[29]

Evelyn reached Paris in October 1646 to find that Charles I's Queen, Henrietta Maria, had established a court in exile, installed in apartments at the Louvre by her sister-in-law, Anne of Austria. A second English court, that of Charles, Prince of Wales, was based at St Germain-en-Laye. His advisers felt it was important that he be kept at a distance from his mother, who was adept at stirring up trouble. A third meeting place for exiles and travellers was the home of Richard Browne, the English Resident, who was to all intents and purposes the ambassador to the French court. Evelyn, who had first made the acquaintance of Browne on his way south to Italy three years before, found him a man after his own heart, a knowledgeable enthusiast for gardens and books. His wife, Elizabeth, made their house 'not onley an Hospital, but the Asylum to all our persecuted & afflicted countrymen'.[30] Now Evelyn enjoyed the hospitality of Richard and Elizabeth Browne, and also noted with interest their accomplished only daughter, twelve-year-old Mary. He was not her sole suitor: his cousin Thomas Keightley had also been drawn to her, but in a letter to Evelyn he ceded his claim, explaining that Mary had taken him into her confidence and 'you would hardly endure to see such deepe symptoms of languishing for your company in your Mistress's face'.[31]

In a piece written around the year 1673, 'The Legend of Philaretes & the Pearl', Evelyn produced this pen portrait of the young Mary:

> Onely daughter ... besides the pretynesse & innocence of her youth ... had something mi-thought, in her that pleasd me in a Gravity I had not observd in so tender a bud; for I could call her Woman for nothing, but her early steadines, & that at the age of playing with babies, she would be at her Book, her needle, Drawing of pictures, casting of Accompts & Undertook to Govern the House. I tooke notice that she began to discourse not Impertinently, was gay enough for my humor & one I believ'd that might one day grow-up to be the agreeable companion of an honest-man.[32]

The couple married quietly on 27 June 1647 in the chapel of the Residency.

Although the age of consent at this period was twelve years for a girl, such a young bride does strike a discordant note today. In the seventeenth century it was not uncommon for heiresses to be promised in marriage at twelve, as this was often a financial arrangement between families. However, that was not the case here, for it was the groom who had the greater fortune. Instead, Evelyn hints in his own words at why he wanted to marry the twelve-year-old Mary now rather than wait for a few years before doing so: he was seeking to mould his wife as she developed. Throughout his life, Evelyn exhibited a controlling tendency, possibly as a result of his lack of self-confidence.

Because of Mary's youth, the marriage was not consummated. Instead, Evelyn left for England to fulfil obligations to his own family, and also to sort out matters for his new father-in-law. Political turbulence is never kind to unworldly people, and Richard Browne had not only mortgaged his estate in England, Sayes Court in Deptford, but also was receiving no salary for his services in Paris. While he was in England, Evelyn had his portrait painted for his bride. The artist Robert Walker produced an image almost in monochrome: his sitter is depicted with flowing black locks, wearing a loose white shirt (Plate 5). Walker's original scheme was to depict Evelyn holding a miniature portrait of Mary, but he was asked to replace this with a skull – the very personification of romantic melancholy. Above Evelyn's head runs a Greek inscription, 'Repentance is the beginning of wisdom', and on the table a paper carries stoical sentiments from Seneca. Evelyn explained to Mary that she must be content with 'la naïfe posture de la Maladie dont je suis tourmenté'.[33]

How Mary responded to this is not recorded, but she took the stoical element to heart during her long marriage to John Evelyn. She early showed her practical character when she ordered a second cabinet of curiosities to add to the one that her husband had already acquired in Italy. Mary probably commissioned it from Pierre Gole, a Dutchman whose shop was near to the Louvre. She chose a restrained exterior of ebony veneer, explaining in a letter to Evelyn, 'I have seene many fine Cabinets this faire butt all sculpture so that I did not much enquire affter the prises because you do not like anything of that kinde.'[34] There was nothing restrained about the price, for Gole was a sought-after ébéniste who charged her the substantial sum of 800 livres. Knowing Evelyn's love of plants, Mary chose as decoration for the exterior the florist's flowers, ranunculi, carnations and tulips, and the pomegranate, all from the Middle East. Once the outer doors were opened, a rich interior was revealed, with the drawers veneered in ivory, stained green, contrasting with the rich golds and browns of cherry, rosewood and snakewood, an exotic hardwood from Surinam, a Dutch colony between the Amazon and the Orinoco in South America. In the centre was a little mirrored stage where a cherished object might be placed and lit by candles. This was overlooked by a strange helmeted figure painted onto ivory, perhaps Gole's idea of a Frisian warrior.[35]

Evelyn returned to France and lived with the Brownes until 1652, when he brought Mary to England to live at Sayes Court. Here she gave birth to their first child, Richard, the first of eight children, of whom only four reached adulthood. Hailed by his father as an infant prodigy, Richard died at the age of six in 1658, along with his brother George. The 1650s – the years of the Commonwealth and the Protectorate of Oliver Cromwell – were described by one Royalist as 'our long winter',[36] and it must have been thus, both politically and personally, for John Evelyn. But, characteristically, he did not sit by the fire, instead applying himself to a whole range of activities.

In 1652, he embarked on the creation of an ambitious garden at Sayes Court, a project that marked the beginning of his serious interest in horticulture and botany. Three years later he began to compile an encyclopaedic history of gardens and garden practices, *Elysium Britannicum*, but the sheer amount of material collected was overwhelming, and it was never published. However, Evelyn did produce several books during the decade. Some were translations of works on subjects that had fascinated him on his travels. His interest in science led to the translation of the first book of Lucretius' *De Rerum Natura*, published in 1656. His horticultural enthusiasm resulted in a translation of Nicolas de Bonnefons' *Le Jardinier François* as *The French Gardiner*, published in 1659. His translation from the Greek of St John Chrysostom's *Golden Book* was produced in the same year, dedicated to the memory of his first son, Richard. He also wrote original books. *The State of France* (1652) was a little book dedicated to Richard Browne, in which he compared Paris with London, to the latter's detriment. Seven years later he followed this up with *A Character of England*, when he adopted the guise of a French visitor despairing of the nation's republican state and nonconformist religious observances. In particular he decried London's congested streets, chaotic housing, noise and overpowering coal smoke: 'Hell upon Earth . . . on a foggy day'.[37] He enlarged upon the theme of the polluted city of London in his third volume, *Fumifugium*, published in 1661, in which he proposed measures to improve the atmosphere both physically and mentally under the restored monarchy.

Meanwhile, Samuel Pepys was completing his education. His headmaster at St Paul's, John Langley, had a particularly good record for getting his pupils into Cambridge, and Pepys proved no exception. The school gave him a leaving exhibition in 1650, and entered his name for Trinity Hall, where his uncle, John Pepys, was a fellow. Later that year, however, he was admitted as a sizar (a student receiving a college allowance towards expenses) at Magdalene College, probably through connections between the college and the Montague family. As at Oxford, Archbishop Laud had seized the opportunity to impose aesthetic and ceremonial innovations on the religious life of the colleges. But a Puritan purge took place in Cambridge in the early 1640s, with the Earl of Manchester empowered by Parliament to eject members of the university deemed unacceptable; at Magdalene, nine out of fifteen fellows were removed, and in 1650, the Master, Edward Rainbow, was ejected and replaced by John Sadler, a radical lawyer who was prone to millenarian flights of fancy and mystical experiences, including prophesying the Great Fire of London.

Pepys clearly enjoyed his time at Magdalene, in later years recalling his favourite walk to Chesterton church, returning by ferry, purchasing stewed prunes from Goody Mulliner, who lived opposite the college, playing music, enjoying bawdy encounters and beer from the buttery. On one occasion, in October 1653, he was reprimanded by his tutor, Samuel Morland, for 'having bene scandalously overseene in drink'.[38] Given the political climate of the times, the classical curriculum was pushed aside in favour of studying divinity. Pepys, however, preferred to read Erasmus and Francis Bacon, and books on English history. He wrote a romance, 'Love a Cheate', but admitted in his diary ten years later:

> This evening, being in an humour of making all things even and clear in the world, I tore some old papers; among others a Romance ... and at this time, reading it over tonight, I liked it very well and wondered a little at myself at my vein at that time when I wrote it, doubting that I cannot do so well now if I would try.[39]

Given the clarity of his subsequent style, would that he had kept it. It was at university that Pepys also taught himself shorthand according to the system devised by Thomas Shelton. He made many lasting friendships, regularly returning to the college and proving a generous donor.

Returning to London after taking his BA in March 1654, Pepys became clerk to his cousin Edward Montague. In the early 1650s Montague had lived quietly in his house in Hinchingbrooke, but returned to the political stage when he became an MP. John Milton wrote of him as being of the 'highest ability and of the best culture and accomplishments', and these qualities were noted by Oliver Cromwell, who made him a councillor of state and commissioner of the Treasury.[40] As Pepys had no home of his own during these early days, he 'perched' in Montague's lodgings in the rambling palace of Whitehall, fulfilling a whole range of duties for his cousin. In 1656 Pepys acquired a more formal position as clerk to Sir George Downing at the Exchequer, which had been resuscitated by Cromwell from its moribund state during the Civil War.

The salary from this job proved timely, for on 10 October 1655 Pepys had married Elizabeth Marchant de St Michel in a civil ceremony, followed three weeks later by a religious ceremony at St Margaret's, Westminster. In between the two events, his bride had celebrated her fifteenth birthday. Elizabeth brought to the marriage no dowry, but rather the negative burden of her impoverished and importunate Huguenot relatives. In 1658 the couple moved into a house in Axe Yard in Westminster and acquired their first servant, Jane Birch.

Pepys refers in his diary to how at this time he went 'clubbing', as he put it, with his fellow clerks to the various taverns and coffee-houses in the area. One such was the Turk's Head in New Palace Yard in Westminster, presided over by its proprietor, Miles. Here were held meetings of the Rota Club, founded by James Harrington. In his book *The Commonwealth of Oceana*, published in 1656, Harrington included the remarkable radical proposal of a republic with a rotating senate, an extended franchise and limitation on property ownership. A specially made oval table was installed, around which members could gather while Miles dispensed coffee and tobacco from a passage along the middle. One member of the club was William Petty, not only a physician but also a polymath, statistician, social planner and inventor. Another was the antiquary and biographer John Aubrey, although he was apparently never much interested in politics. Pepys joined the Rota Club in January 1659, and a copy of Harrington's *Commonwealth of Oceana* was added to his library. An interest in the kind of politics being advocated by Harrington was becoming perilous, however, for the political climate was undergoing a fundamental change. Nevertheless, Pepys continued to show just such an interest, as his library also contains treatises by Harrington, including one entitled 'A discourse shewing that the spirit of parliaments . . . is not to be trusted for a settlement: lest it introduce monarchy'.[41]

When Oliver Cromwell died suddenly in September 1658, apparently at the height of his power, his son Richard was named as his successor, but he had neither the will nor the ability to hold the balance between the many conflicting forces. Parliament was at odds with the army, and the turbulent nature of the regime had divided them both from the people they governed. Suddenly people began to think the unthinkable and talk of the return of the Stuarts: Pepys observed how toasts to the King were no longer drunk in secret, but openly in taverns. His cousin, Edward Montague, now in charge of the fleet, had tried to give support to Richard Cromwell, but this came to nothing with the latter's abdication in April 1659. Ceasing his command at sea, he retired to his estate at Hinchingbrooke, and was kept informed by Pepys of the bewildering political changes taking place in London.

John Evelyn had watched Oliver Cromwell's funeral as it passed through the streets to Westminster Abbey, writing in his diary how it was the 'joyfullest funerall that ever I saw, for there was none that Cried, but dogs, which the souldiers hooted away with a barbarous noise; drinking, & taking Tabacco in the streetes as they went'.[42] He tried to persuade a former schoolfellow, Colonel Herbert Morley, to stage a Royalist coup. Morley was a commissioner for the army, and therefore a key player in the complex situation. However, the person who cut the Gordian knot was General George Monck, a canny operator who on the first day of 1660 marched with his troops from Scotland to London, arranged for the dissolution of Parliament and for the creation of a 'Free Parliament', which voted for the restoration of the monarchy. Four months later, Charles II, advised by his chief counsellor, Edward Hyde, issued a reassuring declaration from the Dutch town of Breda. He pardoned his enemies and, although he promised to uphold the Anglican Church, granted liberty to 'tender consciences', agreeing to leave all difficult questions to the will of Parliament.

Disappointed that Monck rather than Morley had carried the day, Evelyn complained that his old friend had been both disloyal and foolish, but he was delighted by the prospect of the return of the King and the end of the long winter. The worlds of Evelyn and of Pepys, which had begun so differently, were now about to converge.

2

THE DECADE OF THE DIARIES

IN DECEMBER 1659, Samuel Pepys took a boat down the Thames from Westminster to the City and bought a paper-covered book from John Cade, a stationer who traded at the sign of the Globe in Cornhill. Ruling margins in red ink down the left of each page and across the top, he began to write his diary in black and brown ink. Longhand was used for names and places but the main body of the diary was in Thomas Shelton's system of shorthand, which Pepys had mastered years before while at Cambridge.

Diary-keeping had become a custom for some by the end of the sixteenth century. Puritan divines particularly encouraged the discipline as a form of moral accounting. John Beadle wrote in *The Journey or Diary of a Thankful Christian*, published in 1656, how the diary should contain an account of all God's gracious dealings with the diary keeper. He or she should be particularly concerned with his or her inner life, but the diary might also contain notices relating to external affairs, and those public events where divine dispensations might be recognised. Margaret, Lady Hoby, kept hers between 1599 and 1605 when living with her irascible husband in Yorkshire. Some precious details about gardening, household routines and medicinal practice are provided, but much of the record is given over to a reiteration of prayers and readings from the Bible, and lapses from the rigorous regime.[1]

In the century that followed there came a positive wave of enthusiasm for keeping a diary. For instance, Ralph Josselin, an Essex clergyman, farmer and schoolteacher, wrote his from the mid-1640s until his death in 1683. Living in a small village, his experience was necessarily confined to topics such as the weather, the state of the crops and the health of his family. And, like Lady Hoby, his language is replete with religious sentiments, constantly repeated, which can become wearisome to read. Another diarist was Roger Morrice, a Puritan clergyman in North Staffordshire who was ejected by the Act of Uniformity of 1662. He became a servant in the household of the politician Denzil Holles, and kept what he described as an 'Entring Book' from 1677 to 1691. This is more like a historical register or newsletter, providing some glimpses of the turbulent politics of the time, but written in an impersonal style.[2]

Like Morrice, John Evelyn included observations of the events and political climate of his time, but combined these with consideration of his spiritual life, notes of church attendance and sermons preached. He began his journal in his twenties, 'in imitation of what I had seene my Father do'.[3] The early parts of his diary often consisted of brief notes, especially those made on his tours in Europe during the 1640s, which were then written up retrospectively. In 1660 he began what he called his 'Kalendarium', and continued this right through to January 1706, shortly before his death. It is a restrained document, conscious of Evelyn's position in society. As he undoubtedly expected that his family might read it, he regularly revised and altered some of the entries to adjust his views on events in the light of hindsight.

Francis Bacon had recommended keeping a diary in his essay on travel: 'It is a strange thing that in sea voyages, where there is nothing to be seen but sky and sea, men should make diaries, but in land travel, wherein so much is to be observed, for the most part they omit it: as if chance were fitter to be registered than observation. Let diaries therefore be brought in use'.[4] Pepys heeded this advice, providing much fascinating material of everyday life, so that his diary can be read with pleasure today, making him perhaps the first modern practitioner of the art. Like James Boswell in the eighteenth century and Alan Clark in the twentieth, he was highly susceptible to female attractions, forgiving almost anything, even spitting on him at the theatre, if the woman was pretty. Frequently he failed in his attempted conquests, but when he did succeed, he noted his experience in a curious form of romantic language. A rather elaborate example of this is his description of an encounter with his actress friend, Elizabeth Knepp: '[I] had the opportunity, the first time in my life, to be bold ... by putting my hand abaxo de her coats and tocar su thighs and venter'.[5] As clerk to the Navy Board, Pepys was also in an ideal position to observe the great affairs of the state, through personal contact with leading ministers and the King and his brother, James, Duke of York.

The diary of Robert Hooke is in some ways similar to that of Pepys. Hooke was the brilliant and disputatious Curator of Experiments at the Royal Society, Gresham Professor of Geometry, and Surveyor of post-Fire London. He knew both Evelyn and Pepys so that his accounts, from 1672 to 1683, and 1688 to 1693, can fill in details of their activities.[6] Like Pepys he included much social detail, such as what he ate and drank, his medical condition (a source of constant fascination to him) and his sexual encounters. However, his frenetic lifestyle comes through in staccato notes written in his cramped handwriting that led his transcriber to note with saintly tolerance that his task was like solving a cryptic crossword.

Pepys kept his main diary from 1660 to 1669, a tantalisingly short period compared to Evelyn's, but an extraordinarily exciting time. It may well be that the incentive to keep a record in the first place arose from the prospect of the return of Charles II to his kingdom. By the end of April 1660 agreement had been reached in secret between Monck and the exiled court on the terms of a Royalist restoration. Edward Montague, returned to office as General-at-Sea, had joined the fleet and sailed to Holland on 11 May, taking with him Pepys as the Admiral's Secretary. Early entries of the diary describe Pepys's life on board the *Naseby*, which was to be renamed the *Royal Charles*, thus expunging the memory of the defining defeat of the Civil War. The entry for 17 May noted the diarist's meeting in The Hague with the King, who was he thought 'a very sober man'.[7] He also met the King's brother, James, Duke of York, reinstated to the title of High Admiral of the Fleet that had been given to him by his father at the age of nine, and Edward Hyde, shortly to be made the Earl of Clarendon and Lord Chancellor. The term 'sober' to describe a man who became known as the Merry Monarch may seem odd, but Charles was the consummate actor, who had been obliged to be evasive in all kinds of ways during his long years of exile. Presenting a grave face to the party come to bring him back to England was a carefully chosen tactic.

Over 50,000 people crowded the shoreline to see Charles leave Holland, Pepys describing how the white sand had turned black with their numbers. Arriving at Dover, Charles received a rapturous welcome, with Pepys again on hand to report the scene: 'Infinite the Croud of people and the gallantry of the Horsmen, Citizens and Noblemen of all sorts ... The Shouting and joy expressed by all is past imagination.'[8] The King's thirtieth birthday, 29 May, was chosen for when he would enter London. On this occasion it was Evelyn who witnessed the scene, establishing himself on the Strand.

> This day came in his Majestie Charles the 2d to London after a sad, & long Exile, and Calamitous Suffering both of the King & Church ... The wayes straw'd with flowers, the bells ringing, the streetes hung with Tapissry, fountaines running with wine: The Major, Aldermen, all the Companies in their liver(ie)s, Chaines of Gold, banners; Lords & nobles, Cloth of Silver, gold & vellvet every body clad in, the windos & balconies all set with Ladys, Trumpets, Musick & myriads of people flocking the streets.

Evelyn reckoned that there were more than 20,000 troops accompanying him. This was an exaggeration, no doubt brought on by the excitement of the day, but Evelyn also reflected the irony that these were the very men who had rebelled against the Crown. He ended his account by declaring 'it was the Lords doing, *et mirabile in oculis nostris*: for such a Restauration was never seene in the mention of any history, antient or modern, since the returne of the Babylonian Captivity, nor so joyfull a day, & so bright, ever seene in this nation; this hapning when to expect or effect it, was past all humane policy'.[9]

The King was so swarthy in complexion that the poet Andrew Marvell used an Old Testament analogy in his doggerel rhyme: 'Of a tall stature and of sable hue, / Much like the son of Kish, that lofty Jew.' His brother James was contrastingly fair: portraits painted at the time show a handsome face, though later depictions are marred by the haughty expression that he tended to adopt. Both men were inveterate womanisers. At the Restoration, Charles had already fathered several children by various mistresses. Lucy Walter gave birth to his eldest child, James, who was to be Duke of Monmouth, in Rotterdam in April 1649, and this boy became a much-indulged figure at the Restoration court. The King's favourite mistress in 1660 was Barbara Palmer, later to be Lady Castlemaine, and gossip had it that he spent his first night in London in her bed. As yet, Charles was not married, and the Duke of York was his heir apparent.

James lacked the graciousness of his brother, and also his judgement. While in exile in Brussels he had become involved with Anne Hyde, one of the maids of honour of his sister, Mary, Princess of Orange, and daughter of the King's senior adviser, Edward Hyde. In late 1659, he put his signature to an agreement of marriage contract, but the restoration of his brother to the English throne altered his horizons: instead of union with a commoner, he could hope for a noble, indeed a royal bride. Anne then informed him that she was pregnant and that he should honour his commitment. A whole series of people stepped in to try to stop the marriage: his mother Henrietta Maria, his sister Mary, his friends who used the old masculine trick of claiming that Anne was a whore with whom they had all slept. Even Anne's father, now Lord Chancellor and Lord Clarendon, appeared to oppose the match, threatening to turn his daughter out of his house and shouting that she should be sent to the Tower. The King, furious at both his brother's foolishness and his indecision, ordered him to marry the girl and honour his contract. The wedding was held in secret on 3 September 1660, and seven weeks later Charles, Duke of Cambridge, was born. Tragically, after all the alarums and excursions, the little boy died as a baby from smallpox, a scourge that swept through the royal family that winter, killing the King's youngest – and favourite – brother, Henry, Duke of Gloucester, and his sister Mary.

One courtier described Anne as having 'a majestic manner, a figure which is pretty good, not much beauty, a great deal of wit'.[10] Although James was constantly unfaithful to her, he needed Anne's strength of character and intelligence, or as Pepys bluntly put it, 'the Duke of York, in all things but in his codpiece, is led by the nose by his wife'.[11] His choice of mistresses was rather maladroit. The King teased him by suggesting that he chose ugly ones for a penance, whilst one of his later mistresses, Catherine, daughter of the poet and playwright Sir Charles Sedley, was reputed to have declared, 'We are none of us handsome, and if we had wit, he has not enough to discover it.'[12] Duchess Anne bore James eight children in all, although the only two to survive beyond childhood were the Princesses Mary and Anne. Charles gained his Queen, the Portuguese Catherine of Braganza, in 1662, but there were to be no legitimate heirs: all her pregnancies ended in miscarriage, so that James continued to hold the key role of heir apparent.

The Restoration was good for Edward Montague. Despite his previous Parliamentarian adherence, he became a Knight of the Garter, Earl of Sandwich, Vice-Admiral of the Kingdom, Master of the Great Wardrobe, and Clerk of the Great Seal. This rise in status was paralleled by that of his kinsman when he became Clerk of the Acts to the Navy Board and a deputy at the Privy Seal. Pepys was thus now one of the principal officers of the navy, with clerks to help him, an annual salary of £350, and the opportunity to make profits beyond his official pay. He moved with Elizabeth and his household from Axe Yard to the navy's official lodgings in Seething Lane in the City.

The Navy Board under the direction of the Lord High Admiral, the Duke of York, dealt with the civil administration – stores, provisions, shipbuilding, ship repair and management of the dockyards. As Clerk of the Acts, Pepys had a large task facing him, made all the larger by the fact that the navy had been starved of funds during the Interregnum. Men had to be paid, good ships repaired, bad ships written off, and corruption in the dockyards wiped out. To make matters even more difficult, a war was begun with the Dutch that was fought almost entirely at sea. The First Anglo-Dutch War had broken out in July 1652 as a result of the passing of the Navigation Act. This had challenged the Dutch mercantile economy by forbidding importation of goods into Britain except in English vessels or vessels of the country producing the goods. Now another war against the Dutch was threatening, again as a result of rivalry for markets and an enthusiasm for colonial enterprise. As a merchant explained to Pepys, 'the trade of the world is too little for us two, therefore one must down'.[13]

In February 1664 a bill was prepared granting to the Duke of York 'lands in America from St Croix to Long Island', ignoring the fact that these territories were occupied by the Dutch. An expedition seized the lands and changed the name of the major trading centre from New Amsterdam to New York in honour of the Lord High Admiral, a provocation that brought forward the threat of war. Pepys and Sir William Coventry, the best-informed officials on the Navy Board, were well aware that the navy was not ready for conflict, with Coventry explaining to Parliament: 'The Dutch are not to be trampled on, if you do they will kick. Their trade is their God, if you depress that by any force, they will venture all for it'.[14] But the blood of both Court and Parliament was up, and the Second Anglo-Dutch War broke out in 1665.

The Battle of Lowestoft took place on 3 June with the English fleet commanded by the Duke of York from his flagship, the *Royal Charles*. Initially the encounter went well for James, who won in open combat the most conclusive victory of all the wars against the Dutch. With the enemy on the run back to Holland, James gave the order to crowd on sail and pursue, then went below to get some sleep after nearly eighteen hours on deck. While he slept, the opportunity for the destruction of the Dutch fleet was snatched away by the extraordinary action of an officer of his household, Henry Brouncker, who persuaded the officer of the watch to shorten sail.[15] When James awoke, he found that the Dutch had got clean away. He was a naval hero, but also the victim of the bad luck that seemed to dog his career. His brother subsequently forbade him ever again to take part personally in battle.

At the beginning of September, news arrived that Lord Sandwich had engaged the Dutch fleet and captured several ships. A celebration supper was held on 10 September in Greenwich at the lodgings of Lord

Brouncker, Pepys's superior at the Navy Board and older brother of the disgraced Henry. Both Pepys and Evelyn were invited, and the evening went very well, with Pepys reporting how Evelyn gave a rendition of some verses on the use of the words 'may' and 'can'. The correct application of these two words can (or may?) still baffle, but Evelyn not only demonstrated this, but did it at such speed that Pepys declared that he 'did make us all die almost with laughing'.[16] It is a fascinating reference, for not only is this the first record of the two men together at a private party, it also provides a highly unconventional portrait of Evelyn, a man not known for his sense of humour.

The war continued for another two years with mixed results, including humiliation when the Dutch broke the chain that guarded the River Medway, burnt the English fleet which had been laid up there to save money, and towed away the *Royal Charles*. A terrified London waited to see what the Dutch would do next. A naval colleague, William Batten, exclaimed to Pepys, 'By God! ... I think the Devil shits Dutchmen'.[17] Fortunately, the Dutch and their allies the French wanted peace on reasonable terms. The Treaty of Breda of 1667 stipulated the relaxation of the Navigation Acts in favour of the Dutch, who also took the nutmeg island of Ram in the East Indies and were ceded all rights to the colony of Surinam in South America. New York was to remain English, along with some strongholds in West Africa.

There was relief in the corridors of power, but as ever in war, ordinary sailors in both fleets paid a high price. John Evelyn had been recruited onto various commissions after the Restoration, but his job serving on the Commission for Sick and Wounded Seamen was surely the most demanding, especially as his area of responsibility was the key counties of Kent and Sussex. He found himself working alongside Samuel Pepys as Clerk of the Acts to the Navy Board. In his diary for 5 October 1665, Pepys noted travelling down to Deptford to meet Evelyn to discuss the plight of the distressed seamen who also included Dutch prisoners of war. The entry is typically Pepysian, for on his way down, he 'did pass some time with Sarah' and then visited Mrs Bagwell, the complaisant wife of a naval carpenter, and 'did what I would con ella'. Sexual encounters were laid aside when he met up with Evelyn, for they were both horrified by the conditions in which the men were living, or 'much put out of order' as Pepys termed it. Evelyn was particularly overwhelmed by the ghastliness of the situation, but the presence of the businesslike Pepys enabled him to keep at the task.[18]

Matters had been made far worse by the outbreak of plague. There had been many epidemics afflicting London over the centuries, and following the Black Death these were usually of the bubonic strain. A serious epidemic had occurred in 1625, when the young John Evelyn was sent to live with his grandfather, but the outbreak of 1665 was far worse than any that had appeared before. It began in London in November 1664, and the winter initially kept the numbers down. However, by the late spring, the bills of mortality recording deaths showed the inexorable grip the disease had upon the capital (Plate 7). The diaries of both Pepys and Evelyn are full of references. Pepys had sent his family out of London for safety – Elizabeth and the household servants to Woolwich, and his clerks to Greenwich – while he stayed with one maid in Seething Lane. Even the Deptford and Woolwich area recorded deaths from the plague, so Evelyn sent Mary and the children to his brother's house at Wotton in Surrey.

June 1665 was very hot, and Pepys noted how in Drury Lane he saw 'two or three houses marked with a red cross upon the doors, and "Lord have mercy upon us" writ there – which was a sad sight to me, being the first of that kind that to my remembrance I ever saw'.[19] In early September, as Evelyn made his way from Deptford to St James's Palace, he saw 'all along the Citty & suburbs . . . a dismal passage & dangerous . . . so many Cofines exposd in the streetes & the streete thin of people, the shops shut up, & all in mournefull silence, as not knowing whose turne might be next'. He was on his way to see George Monck, now Duke of Albemarle and a joint commander of the fleet, about a 'pest ship' in which to accommodate the sailors who had been infected.[20]

Just three days before Evelyn made his way through the silent streets of London, Pepys wrote from Woolwich to Elizabeth Carteret, wife of Sir George, Treasurer of the Navy. He gave her a vivid picture of the terrible strain that fear of the disease was having upon the city's population. The plague had spread to Greenwich, he said, 'but we are by the command of the King, taking all the care we can to prevent its growth',

> meeting to that purpose yesterday after sermon with the town officers, many doleful informations were brought us, and among others this which I shall trouble your Ladyship with the telling. Complaint was brought us against one in the town for receiving into his house a child newly brought from an infected house in London. Upon enquiry we found that it was the child of a very able citizen in Gracious Street, who, having lost already all the rest of his children, and himself and wife being shut up and in despair of escaping, implored only the liberty of using means for the saving of this only babe; which with difficulty was allowed, and they suffered to deliver it, stripped naked, out at a window into the arms of a friend, who, shifting it into fresh clothes, conveyed it thus to Greenwich, where . . . we suffer it to remain. This I tell your Ladyship as one instance of the miserable straits our poor neighbours are reduced to.[21]

The final death toll according to the bills of mortality was 68,576, but in reality around 100,000 perished, about one-fifth of the city's population. Pepys was told by the clerk of his parish, St Olave's, that '"there died nine this week, though I have returned but six" – which is a very ill practice, and makes me think it is so in other places, and therefore the plague much greater than people take it to be'. The disparity in numbers was probably caused by the fact that the 'searchers of the dead', usually old women employed by parishes to examine corpses and ascertain the cause of death, had little or no medical knowledge and therefore could only give unreliable diagnoses.[22]

By the end of 1665 the number of cases had dropped. In another letter to Elizabeth Carteret, John Evelyn allowed himself to be rather more light-hearted, flirtatious almost, teasing her about holding some rue (the herb said to be efficacious against the plague) under her nose when a pair of slippers had arrived from London. Nevertheless, he did add sober details of how some of his neighbours in Deptford were shut up in their homes, and how lonely he was because his family was away in Surrey.[23]

Life was indeed returning to normal. On Christmas morning, Pepys remarked upon a wedding in his church, 'which I have not seen many a day, and the young people so merry one with another', though he went on rather sourly to add 'and strange to see what delight we married people have to see these poor fools decoyed into our condition, every man and wife gazing and smiling at them'.[24]

The following summer was again very hot, and Londoners were concerned that the plague might return, but it was a different calamity that hit the city. At a little before two o'clock in the morning of Sunday, 2 September 1666, a fire broke out in Thomas Farriner's bakery in Pudding Lane, just by the northern end of London Bridge. Fire was an ever-present hazard in overcrowded cities, and at nine o'clock in the evening households were expected to use a *couvre-feu* or curfew to stifle their fires: the bell of St Mary-le-Bow was rung daily as a signal for Londoners.[25] So the initial response of the Lord Mayor, Sir Thomas Bloodworth, when roused from his bed to be given news of the fire in Pudding Lane, was dismissive: 'Pish! A woman might piss it out!'[26] But Bloodworth did not reckon with the dryness of the season and the exceptionally strong winds blowing from the east.

Pepys reacted very differently when his maid, busy preparing for the Sunday feast, woke him at three to tell him of the fire. Recognising that the flames were indeed taking hold, he set out to Whitehall to inform the King and the Duke of York, who sent him back to command Bloodworth to pull down houses in the path of the fire. Pepys came upon him in Canning Street, 'like a man spent, with a handkercher about his neck'. When told of the royal command he exclaimed 'like a fainting woman, "Lord what can I do? I am spent, people will not obey me. I have been pulling down houses but the fire overtakes us faster than we can do it".'[27] The houses of London, packed tightly together, were mostly half-timbered so were highly combustible, and the fire spread inexorably. After their dinner, Evelyn with his wife and son 'took Coach and went to the bank side in Southwark, where we beheld that dismal speectaccle, the whole Citty in dreadfull flames neere the Water side'.[28]

Over the next five days both diarists give us a vivid picture: the great arch of fire like the top of a burning oven; the thunderous noise of the flames and the shrieking of people; the ground underfoot so hot that it burned the soles of feet; the sad encampments of the homeless. Pepys adds some touching details. Pigeons, reluctant to leave their perches, hovered about until their wings were burnt and they fell from the skies. A cat, rescued from a hole in a chimney by the Royal Exchange, had lost all its fur, but was still alive. This was an especially remarkable survivor, for there had been a severe cull of cats and dogs the previous year as they were considered to be carriers of the plague. Such was the size of the fire that it could be seen as far away as Oxford, where one witness described the night sky being lit up by reddish sunshine. Unlike Evelyn, whose house and family were safe in Deptford, Pepys had to deal with the very strong possibility that his home in Seething Lane might be destroyed. Dressed only in his nightshirt, he drove most of his valuables to a friend's house in Bethnal Green. His family and furniture were sent by boat to Woolwich, and Pepys completed his precautions by burying his papers, his wine and a prized Parmesan cheese in the garden of his City home.[29]

In the event, his house survived thanks to the measures organised by the King and the Duke of York. The royal brothers established eight firefighting bases, each with thirty soldiers and a hundred volunteers. The Duke also brought in the navy to blow up houses with gunpowder, halting the eastward spread of the fire towards the Tower of London. At last, after five days, the strong wind dropped, but a blaze still raged at the Temple, Holborn and Cripplegate, where the King was seen helping the soldiers. By the night of 6 September the worst was over. Nearly 400 acres had been burned within the city walls and a further 63 acres beyond (Plate 8). Eighty-seven churches had been destroyed, together with forty-four livery halls and 13,200 houses. Officially, only nine deaths were recorded, although there were probably others. Thousands had lost their homes and were camped on any area of open ground around the capital, as noted by Evelyn: 'the poore Inhabitants dispersd all about St Georges [Lambeth], Morre filds, as far as higate, & severall miles in Circle. Some under tents, others under miserab[l]e Hutts and Hovells, without a rag, or any necessary utiinsils, bed or board.'[30]

Thoughts inevitably turned to blame. Whilst the Lord Mayor was accused of incompetence in not containing the fire in the first instance, the actual cause was attributed by some to malevolent acts by the French or the Dutch, with whom England was at war. Even as the fire took hold a rumour had spread that 50,000 enemy troops were about to invade the city. Charles sought to quell such fears by telling the homeless refugees that the calamity was 'the hand of God and no plot'. Evelyn agreed with him, although the King would not have appreciated the fact that he wrote in his diary that 'the late dreadfull Conflagration, added to the Plage & Warr' were judgments inflicted 'for our prodigious ingratitude, burning Lusts, dissolute Court, profane & abominable lives'.[31] A demented Frenchman, Robert Hubert, confessed to setting fire to the baker's shop and was hanged at Tyburn after the baker Thomas Farriner signed the 'True bill' that sentenced him.

Two monuments commemorate those times of calamity and confusion. The Golden Boy of Pye Corner is a small statue built into the corner of Giltspur Street and Cock Lane in Smithfield, where the fire was stopped. Its inscription notes that the conflagration was 'occasion'd by the Sin of Gluttony': Evelyn was by no means the only person to attribute the fire to divine wrath. The Monument, designed by Christopher Wren and Robert Hooke, was constructed during the 1670s close by Pudding Lane, where the fire had started. The inscription in Latin begins in translation: 'In the year of Christ 1666, on 2 September, at a distance eastward from this place of 202ft, which is the height of this column, a fire broke out in the dead of night which, the wind blowing, devoured even distant buildings'. A significant addition was made in 1681: 'But Popish frenzy, which wrought such horrors, is not yet quenched'.

With the Great Fire, many of the places of Pepys's childhood had gone. On the morning of 7 September he walked up from Paul's Wharf on the Thames 'and saw all the town burned, and a miserable sight of Pauls church [the cathedral], with all the roofs fallen and the body of the Quire fallen into St Fayths [the crypt] – Paul's school also – Ludgate – Fleet street – my father's house and the church [St Bride's], and a good part of the Temple the like'.[32]

The largest victim of the fire was the medieval cathedral. Only a week earlier a meeting had been held at St Paul's 'to survey the generall decays of that antient & venerable Church'. In attendance were members of the commission that had been set up in 1663 to oversee the refurbishment of the cathedral. These included John Evelyn, newly appointed by Lord Clarendon as surveyor of the repairs, along with the architects Christopher Wren, Hugh May and Roger Pratt. Wren presented his plans for what could be done to prevent the cathedral's collapse after years of neglect and vandalism. A heated discussion ensued, with Wren and Evelyn arguing hard for the building of a dome over the crossing, 'a form of church-building not as yet known in England, but of wonderful grace'.[33]

This debate became academic with the fire's outbreak. The fact that St Paul's was being repaired sealed its doom, for the wooden scaffolding erected to support the crumbling central tower encouraged the spread of the flames. When these reached the roof, they caused molten lead to pour down on St Faith's in the crypt, fondly described by the Stationers' Company, whose chapel it was, as the 'babe in the womb'. Here the booksellers had taken some of their stock for safe keeping, considering the massive stone walls to be more than adequate protection from the flames. Tragically, they were not, and all the Company's books and journals had gone up in a massive bonfire. When Evelyn went to look at what remained of the cathedral on 7 September, he found that the west front and Corinthian portico built earlier in the century by Inigo Jones had survived remarkably unscathed, although the intense heat had 'in a manner Calcin'd, so as all the ornaments, Columns, freezes, Capitels & proje(c)tures of massie Portland stone flew off, even to the very roofe . . . Thus lay in ashes that most venerab(l)e Church, one of the (antientiest) Pieces of early Piety in the Christian World.'[34]

Once the fire was completely extinguished, the King and Parliament were eager to start rebuilding the city. Evelyn wrote to his wife's kinsman, Samuel Tuke, in Paris: 'I believe it will universaly be the employment of the next Spring. They are now buisid with adjusting the claimes of each proprietor, that so they may dispose things for the building after the noblest Model.'[35] Evelyn had been criticising the state of London for several years, as he made clear in his books. In *Fumifugium*, published in 1661, for instance, he deplored the fact that 'the Buildings should be compos'd of such a Congestion of misshapen and extravagant Houses':

> That the Streets should be so narrow and incommodious in the very Center, and busiest places of Intercourse; That there should be so ill and uneasie a form of Paving under foot, so troublesome and malicious a disposure of the Spouts and Gutters over head, are particulars worthy of Reproof and Reformation.[36]

Now it would seem that he had a wonderful chance to do something about the inadequacies.

Evelyn's 'noblest model' was an amalgam of the ideas about the layout of cities that he had assembled over the years, which he gathered into a report, *London Redivivum* (London Revived). He was able to call upon his experience of Rome, laid out in the 1580s by Pope Sixtus V and his architect, Domenico Fontana, with obelisks, fountains and churches to catch the eye. To this he could add the urban features of Paris, with city gates in the form of 'triumphal arches, adorned with Statues, Relievos, and apposite Inscriptions, as Prefaces to the rest within'.[37] In this period the gates of the City of London were closed at night from ten o'clock; indeed, Pepys recorded in his diary on one occasion being locked out after a day spent in Chelsea. Fortunately for him, the gate in question was Newgate, and the custodian was distracted by a breakout at the gaol, so the coach was allowed through.[38] Evelyn felt that such gates should be of appropriate stateliness.

In his scheme, St Paul's Churchyard would act as the hub of the city, oval in shape, with the cathedral at the centre, its grammar school, library, deanery and stationers' shops gathered around it. He identified the next most important focal point as the College of Physicians – healthiness after godliness – 'encircled with an handsome piazza for the dwelling of those learned persons with the Chirugeons, Apothecaries and Druggists in the streets about them; for I am greatly inclined to wish that of a mystery should not be destined to their several quarters'. Thoroughfares of varying widths would cut through the layout, linking other key buildings such as livery halls and the Guildhall, whilst visual breathing spaces would allow for 'breakings, and enlargements into piazzas'. Here, markets and 'the better sort of shopkeepers' would be allotted their locations, with craftsmen tucked away in streets and passages behind. Remembering his visit to Holland in 1641, Evelyn proposed that the residential areas of the city would have wide, paved streets of stone or brick, with sleds rather than heavy carts to service the houses. An ample quay would be built all along the north bank of the Thames, 'the goodliest river in the world', while the River Fleet would be broadened and channelled, with wharves for substantial vessels. Where it met the Thames, its waters would be filtered and 'preserved sweet . . . through flood-gates'.[39]

Evelyn presented his plan and report to the King and Queen and the Duke of York at Whitehall just a week after the fire, but found that Christopher Wren had moved even more quickly, getting his scheme to them two days earlier on 11 September. In many ways Wren's proposal resembled Evelyn's, with a series of wide, straight streets radiating from central points, although unsurprisingly, given that Wren had already begun to design buildings, it was more sophisticated. A plan proposed by Robert Hooke, based on a grid pattern with boulevards and arteries, was shown first to the Royal Society, and then to the King (Plates 10–12). Two schemes recommended simple rectangular sites. The first, by the cartographer Richard Newcourt, consisted of a series of identical blocks, each centred on a church and churchyard.[40] The second, by Captain Valentine Knight, had two main streets running west to east, and eight running north to south, interconnected by smaller lanes. A new canal was proposed, running in a loop from Billingsgate to the Fleet, which Knight suggested could charge tolls towards the financing of the whole project. Unfortunately, Charles was so offended by this proposal, accusing Knight of trying to make financial gain at the expense of the calamity that had befallen Londoners, that he ordered his immediate arrest. The dramatist Thomas Shadwell, who liked to satirise current events in his plays, included reference to the many schemes in *The Sullen Lovers* performed in 1668.

The King, recognising the importance of speedy resolution, proclaimed the principal outlines of the new city on 13 September. Rebuilding was forbidden until owners had cleared their debris from thoroughfares and established their claims. All the redevelopment schemes that had been submitted were soon rejected on the grounds that they were impractical. John Evelyn was ruefully to write in his commonplace book how 'London since the Conflagration might so have been made the most beautiful, uniforme and usefull and stately Citty in Europe, had K. Chas II taken any care about it; But the Women and his love of ease broke up all his Thoughts; so he minded nothing'.[41] Here he was being unfair to the King, for rather than indulgence, idealism had to give way to reality. The nation was at war with both the Dutch and the French, and it was vital that London returned as rapidly as possible to being a functioning commercial city. It was decided therefore that rebuilding would take place on previously occupied sites, although some streets should be widened and the houses be constructed in brick and stone. Regulations stipulated that public buildings should be reconstructed with revenue from a coal tax, while private houses were to be rebuilt with 'two storeys for bylanes, three storeys along the river and for streets and lanes of note, four storeys for high streets and mansion houses for citizens of extraordinary quality'. Two of Evelyn's suggestions were initially retained: that there should be a quay on an embankment stretching from the Temple to the Tower of London; and that noxious but necessary industries, such as brewing, dyeing, and the boiling of salt, sugar and soap, were to be moved to special quarters, such as Bow to the east, or Wandsworth to the west. However, in the course of time, even these plans were abandoned.

The City authorities met with the King's Council and agreed that a small commission of experts be appointed to survey and map all the properties and establish a set of building rules. The King's three nominees to this commission were Christopher Wren, Hugh May and Roger Pratt, the three architects who only a few weeks earlier had debated the plans for refurbishing St Paul's. The City chose two experienced craftsmen, Peter Mills and Edward Jerman, plus Robert Hooke, whose redevelopment plan had greatly impressed them. Wren and Hooke were already good friends, and this must have been a factor in the City's decision to nominate the latter. The combination proved a masterstroke, for in an extraordinarily short space of time the City was being rebuilt.

Evelyn's hopes of being involved were dashed, although he kept a careful watch on progress. Indeed, he even planned to make suitable bricks at Sayes Court for the building of the embankment on the north side of the Thames. He had been impressed by the bricks or clinkers that he had observed in Amsterdam a quarter of a century earlier, so went into partnership with Sir Jan Klevit, a Dutch political exile. But the Deptford clay proved unsuitable and the project foundered, along with the embankment itself. In a letter to a friend, Mary wrote that the advantage of the enterprise was only in prospect, whilt the expense was certain and immediate. Pepys was less charitable, noting in his diary in September 1668:

> at noone comes Mr. Eveling to me about some business with the office, and there in discourse tells me of his loss, to the value of 500l, which he hath met with in a late attempt of making Bricks upon an adventure with others, by which he presumed to have got a great deal of money – so that I see the most ingenious men may sometimes be mistaken.[42]

The 'business with the office' is a reference to the commission for the sick and wounded that Pepys and Evelyn had been engaged upon during the Anglo-Dutch War. They had begun to correspond with each other over the many practical difficulties, and these early letters, often expressing despair at the lack of funds available and the plight of 'these miserable Creatures', are mostly brief and businesslike.[43] But on 21 August 1669, John Evelyn wrote a letter of a very different kind. Pepys had decided to take a holiday in France with Elizabeth. He was very concerned about his eyesight, which had been increasingly troubling him. At the end of May of that year he wrote in his diary:

> And thus ends all that I doubt I shall ever be able to do with my own eyes in the keeping of my journal, I being not able to do it any longer, having done now so long as to undo my eyes almost every time that I take a pen in my hand; ... And so I betake myself to that course which [is] almost as much as to see myself go into my grave – for

which, and all the discomforts that will accompany my being blind, the good God prepare me.[44]

In a long letter, Evelyn provided Pepys with what he called his 'Rhapsodies' on the forthcoming 'Running Voyage'. Using his diary from the time that he had visited and lived in France, he gave Pepys a detailed list of places to see on his way to Paris, and the sights of the capital itself.[45] Appreciating that Pepys had a shared interest in books and prints, he told him where he might purchase them, and gave him letters of introduction to people who would help him. Elizabeth Pepys was, in fact, already familiar with Paris because she had spent some of her childhood there. This was a tour itinerary full of exciting places for the couple to enjoy, which makes all the more poignant the next letter in the correspondence with Evelyn. It is from Pepys, dated 2 November, explaining that they had arrived home in London ten days earlier, but that his wife had contracted an illness in Flanders and 'hath layne under a fever soe severe as at this houre to render her recoverey desperate'.[46]

Frantic efforts were made to save her, but Elizabeth Pepys died on 10 November, aged just twenty-nine. She was buried three days later in their parish church of St Olave's, Hart Street, with Evelyn among the mourners at the night-time ceremony. Pepys commissioned a memorial bust from the sculptor John Bushnell that shows her animated as if in mid-sentence, which still looks down from high up on the church wall (Plate 13).

Despite their many years of quarrels as chronicled in the diaries, Pepys was devastated by the death of his wife, and this may well be one of the reasons that he never seriously took up his diary quill again. His eyes did recover, and he was able to make shorthand notes for reports, although he found too much brightness painful. Perhaps a few months of not undertaking the very considerable chore of keeping a daily record came as such a welcome relief that he felt he could not go back to it. Whatever the reason, or reasons, a wonderfully vivid and detailed record of the time was lost, and henceforward we are dependent on the diaries of Evelyn and of others, along with the correspondence that shows the development of the friendship between the two men.

3

PRODIGIOUS REVOLUTIONS

T HE END OF the 1660s not only marked a watershed as far as Samuel Pepys's life was concerned, it also signalled a turning point in the national political scene. The fall of Lord Clarendon, Charles II's powerful minister, came in 1667, partly as a result of the Dutch Medway disaster. Instead, England was governed by a group of five ministers whose initials spell out 'Cabal': Lord Clifford of Chudleigh, a Roman Catholic; Henry Bennet, Earl of Arlington, also a Catholic; George Villiers, Duke of Buckingham, one of the court's most outrageous rakes who nevertheless represented the Puritan interest; Anthony Ashley Cooper, Earl of Shaftesbury, strongly anti-Catholic; and John Maitland, Duke of Lauderdale, who ruled Scotland with a heavy hand. A totally disparate group, they were regularly deceived by the King, even though they were carrying out his policies.

Religion became once more the centre of dissension. At some time around 1668 the Duke of York converted to Roman Catholicism, possibly led to the decision by his strong-minded wife, Anne Hyde. This move was not made public, but seems to have been known, for when in July 1669 Pepys decided to stand as a parliamentary candidate for Aldeburgh in Suffolk, with the Duke's support, he was accused of being a Catholic. Apparently one of those in the dark about James's conversion, Pepys protested in a letter to the bailiff in charge of the election:

I do wonder from what ground any question could be raised, my education at the University ... and the whole practice of my life, both past and present, giving testimony of my being no Papist, besides the duty of my place, which obliges me not only to take the Oaths of Allegiance and Supremacy but to administer it myself to every man that takes the charge as master of any of the King's ships.[1]

He duly lost the by-election, unable to find time to visit the town and damned by the accusations of his opponents. His association with the Duke of York was going to make life very difficult for him.

Although the Anglo-Dutch War of 1664–7 had been fought against not only the United Provinces, but France too, the royal family's links with France were strong. Louis XIV was first cousin to the Stuarts, while Charles's sister, Minette, was married to the Duc d'Orléans, the Sun King's brother. With Minette acting as a go-between, Charles signed the secret Treaty of Dover in 1670. As one historian has put it, 'This is one of the most startling obligations ever imposed on a fortunately ignorant nation'.[2] Louis XIV undertook to give a substantial subsidy to his cousin so that he could raise an army and re-equip the navy. In return Charles was to co-operate with the French in the destruction of the Dutch Republic and the partition of its overseas possessions. He was also to declare his Catholicism and lead England back to the Church of Rome; in the event of disturbance following such an attempt, he could depend on Louis to support him with French troops.

So breathtaking was the perilous ambition of such an agreement that most historians assume it represented a confidence trick on Charles's part, to acquire the subsidy that would enable him to avoid asking for money from Parliament. The few that were let into the secret included James and the two Catholic sympathisers of the Cabal, Arlington and Clifford. Somehow the rest of the nation was kept blissfully ignorant and the treaty remained a secret for over a century. Charles, with characteristic guile, allowed Buckingham to make a second treaty with France, similar to his own, but without the clauses concerning religion.

Adding a frisson to the whole proceedings, Louise de Kéroualle was dispatched by Louis XIV to England, and became Charles's mistress.

John Evelyn reported with grim disapproval the story of this aid to the alliance:

> It was universaly reported that the faire Lady – was bedded one of these nights, and the stocking flung after the manner of a married Bride: I acknowledge she was for the most part in her undresse [informal dress] all day, and there was a fondnesse, & toying, with that young wanton: however twas with confidence believed that she was first made a *Misse*, as they cald those unhappy creatures, with solemnity, at this time.[3]

This mock marriage took place at Arlington's Suffolk home, Euston Hall. Louise's arrival into the group of royal mistresses was greeted with hostility, especially from Nell Gwyn, the 'Protestant whore', who made many quips at her expense, including calling her 'Squintabella' and 'Weeping Willow'.

In 1672 Charles began to implement the policy of the agreement by issuing a Declaration of Indulgence, a royal command for religious toleration in the kingdom, followed shortly by a declaration of war on the Dutch. At first things went well for the allies: in May the English fleet scored a success against the Dutch at Southwold Bay off the Suffolk coast. The battle, however, claimed the life of Edward Montague, Lord Sandwich, in command on the *Royal James*. He seems to have had a premonition of what was to come, for when news arrived that the Dutch were approaching he bade his valet tie back his long hair and dress him in his full regalia as a Knight of the Garter. During the battle the *Royal James* was set alight by a fireship, killing almost everyone on board: Sandwich's body was found two weeks later, still wearing his Garter ribbon. Pepys, who owed so much to his cousin, took part in the state funeral in Westminster Abbey, having charge of one of the banners displaying the dead man's arms, which were carried alongside the coffin and then laid over his resting place.

While the English were fighting the Dutch at sea, the French swept into the United Provinces, forcing the inhabitants to breach dykes to flood the countryside and halt the onslaught. The Dutch responded by murdering their leader, Johann de Witt, and placing themselves under the control of Prince William of Orange, Charles II's nephew, who managed to stem the tide and keep the French at bay.

The Third Anglo-Dutch War brought Pepys and Evelyn together once more to try to alleviate the plight of distressed seamen, as graphically shown in their correspondence. In one letter Evelyn told Pepys how he had scarcely been to bed for days, as he was totally taken up with visits to Chatham, Rochester and the Fleete, where he found that

> unlesse you be pleasd to allow some Covering to the poore Creatures, who are (many of them) put stark naked and mortified, on the shore: multitudes of them must perish; and therefore (presuming on your Charity, and indeede humanity) I have adventur'd to give way, that some of the most miserable should have shirts or stockings (according to their needes) to preserve them from perishing ... That his Majestie may not loose his Subjects for want of so slight and yet necessary supply.[4]

There were to be no more victories for the English fleet, and the King faced a hostile Parliament when it met in February 1673. Members were furious that he had declared war during their absence and issued the Declaration of Indulgence without consultation. The declaration was duly rescinded, and instead the Test Act was passed, obliging all office holders under the Crown to affirm their loyalty to the Church of England, forcing the Duke of York to resign as Lord High Admiral. His Duchess, Anne, had died two years earlier, and with the classic bad timing that only James could muster, he announced that he was going to remarry, choosing Mary of Modena, a Catholic princess of fifteen. This decision caused uproar, for Mary could be expected to provide him with sons, heirs to the throne in precedence over Mary and Anne, his daughters by Anne Hyde. Mary of Modena arrived in London on 4 November, the eve of Guy Fawkes Night, already established as the occasion for anti-Catholic celebrations. John Evelyn duly noted in his diary: 'This night the youths of the Citty burnt the Pope in Effigie after they had made procession with it in great triumph:

displeased at the D: [James] for altering his Religion, & now marrying an Italian Lady'.[5]

For Pepys, these were roller-coaster times. Recognising his ability and loyalty, the King promoted him, at the age of forty, to the post of Secretary to the Admiralty Board. But when Pepys decided to stand again for Parliament, this time for Castle Rising in Norfolk, with support from the Duke of York, he was once more accused by the crowd at the election of being a 'bluddy Papist', while the Earl of Shaftesbury lent secret support to his rival. Although Pepys submitted testimonials of his Anglican faith to the voters, and won the election, the accusations of papism stuck. Arriving in Westminster in January 1674, he found himself again under attack, having to answer charges sent to the Commons by Shaftesbury to the effect that he had seen Catholic objects of worship and books in Pepys's home. Pepys stood up in the House and 'did heartily and flatly deny, that he had any Altar, or Crucifix, or the Image of a Picture of any Saint whatsoever in his House, from the Top to the Bottom of it'.[6] He was certainly being economical with the truth, for the catalogue of his library shows that there were such books and religious prints in his collection. Rescue came when the King prorogued Parliament and sittings were discontinued until the end of the year.

Instead, Pepys got on with bringing reform to the administration of the navy. At this time it was not a recognisable or permanent force, nor was there a distinction drawn between the military and mercantile sections. Pepys, with his genius for organisation, set about the immense task of bringing some order and regularity to a wide range of areas, from the running of dockyards and the construction and fitting out of ships, to their armament and stores, and the standards of diet and health for the seamen.

One of the areas to which he attached great importance was the officer structure. At the time of the Restoration, the majority of the naval officers were what Pepys called 'bred seamen', sometimes given the disparaging nickname of 'tarpaulins'. But the King and the Duke of York soon brought in a number of new officers drawn from court circles, known as 'gentlemen'. Whilst some of the latter had military knowledge, they were not experienced in seamanship. Along with his naval colleagues, Pepys had become a Brother of Trinity House, the public authority for lights, beacons and buoys, with membership drawn mostly from masters and pilots working on the Thames. In 1676, when Pepys became Master, here too he began to reform record keeping and working methods, and to push for 'reformadoes', prospective lieutenants and captains of sixth-rate warships, to be subject to tests of competence by the Trinity House brethren. He also arranged for them to examine boys from Christ's Hospital School, founded in the sixteenth century and located in Newgate Street. In 1673 he had taken a leading role in the establishment of the Royal Mathematical School at Christ's Hospital for forty boys to be trained in the science of navigation for both the royal and the mercantile services.

By the mid-1670s two political factions were emerging. The first, led by Shaftesbury, was the Country Party, which campaigned against the Duke of York and Queen Catherine, and for the Dutch. Nicknamed 'Little Sincerity' for his diminutive stature and alacrity at changing sides, Shaftesbury drew his strength from the City, coffee-houses and the mob. His supporters were known as Whigs, a name given to Scottish outlaws. Opposed to him was Thomas Osborne, Earl of Danby. He built up support in Parliament through judicious bribes, and his followers were dubbed Tories, the name given to Irish thieves and outlaws. Danby was strongly loyal to the Anglican Church. He was the patron of Henry Compton, Bishop of London, who as dean of the Chapels Royal was responsible for the spiritual education of the Princesses Mary and Anne, defying their father, the Duke of York, by having them confirmed into the Church of England. In 1677 Danby managed to persuade the King to agree to the marriage of Mary with her cousin, William of Orange. This further infuriated the Duke and Louis XIV, who was fighting head to head with William in Europe, but it did strengthen the possibility of a Protestant future for the English monarchy.

The uneasy equilibrium of the country was thrown into turmoil once again with the revelation of the Popish Plot. In 1678 two men – Israel Tonge, a cleric who specialised in the discovery of Jesuit conspiracies, and Titus Oates, who had been both an Anglican clergyman and a

Jesuit priest and who made his living by swearing testimony to bring culprits to justice – claimed evidence of a Catholic conspiracy to murder the King and supplant him with James. The unsavoury pair announced that the Pope was in the plot along with Louis XIV, and that English Catholics were preparing to rise up, murder Protestant citizens and burn the City of London. The King initially refused to take this claim seriously, until Edward Coleman, Secretary to the Duchess of York, was discovered to have had potentially treasonable correspondence with prominent European Catholics. Shortly after, the dead body of Sir Edmund Berry Godfrey was discovered on Primrose Hill: Godfrey was the London magistrate to whom Oates and Tonge had sworn their testimony. His corpse showed signs of murder, though the case remained unsolved. The conclusion drawn was that a Catholic plot was afoot, and mass hysteria ensued. Evelyn captured the atmosphere in one of his letters, in which he described himself as battered by 'the publique Confusions in Church and Kingdome (never to be sufficiently deplor'd) and which cannot but most sensibly touch every sober and honest man'.[7]

Coleman was tried and executed, and five Catholic peers were sent to the Tower of London along with many other suspects, including Samuel Pepys. He considered himself a Tory, as he later made clear in a letter to a friend, whom he addressed as 'Your Whigship'.[8] In February 1679, when Shaftesbury compiled a list of MPs, he marked his supporters with a w, denoting worthy, while his opponents had a v, for vile. Pepys was marked v.[9]

In the weeks before his imprisonment, the 'vile' Pepys had in fact been striving to ensure that the navy was not infiltrated by Catholics, writing of 'the whole government seeming at this day to remain in such a state of distraction and fear, as no history I believe can parallel'.[10] He did have in his household a Catholic, Cesare Morelli, who helped him with his music. When Catholics were banned from coming within a thirty-mile radius of London, he got Morelli away to Brentwood in Essex. However, one of his clerks, Samuel Atkyns, was then arrested, accused of being an accessory to the murder of Godfrey. Despite intense pressure being applied by Shaftesbury, Atkyns refused to implicate Pepys, and in his turn Pepys undertook some detective work that provided an alibi for his clerk for the time of Godfrey's murder, which led to his acquittal. But the attacks on Pepys in Parliament increased in strength, and his opponents found men prepared to accuse him of selling naval secrets to France. One was his ex-butler, John James, who bore a grudge because he had been dismissed after Morelli found him in bed with the housekeeper. Although once again Pepys mounted a strong defence, he was borne down and, resigning as Secretary to the Admiralty, was committed to the Serjeant at Arms and taken to the Tower.

Pepys's sojourn, first in the Tower and then in the Marshalsea in Southwark, was not too uncomfortable. He was able to dispatch his brother-in-law, Balthasar St Michel, to France to gather evidence for his defence. He also received visitors, including John Evelyn. On 4 June 1679 Evelyn noted in his diary: 'Din'd with Mr Pepys at the Tower, whither he was committed by the house of Commons, for misdemeanors in the Admiralty, where he was Secretary; but I believe unjustly'.[11] When Pepys was transferred to the Marshalsea, Evelyn sent him some venison, and then went to dine with him, presumably sharing the joint. On 9 July Pepys was released on bail as no charges had been preferred against him – somewhat to his chagrin, as he had gone to great lengths to prepare his defence and to unmask his accuser and their agents as dupes. The following March, on his deathbed, John James admitted that he had been lying, and eventually Pepys was released from his bail. Recognising that he had been in real danger, and that others had been executed as a result of the Popish Plot, Pepys compiled a huge book of the documents, letters, journals, verbatim statements and court proceedings, which is still in its manuscript form in the Pepys Library at Magdalene College, Cambridge. He called it 'my Book of Mornamont', after a bogus French estate claimed by one of his other accusers, a supreme fantasist, 'Colonel' Scott.

Pepys went to live with his former manservant and clerk Will Hewer, who had become a man of substance; Evelyn was to describe him as having gained a 'very considerable Estate in the Navy'.[12] Although Pepys's home in Seething Lane had been spared by the Great Fire of London, it succumbed to flames seven years later, and he lost all his personal possessions and mementoes of his life with Elizabeth. The

Crown had been obliged to rehouse him, but now he was to have a home of his own again with Hewer, in York Buildings in Buckingham Street, off the Strand. York Buildings was the general name for the houses erected on the site of York House, sold to a syndicate by the Duke of Buckingham in 1672. Three years later waterworks were built on the west side of Villiers Street to provide a supply to the surrounding houses. This was a prime site for a London residence, close to Whitehall and Westminster, with easy access to the river: John Evelyn was to take one of the houses in Villiers Street when his daughters were presented at court.

The threat of a Catholic succession to the throne was not going to go away. Shaftesbury whipped up resistance in what are termed the Exclusion Crises, proposing that James should be excluded from the succession in favour of the King's eldest illegitimate son, the Duke of Monmouth. Charles was adamantly opposed to this, and engineered Shaftesbury's fall in 1681. Prompted by the King, John Dryden poetically rendered Shaftesbury as the duplicitous adviser Achitophel in his allegorical poem *Absalom and Achitophel*: 'In friendship false, implacable in hate / Resolv'd to ruin or to rule the state.'[13] Shaftesbury went into exile, but did not give up his determination to secure a Protestant succession. He urged Monmouth, along with Whig aristocrats including William, Lord Russell, Henry Sidney and Arthur Capel, Earl of Essex, into a conspiracy that Evelyn called the 'Protestant Plot'. Meanwhile, a small group of fanatics, led by an old Cromwellian soldier, planned to ambush the King and the Duke of York at Rye House on their way back to London from Newmarket. When this was foiled, it was used as the opportunity to eliminate the Protestant plotters. Russell and Sidney were executed, Essex committed suicide and Monmouth was allowed to escape to Holland. A kind of calm was finally established, with the King ruling without Parliament until the end of his reign.

Charles continued to look kindly upon Pepys, and in August 1683, at two days' notice, he was bidden to Portsmouth 'without any account of the reason for it', ready to embark for an unknown period of time and destination under the command of George Legge, Earl of Dartmouth.

Once aboard ship, Pepys was informed by Dartmouth that their mission was to oversee the abandonment of the British settlement in Tangier, or as he put it in a letter to his friend James Houblon, 'withdrawing . . . all forces and subjects from this place, rendering it desolate'.[14] Pepys had longed to travel abroad, but his desire would have been to see the great cities of Europe, so this must have come as a disappointment. It was made worse by the irony that his late cousin, Lord Sandwich, had conceived the idea of Tangier as a naval base when it was given to England as part of Catherine of Braganza's dowry in 1662. Sandwich had chosen a site to build a mole to provide sheltered mooring, and now Pepys was to be a 'sulphur-monger' to demolish it, working alongside the engineer Henry Sheeres, the very man who had built the structure twenty years earlier.

The Tangier project took approximately six months, and during this time Pepys kept what is now called his Second Diary. This stands in marked contrast to what might be described as his First Diary of the 1660s. There is none of the *joie de vivre* of the latter, and even the details of local life in Tangier are not particularly vivid. Instead it dwells upon considerations of social class within the navy, and charts with dismay the corruption of officials. Pepys reflected at Cadiz on his journey home, 'On the whole, it is plain this business of money, which runs through and debauches the whole service of the navy, is now come to the highest degree of infamy, and nobody considers it.'[15] It is in his letters to his friends that Pepys provides some sparkle and wit. For instance, in a letter to John Evelyn, written just as he was about to set off from Portsmouth, he describes his fellow passengers as being like a high table of a university college in miniature:

as delightfull as companions of the first forme in Divinity, Law, Physick, and the usefullest parts of Mathematics can render it, namely Dr. Ken [Thomas, chaplain to Lord Dartmouth], Dr. Trumbull [William, Judge Advocate], Dr. Lawrence [physician to Lord Dartmouth], and Mr. Shere [Henry, engineer]; with additionall pleasure of concerts (much above the ordinary) of Voices, Flutes and Violins; and to fillings (if any thing can do't where Mr Evelyn is wanting), good humour, good Cheere, good books, the company of my neerest friend Mr. Hewer, and a reasonable prospect of being home againe in lesse than two months.[16]

In fact, Pepys's hope to be back in two months was not fulfilled, but when he did return to London in the spring of 1684 Charles II gave him a very important job. As Secretary for the Affairs of the Admiralty of England, Pepys had in effect been accorded ministerial powers, with a handsome annual salary of £2,000 plus additional payments for passes and appointments. He had access to the King and the Duke of York at least once a week, and began to prepare for them a report on the state of the navy, including the 'disorders and distresses' into which he found it had fallen.

For John Evelyn, the early 1680s provided a period of reflection. Unlike Pepys, whose medical problems were so manifold that it is a miracle he survived into old age, Evelyn usually enjoyed good health, but in 1682 he suffered a scare with a series of fits. He dealt with these by sitting in what he described as a 'deepe Churn or Vessell', drinking an infusion of thistle, and going, heavily swaddled, to bed. Taking note of 'this Warning & admonition', he put his papers in order, made an inventory of Sayes Court and a new will, and looked back through his diary, working it into a continuous narrative.[17] The diary is also increasingly filled with notes of the sermons that he heard. He had become close to a group of Anglican divines known as Latitudinarians, men who hoped that by making concessions in those rites and ordinances that were of purely human institution, the Church of England might attract back some nonconformists. In particular, Evelyn developed a friendship with Thomas Tenison, vicar of St Martin-in-the-Fields.

Evelyn had been concerned with financial difficulties arising from the encumbrance of the estate of his father-in-law – the 'tedious Chancery Suit' as he called it. Pepys had nominated him for a post on the Navy Board, and although this did not materialise, a project dear to his heart did in the autumn of 1681: the creation of Chelsea Hospital. A theology college established on the site in 1618 had not prospered, and during the Second Anglo-Dutch War it was intended to house prisoners of war under Evelyn's supervision. Although in 1666 it was granted to the Royal Society, the buildings were too dilapidated for use. Now the Paymaster-General, Sir Stephen Fox, asked Evelyn as a council member of the Royal Society to persuade the fellows to sell their interest in the site. Fox was prepared to pay the substantial sum of £1,300 out of his own pocket so that a barracks could be built for elderly ex-combatants. His generosity was prompted by shame at seeing honourable ex-soldiers reduced to begging in the street, which he thought 'a scandal to the kingdom'.[18]

Evelyn must have been doubly pleased, for not only was the money badly needed by the Royal Society, which had got itself into a financial pickle, but he had long cherished such a project. During his visit to Amsterdam in 1641 he had visited various hospitals including 'one appointed for the Lame, & disabled Soulders & Seamen; where the accomodations are very greate, the building answerable, and indeed for the like publique Charitys, the provisions are admirable'.[19] In the 1660s he had tried to get such an establishment founded at Chatham. Pepys noted in his diary taking a coach journey with him in 1666 to Clapham, during which Evelyn 'perticularly ... intertained me with discourse of an Infirmery, which he hath projected for the sick and wounded seamen against the next year, which I mightily approve of – and will endeavour to promote it, being a worthy thing – and of use, and will save money'.[20] Unfortunately, Pepys's wise counsel did not prevail, and the project had lapsed.

The Chelsea scheme had the great advantage of the King's support, for he was well aware of Louis XIV's Hôtel des Invalides in Paris, and Evelyn became involved in the planning. He recommended that 400 men be housed in thirty-two dormitories with regulations which were to be 'as strickt as in any religious Convent', and that a library be established 'since some souldiers might possibly be studious, when they were at this leisure to recolect'.[21] Christopher Wren was appointed architect, and the King laid the foundation stone in 1682. Within seven years, 476 old pensioners were admitted, and the buildings were completed in 1692.

Evelyn's intimations of mortality proved unfounded, but it was not so for Charles II, who unexpectedly suffered a stroke on 1 February 1685.

John Evelyn recorded in detail in his diary the efforts of the royal physicians to save the King, but it was in vain. Five days later, Charles II died. Evelyn composed a measured summation of the Merry Monarch: 'A prince of many Virtues, & many greate Imperfections, Debonaire, Easy of accesse, not bloudy or Cruel'. Among those 'imperfections' mentioned by Evelyn was the addiction that Charles had to 'Women, which made him uneasy & allways in Want to supply their unmeasurable profusion, & to the detriment of many indigent persons who had signaly serv'd both him & his father: Easily, & frequently he changed favorites to his greate prejudice'.[22]

Evelyn recorded that the King's deathbed had been attended by the Archbishop of Canterbury, William Sancroft, and other bishops including Thomas Ken, now Bishop of Bath and Wells, who offered him the sacrament according to the Church of England. Although he hoped it was not correct, Evelyn also noted that a Benedictine monk, John Huddleston, 'had presum'd to administer the popish Offices'.[23] This was, however, precisely what happened, with the priest smuggled in by Charles's mistress, Louise de Kéroualle, aided by the Duke of York, thus enabling the dying King to make his peace with the Catholic Church. Samuel Pepys soon heard a rumour of this and, greatly daring, asked the new King, James II, to confirm it. Later he met up with Evelyn and passed on the information. The deception clearly shocked Evelyn, who turned it over at length in his diary entry for 2 October, and interestingly wrote that he preferred James's open Catholicism to Charles's secrecy. His view of the new King was that he was possessed 'of a most sincere and honest nature, one upon whose word, one may relie', and he expressed his confidence that 'the Church of England may yet subsist; & when it shall please God, to open his Eyes, & turne his heart (for that is peculiarly in the Lords hande) to flourish also'.[24]

Many shared Evelyn's desire to find the best intentions in the new King. Shortly after his accession, James told the nation that he intended to preserve the government 'in Church and State, as is now by law established. I know the principles of the Church of England are for monarchy and the members of it have shewed themselves good and loyal subjects, therefore I shall always take care to defend and support it'.[25] Pepys had merely been one of the crowd at Charles II's coronation in 1661, but now for James's crowning he played an important role as senior Baron of the Cinque Ports, carrying one of the poles of the royal canopy (Plate 15). Although the music was magnificent, James's coronation was considerably truncated, for he did not wish to communicate with the Church of which he was the Supreme Governor. Moreover, the crown slipped on his head and the royal canopy broke, incidents that were later regarded as omens of significance.

When the Duke of Monmouth landed in the West Country and raised the flag of rebellion, the country did not rally to his cause. Instead, he was totally defeated at the Battle of Sedgemoor on 5 July 1685. Pulled ignominiously out of a ditch in the New Forest by the King's troops, and suffering from a heavy cold, he cannot have been reassured by his companion, Lord Grey, who told him that if his cold was troubling him, his uncle had a ready cure for it. Monmouth had been able to secure forgiveness from his father for plotting against him in the summer of 1683, but this was a very different scenario. Enraged by the publication of Monmouth's declaration that branded him responsible for all the ills of the kingdom from the Fire of London to the death of Charles II, James withheld all hopes of mercy, and the young man was executed on 15 July. Evelyn noted in his diary, 'Thus ended this quondam duke, darling of his father and the ladies, being extraordin[ar]ily handsome, and adroit: an excellent souldier, & dauncer, a favorite of the people, of an Easy nature, debauch'd by lusts, seduc'd by crafty knaves. He failed and perished.'[26]

His followers suffered terrible fates. Many received summary executions at the hands of the troops who had been recalled from Morocco and were ironically dubbed the Lambs. They were led by Colonel Kirke, a man singled out by Pepys in his Tangier diary for his brutality and corruption.[27] Those who survived were handed over to the judgement of the Bloody Assizes presided over by Judge Jeffreys. Around 300 were hanged, drawn and quartered and their bodies displayed as a warning against further thought of rebellion. On his return to London, the judge was rewarded by James with the office of Lord Chancellor. Evelyn noted in his diary how Jeffreys 'has serv'd the Court Interest upon all the hardiest occasions', adding later, 'of nature cruell & a slave of this Court'.[28]

Evelyn was able to observe Jeffreys at first hand because he was about to be sworn in as a commissioner of the Privy Seal, one of three appointed to take the place of the King's brother-in-law, Henry Hyde, Earl of Clarendon, who had gone to Ireland as Lord Lieutenant. Whilst Pepys had spent almost all his working life as a servant of the Crown, Evelyn had only done so intermittently, cushioned by his independent means. Now, with his estates encumbered by financial problems, he had to deal with the moral dilemma of serving under a monarch whose agenda could clash with his own strong Protestant principles.

The King's success at quashing Monmouth's rebellion served as encouragement for him to push forward with his Grand Design: a strong army on the French model, a powerful navy, becoming a major player in European affairs, the expansion of trade and empire, complete liberty of conscience and, last but not least, rule through his own choice of ministers and bureaucracy without the advice of Parliament, whose role should be to approve his policies. The man who emerged as James's chief minister was Robert Spencer, Earl of Sunderland, whose main interest was to stay in power. As other ministers fell by the wayside, dismissed for resisting the King's push towards Catholicism, Sunderland stayed the course, eventually himself converting. Evelyn, who had given the King the benefit of the doubt at his accession, was horrified by the turn of events, writing in his diary of Sunderland, 'by a fatal Apostacy, & Court ambition he has made himself unworthy'.[29]

Despite the continued existence of the Test Act, Roman Catholics were now introduced into corporations, the navy and the standing army. High officials were sacked when they refused to convert, judges were intimidated. James was also interfering in the affairs of the universities. A vivid personal example is provided in a letter written in February 1687 to Pepys by Dr John Peachall, Master of Magdalene and Vice-Chancellor of Cambridge University. Pepys was a generous bene-factor to his former college, and Peachall knew that he had the ear of the King. Peachall explained to him: 'I must not conceale from such a friend as you what before this comes at you will be known in Court and City. His Majesty was pleasd to send a letter directed to me, as Vicechancellor to admit one Alban Francis, a Benedictine Monk Master of Arts without administering any oath or oaths to him.' He then explains his dilemma: 'I could not tell what to do, decline his Majesties Letter, or his Lawes.' Pepys's immediate response is not known, and in May 1687 Peachall was suspended from the mastership and deprived of the vice-chancellorship.[30]

John Peachall was one of many officials who were caught up in the testing of the anti-papal laws. In July 1686, Henry Compton, Bishop of London, was tried before the new Ecclesiastical Commission Court for refusing to dismiss a rector who had preached an anti-papal sermon, and was suspended from his office. He retired to tend his famous garden at Fulham Palace, but he was to prove the vanguard of an episcopal resistance. In 1687, James issued his first declaration of liberty of conscience, granted to all denominations in England and Scotland, and in April of 1688 he followed it with a second declaration, which he ordered to be read in all churches. Archbishop Sancroft and six other bishops petitioned the King not to insist on the reading of what they held to be an illegal order, and were summoned to his presence. Pepys was in attendance when the King questioned them and was advised by his chief minister Sunderland and Judge Jeffreys to let them off with a warning. He decided instead to arrest them on a charge of seditious libel and send them to the Tower. The febrile atmosphere of London was captured by Evelyn in his diary: 'Wonderfull was the concerne for them [the bishops], infinite crowds of people on their knees, begging their blessing & praying for them as they passed out of the Barge; along the Tower wharfe'.[31]

Pepys was also called as a witness at the trial in Westminster Hall in June 1688. He was in a quandary, for one of the accused was his friend, Thomas Ken, whom he had got to know during their voyage to Tangier. Treading a careful path, he said nothing that could help either side. Although under pressure from the King, two of the four judges summed up clearly in the bishops' favour, and the jury, who had been kept up all night without light or water, found them not guilty. Jubilation broke out with the London mob cheering the bishops as they left the court. Most ominously for the King, those cheers were echoed by his soldiers encamped west of the city, at Hounslow.

The very next entry after Evelyn's description of the crowd supporting the bishops as they arrived at the Tower was his note of the birth of a son to James and Mary of Modena. Later he added the classic understatement, 'which will cost dispute'. Mary had undergone six previous pregnancies, two resulting in miscarriage, four in children who had died in infancy. Despite this history, James was jubilant and, convinced that the child would be a boy, pressed on with his Great Design, including the second declaration just mentioned. Mary went into labour a month earlier than expected, so that it was suspected that a changeling Prince of Wales was to be foisted on the nation. The Queen had added to this idea by refusing to allow anybody to see her belly or feel the baby during her pregnancy. Anne, her hostile stepdaughter, wrote to her sister Mary in Holland: 'I believe when she [the Queen] is brought to bed, nobody will be convinced it is her child, except it prove a daughter. For my part, I declare I shall not, except I see the child and she parted.'[32] Mary could not avoid the custom of giving birth before a number of witnesses, and over thirty people crowded into her bedroom in St James's Palace to listen to her cries in labour. It was claimed afterwards that a warming pan was slipped into her bed with a baby concealed inside, but there is no doubt that Mary gave birth. Another claim was that the new baby was taken into an adjoining chamber by the midwives and Lady Sunderland before being shown to the assembly. So rumour swirled around the birth of James Francis Edward Stuart, later to be known as the Old Pretender.

Whatever the truth, the nation was seriously alarmed by the prospect that the King's pro-Catholic policies might become a permanent fixture under a Catholic heir. Characteristically, the King blundered ahead, inviting the Pope to be his son's godfather. John and Mary Evelyn watched a spectacular firework display that celebrated 'the Queen's upsitting', her recovery after childbirth: 'We stood at Mr. Pepys's Secretary of the Admiralty to greate advantage for the sight, & indeede they were very fine, & had cost some thousands of pounds about the pyramids & statues &c: but were spent too soone, for so long a preparation' (Plate 19).[33] More fireworks of a very different kind were to follow.

Totally different sections of the kingdom were coming together in opposition to James. Tory gentry and Anglican clergy, disillusioned by the promises made by the King at the beginning of his reign, were now joined by moderate Catholics worried about the future and dissenters who suspected that the declarations of tolerance represented a snare. In January 1687, William of Orange dispatched to England his agent Everard van Weede, Lord of Dijkvelt, to assure James II, both his uncle and his father-in-law, that he wanted to support him, so long as he abandoned attempts to alter laws against Catholics without the consent of Parliament. Foolishly, James denied Dijkvelt an early audience, and instead the Dutchman made contact with influential politicians right across the spectrum to tell them that the Prince was backing their efforts against the King's policy.

The idea that he might actually attempt an invasion of England probably formed in William's mind in the late spring of the following year. First, he had to make careful preparations, and ensure that his European allies would keep Louis XIV busy. James played into his hands when he refused the French King's offer of troops, fearful of the effect this might have on English opinion, and mindful of his brother Charles's underhand dealings in the secret Treaty of Dover. This position of principle was a disastrous one, and when James realised his mistake, it was too late: Louis could not respond, bogged down as he was on his eastern front in Germany. Princess Mary, meanwhile, was seeking friends in high places at the English court, maintaining correspondence with her sister using code names. One friend who responded was John Churchill, husband of Sarah, Princess Anne's bosom companion. He wrote to William 'to give you assurances under my own hand that my places and the King's favour I set at nought in comparison of being true to my religion'.[34] William could also boast possibly the best propaganda machines in Europe. A manifesto entitled *Declaration of Reasons for Appearing in Arms in England*, written by William's adviser Caspar Fagel, pronounced that the Prince opposed persecution, and suggested that the British nation should look to him to stop King James attacking their liberties. Copies poured off the Dutch printing presses.

A huge fleet was assembled in Holland, the largest ever to engage in an invasion of England, with 200 or 300 transports and 50 fighting ships. These would carry 13,000 troops, a mixture of Dutch, English, Scots, Brandenburgers and Scandinavians. This force was much smaller than James could muster, but far better commanded and not weakened by religious dissension. Just twenty years earlier, Sir William Batten had exclaimed to Pepys that the Devil was shitting Dutchmen (p. 31), but now Evelyn recorded in his diary that people were 'praying incessantly for an easterly wind' to blow William to English shores.[35] In response, James replaced Sir Roger Strickland, the Catholic in command of his navy, by Lord Dartmouth, like Pepys a Protestant but loyal to the Crown. The army was put under the command of the apparently loyal John Churchill. Pepys reassured Dartmouth about the strength of the fleet in readiness to defend the east coast. At the end of October William did indeed set out for Yorkshire, but was driven back by bad weather. The wind then changed direction and he sailed westwards through the Channel, avoiding the English fleet that was bottled up in the mouth of the Thames, and landed at Torbay in Devon on 5 November. This date held special significance for Protestants, as did the wind, a reminder of the one that had scattered the Spanish Armada.

News of William's progress quickly reached London. Robert Hooke described in his diary for 5 November a frenetic shuttling around the City's coffee-houses with Christopher Wren, picking up the latest news. At Jonathan's in Exchange Alley he learnt of the sighting of the Dutch fleet off the Isle of Wight, followed by a second, later visit when the news – incorrect – came through that William had landed at Poole in Dorset. The fact was that the arrival of the Dutch, although much desired, had happened so easily that everybody, including possibly William himself, had been taken by surprise. He encountered little resistance once landed, and although at first not many rallied to him, support began to build.

Pepys had spent the day with the King, who was sitting for a portrait by Godfrey Kneller that Pepys had commissioned. Ten days later Pepys witnessed the King's will and travelled westwards with him as he prepared to face William. At Windsor he presented James with a document acknowledging that nearly £28,000 was owing to him for his service in the Admiralty and as Treasurer of Tangier. Back in 1679 when James had been excluded from office through the Test Act, Pepys had written to him, 'so long as Mr Pepys should be there his Royall Highness remains in effect Admiral'.[36] James must have been well aware of Pepys's long and unswerving loyalty to him, so duly signed the IOU twice: of course, it was never paid.

As he approached Salisbury, the King learnt of defections, perhaps the most hurtful of which was that of John Churchill. Suffering from uncontrollable nosebleeds, he decided to avoid immediate battle, and instead returned to London to find that Princess Anne had fled from Whitehall, along with Sarah Churchill, helped in their escape by Henry Compton and his head gardener, George London. Forsaken even by his own daughter, James sent Mary of Modena and their baby son off to France, and on 10 December made the fatal decision to take flight himself. While his wife, his Catholic priests and his ministers all made their way safely, James was intercepted at Faversham in Kent and brought back to London. William, who had been invited by the Corporation into the City to maintain order, would have much preferred his uncle to have left the country, so now sent him to Rochester, knowing that he would make a second attempt at escape. This time it was successful, and James left England for ever. Evelyn wrote to Pepys 'upon the great Convulsion of State upon the King's with-drawing'. Recognising that Pepys would remain loyal to James, he offered 'to know if in any sort, I may serve you in this prodigious Revolution: You have many Friends, but no man living who is more sincerely your servant, or that has a greater value for you.'[37] After William entered London, becoming de facto ruler of the country, Pepys began to refer to contact with him on naval matters, though he was well aware that he was not going to be in office much longer and ended a letter to Lord Dartmouth: 'If I may be able by any means to be of use to your lordship, though I have given over even thinking on't for myself.'[38]

Pepys had first met the Prince nearly thirty years earlier, when he went to Holland as part of the entourage to bring Charles II back to England at the Restoration. He had noted in his diary that William was 'a very pretty boy'. He expressed surprise at the very small group of attendants 'for a prince', but this reflected the particular situation of the House of Orange within the republican constitution of the United Provinces.[39] The Prince was in fact a dynastic miracle, for he was the only child of William II and Mary Stuart, born eight days after his father succumbed to smallpox in 1650. He also proved a miracle for the independence of his nation by combating over the years the mighty threat posed from the French under Louis XIV. The 'pretty boy' had grown into a puny man, with a body that was almost deformed, a white face pitted by smallpox, and suffering from chronic asthma. His upbringing, moreover, had imbued in him solid Calvinist beliefs combined with a sense of Orange historical destiny, which, as one biographer points out, did not encourage affability.[40] His dour character was witnessed by John Evelyn's son, also called John, who joined the Prince on his way to London from the West Country. As he observed to his father, William's chilly reserve was not the ideal way to win 'us English-men, who are sooner vanquish'd with kind words and good looks, than with Armies, and at a cheaper rate'. When his difficult manner was pointed out to William, he tried to correct it, but it was not a propitious start.[41]

William had invaded England not as a rival claimant, but rather to protect the Protestant religion and the liberties of its subjects. If James had not chosen flight, he could well have kept his crown, but instead there was a constitutional vacuum, and throughout January 1689 debates raged about how to fill it. Should William become the consort of his wife, Mary, who held the right of succession to the throne; should he act as Regent or as King; or should there be a joint monarchy? Moderate Tories favoured the consort solution, though William objected to being his wife's 'gentleman usher'. High Tories preferred a regency, governing on behalf of the anointed King, James. Exclusionist Whigs were in support of William becoming King. In the event, it was the fourth solution that was chosen, and the crown was offered jointly to William and Mary on 13 February.

Mary now came over to join her husband. She had not been in England since 1677 when, at the age of fifteen, she had married William and departed, weeping inconsolably, for Holland. The weeping continued for many years, as the marriage was not a happy one. Whilst she was tall and beautiful, he was short and so unprepossessing that her sister Anne nicknamed him Caliban. After two miscarriages, Mary had ceased to conceive, and William took her childhood friend, Elizabeth Villiers, as his mistress. Nevertheless, a modus vivendi was established, and Mary pined when William was away fighting, which he perpetually was.

Mary's position on her return to London in 1689 was a delicate one, for she was taking the throne of her own father. As Evelyn explained, it was thought that 'the Princesse, would have shewed some (seeming) reluctancy at least, of assuming her Father's Crowne & made some Apologie, testifying her regret, that he should by his misgovernment necessitate the Nation to so extraordinary a proceeding'. Instead she behaved 'as to a Wedding, riant & jolly, so as seeming to be quite Transported'.[42] In fact, Mary had been told by William to put on a cheerful face, especially as he was aware of his own dour nature. Whatever family feelings Mary may have held for her father were far outweighed by the importance of her religious conviction. When James had become King, she had written anxious letters to her sister asking for her assurance that she was remaining loyal to the Anglican Church. Anne replied in no uncertain terms that she abhorred the principles of the Church of Rome as much as it was possible to do, and accused her father's wife of encouraging him 'to be more violent than he would be of himself . . . for she is a very great bigot in her way'.[43] Now the Anglican succession had been re-established, and the new Queen continued to present an open and cheerful presence that proved a huge asset to William. In time he came to recognise the important role she played, and when Mary died from smallpox in December 1694, he was devastated by the loss.

Within a week of William and Mary assuming the throne, Pepys resigned from his position at the Admiralty. His loyalty to James meant that he was a non-juror, refusing to swear an oath of allegiance to the new monarchs. In this he was not alone, for more than 300 clergy, including Archbishop Sancroft and the Queen's own childhood spiritual counsellor, Bishop Compton of London, were also non-jurors, along with other laymen with tender consciences. As a result, Pepys was doubly taxed and came under the surveillance of William's efficient security service. Twice he stood for Parliament, but failed, with the old accusations of papism levelled against him. Twice he was arrested and imprisoned in the Gatehouse in Tothill Street in Westminster, accused of 'dangerous and treasonable practices against His Majesty's government'. With James in exile at the court of William's arch enemy, Louis XIV, Pepys was deemed guilty of what he himself described as the 'Sin of Jacobitisme', and would be vulnerable when conflict threatened between England and France.[44]

In October 1689 his naval colleague and close friend Sir Anthony Deane, who had also lost his job, wrote to Pepys saying that he expected nothing more than 'the old soldiers request, a little space between busines and the grave'. The response from Pepys showed no such indication of dejection. Instead he wrote, 'the worse the world uses me the better I think I am bound to use my self; nor shall any solicitousness after the felicities of the next world . . . ever stifle the satisfactions arising from a just confidence of receiving such unaccountable usage as I have sustained in this'.[45] He threw himself into entertaining his friends, holding open house on Saturdays, and the list of his guests reads like a roll call of the distinguished men of London (pp. 127–8).

Urged on by Evelyn, Pepys returned to working on a history of the navy. This had been first mooted in 1680 when Pepys was 'resting' from his work at the Admiralty. Letters from Evelyn at that time had been filled with ideas and references, many of them historical and classical quotations, and even notes about the martial performance of dogs, drawing on the notes he had made for a history of the Third Dutch War that Charles II had commissioned and then aborted. Some letters were extremely long, one reaching nearly 7,000 words, and Pepys must have felt that he was under bombardment.[46] In the end the task proved too much for him, and instead of a naval history, he produced a polemic in defence of his own work and a critique of the conduct of the navy commissioners in the period between 1679 and 1684. Uncertain of its merits, he read the text to Evelyn, who wrote him an encouraging note:

When I Reflect . . . upon what you were pleas'd to communicate to me Yesterday; so many, and so different passions crowd on my thought, that I know not which first to give vent to: Indignation, pitty, Sorrow, Contempt and Anger: Love, Esteeme, Admiration, and all that can express the most generous Resent'ments of One, who cannot but take part in the cause of an Injur'd and most worthy Person! With what Indignation for the Malevolence of these men, pitty of their Ignorance and Folly, Sorrow and Contempt of their Malice and Ingratitude, do I looke upon and despise them![47]

Pepys's *Memoires Relating to the State of the Navy* was published in 1690. Until recently his assertions have been regarded as justified, but a study by a naval historian has shown that he probably exaggerated the incompetence of the commissioners in a desire to mask the arbitrary and capricious behaviour of Charles II. Although Pepys planned to publish more on naval history, instead he helped a young scholar, Edmund Gibson, to produce a new edition of *Britannia*, a guide to the British Isles.[48]

Evelyn's response, quoted above, is interesting in two ways. First, it is typical of his dramatic, over-the-top style, the literary equivalent of the elaborate bows that etiquette demanded a gentleman should make in greeting. In a later letter Pepys pointed out to Evelyn that he turned all his geese into swans.[49] Second, it shows how the friendship between the two men had deepened, and that there was a real affection and intimacy between them. Moreover, Pepys's letters, so businesslike a generation earlier, had now taken on a more flowery style, though never quite reaching Evelyn's level.

In 1691, Evelyn's older brother George offered him an apartment in Wotton, 'a Retreate (with my sole companion) in the place that gave me Birth, & most shortly Burial'.[50] Warming to the idea, which would ease their financial problems and the growing burden of maintaining a large house and garden, John and Mary resolved to let Sayes Court. Mary told her husband that she wished his friend 'had occasion for a countrie house' for he would be the ideal tenant 'prefferred to any other for his Neatnesse and friendship'.[51] The friend is not named, but Pepys has been suggested as the most likely candidate. By this time, however, Pepys had made it his custom to spend his summer months at William

Hewer's country retreat in Clapham, so did not take up the invitation, if indeed it was ever made. Instead, Sayes Court was to be let to a much less neat individual, Czar Peter of Russia, when he came to London to study the naval dockyard at Deptford. It has been suggested that the well-known story of the Czar and his Cossack attendants having wheelbarrow races through Evelyn's much-prized holly hedges might be apocryphal, but one of Evelyn's servants complained to him that the house was 'full of people, and right nasty', and Evelyn received compensation for damage sustained during the Russians' stay.[52] Among Evelyn's papers, moreover, are some verses in which he referred to Peter as 'the barb'rous Czar, sprung from ye Scythian Huns', who had wrought more havoc in his garden than a recent hurricane.[53]

In a letter from Wotton to Pepys in August 1692, Evelyn bemoaned his rural life, describing it as insipid and contrasting it with Pepys's busy London existence: 'O Fortunate Mr Pepys! who knows, possesses, and Injoyes all that's worth the seeking after. Let me live among your inclinations and I shall be happy.'[54] But now a new project arrived to keep Evelyn busy, the fulfilment of his long-desired plan to establish an institution for wounded and impoverished seamen. The Tudor palace at Greenwich had fallen into disrepair during the Civil War, and in the 1660s a classical building was designed and built by John Webb for Charles II. When the monarch lost interest and the money ran out, the scheme was abandoned, but James II earmarked the site for a naval hospital. His daughter Mary confirmed that it should be so used, for her consort much preferred to live upstream at Hampton Court, where Christopher Wren created magnificent apartments for them.

In 1692 the English fleet won a great victory at La Hogue off the Normandy coast, humiliating the French and putting paid to James II's plans to invade and regain his kingdom. The suffering endured by the British sailors so horrified the Queen that it served as an impetus for the naval hospital. Wren gave his services as architect free of charge, with Nicholas Hawksmoor as his assistant. The original plan was to build a corresponding wing to the east of Webb's building, and a connecting block topped by a dome, echoing the form of Les Invalides in Paris. Queen Mary objected to this scheme, as it would block the view to the river from Inigo Jones's Queen's House. Although the resulting solution, splitting the hospital into two, is neatly summed up by Samuel Johnson, who declared it 'too much detached to make one great whole', the Baroque ensemble is still magnificent.[55]

John Evelyn became involved in the planning of the hospital, and in 1695 was made the Treasurer. Almost certainly it was Evelyn who brought Pepys into the discussions. Writing down his thoughts in a letter in November 1694, Pepys expressed bewilderment at the various schemes and questioned the primary purpose of this 'Invalides with us for the sea': was it for widows and orphans, as well as 'persons of such as age, infirmities, or wounds, shall have rendered incapable of farther services'? He wisely advised that the money must be voted by a Parliament which was 'as little disposed to deny as any I sat in'.[56] The Queen's sudden death at the end of the year did not delay the project, but it was fraught with financial problems as enthusiasm waned and the King's promised contribution became difficult to extract. A grand committee meeting, attended by both Evelyn and Pepys, was held in April 1696 to inspect the plans, and two months later, at 5 pm, 'Mr Flamsted the Kings Astronomical Professor observing the punctual time by Instruments', Wren and Evelyn laid the foundation stone.[57]

Although the building of the Royal Naval Hospital was now under way, the money was still difficult to collect. Would-be subscribers reneged, and Evelyn as Treasurer wrote to the minister, Sidney Godolphin, that when he approached them for money, they 'avoid me, as one Carying the Pest about me'.[58] Mary Evelyn, who knew her husband's temperament well, advised him: 'you are generally aprehensive of the worst, when all is don, wee must submit and acquiesce in what Almighty God determines for us'.[59] The financial difficulties were solved when Wren suggested some of the duties on coal voted for the rebuilding of the City churches after the Great Fire should be diverted to the 'Charity', while the Paymaster, Sir Stephen Fox, proposed that funding could be provided by levies on the wages of seamen. Thus these future pensioners were paying towards their own charitable foundation. When Evelyn resigned from the treasurership in 1703, at the age of eighty-three, the hospital was in sound financial health.

It is remarkable how both Evelyn and Pepys continued to be busy. For several years Pepys had been waging a single-handed campaign against what he had identified as financial maladministration and poor teaching at the Mathematical School that he had been instrumental in establishing two decades earlier. When the governing body ignored his warnings, he turned to the Lord Mayor of London, who also ignored him, assuming him too old and frail to cause much trouble. He found he had made a grave miscalculation, for Pepys then printed his warning letters in a pamphlet targeted at the aldermen of the City, and in a second informed them that the affair was the talk of the coffee-houses. Altogether he produced six pamphlets in what became a slanging match. Thomas Gale wrote to Pepys, 'you have mett with what was to be expected from men whose education is vile', adding that they were a 'generation of caterpillars!'[60] Pepys ultimately won through, with the aldermen and a new mayor ensuring that Christ's Hospital was reformed. Pepys himself was appointed Vice-President, a post that could only be held by a freeman of the City of London – an honour that, despite having lived in the City almost all his life, and having been involved with many London institutions, he had not received. That all changed in 1699 when Pepys was given the freedom of the City for his services to Christ's Hospital.

Pepys was sixty-six when he made the journey to the Guildhall. This may not seem very old by today's standards, but Pepys had suffered from ill-health all his life, and was now finding it difficult to leave his house in Buckingham Street. Whether he travelled by road or by river, he must have been fascinated to see how London had been transformed in the years since the Great Fire. Christopher Wren and Robert Hooke had designed fifty-one parish churches in a variety of styles and layouts. They were not, however, working on a *tabula rasa*, for they were obliged to follow the footprint of the medieval predecessors of these buildings, which from the outset had been erected on constricted urban sites. Thus, Wren had adapted the traditional Gothic nave and aisle plan at St Bride's, next to Pepys's old home, and at St Stephen Walbrook the transepts were contained within the rectangular scheme. For St Martin's Ludgate, Hooke used a Greek cross, but once again with no projecting transepts. For St Benet's, Paul's Wharf, Hooke drew on Dutch influences, as with the civic buildings that he had designed for the City. Above these churches a skyline was taking form, a combination of towers, lanterns, pinnacles, cupolas and spires, some of them designed by Wren's ingenious assistant, Nicholas Hawksmoor. Wren's supreme achievement, the new cathedral, was still in progress in 1699 and without its dome and towers, but the proud Baroque building was rising above St Paul's Churchyard, so familiar to Pepys in his childhood (Plate 20).

Pepys took great delight not only in his old friends, but also in the younger generation, offering them help and encouragement. He had designated his nephew, John Jackson, as his heir, and resolved to send him on the Grand Tour. With the help of his friends, the Houblon family, who had good trading links with the Continent, Pepys drew up itineraries and organised introductions. The tour, which began in 1698, was to take in France, Switzerland, Italy, Spain and Portugal. One interesting detail is that Pepys ensured that Jackson would go nowhere near St Germain-en-Laye, where James II had his court in exile – there was to be no suspicion of Jacobitism countenanced.

In a letter written on Christmas Day from Rome, John Jackson described to his uncle the celebrations ushering in the new century. He told him how through contacts he had been given a seat in St Peter's, in the area reserved for the clergy and 'persons of the first quality', to watch the papal procession. This included the Swiss Guard, bishops and cardinals, but not the Pope himself, who was too ill to attend. He also observed the cardinals at supper in the Vatican Palace and, knowing Pepys loved music, attended a concert to hear a young eunuch sing and Corelli, 'the famous violin', playing in a consort. Perhaps aware of the danger of appearing pro-Catholic, he dismissed the rumour that Pope Innocent XII had died by commenting facetiously: 'He ... could not do a greater piece of service to the strangers than to dropp off at this juncture, to compleat their shew by a *Sede Vacante* to which some are of the opinion will be added a Canonization this Holy Year; and after that I think there should remain nothing more to be wished for us.'61

Pepys's desire to open up horizons for his young relative stands in total contrast to John Evelyn's attitude to the idea of travel for his

grandson, known as Jack. Evelyn had found Jack's father a disappointment, which he did not scruple to make clear, and their relationship had
been a troubled one, as will be shown in the next chapter. The young
Jack became the focus of his grandfather's hopes and dreams, a focus
that became magnified when John Evelyn junior died in 1699 at the age
of forty-four. Jack was clearly a charming young man, whose company
Pepys much appreciated. In a letter to Evelyn in 1694, Pepys described
how Jack, 'our pretty ætonian', had come to visit but would not stay for
dinner, 'the little knave'.[62] In a later letter, after Jackson's return, Pepys
talks of some Latin verses composed by Jack, declaring that there was no
need to travel to Rome as its pleasures could be enjoyed in Pepys's own
home, where the garnered treasures were now on display.[63] But Jack may
have been putting on a brave face, for another letter, written on Christmas
Eve 1701, represents a passionate plea on Pepys's part for Evelyn to let
his grandson travel. In this letter, Pepys reminds Evelyn that it was his
encouragement back in 1669 that had persuaded him to travel to France
with his wife, Elizabeth, 'to a degree of satisfaction and solid usefull-
nesse that has stuck by mee through the whole Cours of my Life and
Businesse since'.[64] Jack had the previous year fought off a bout of
smallpox while at Oxford, and his grandfather felt, as his sole male heir,
his life was too precious for him to travel abroad.

This letter is the last one that survives from Pepys to Evelyn. By this
time Pepys had become very ill, and had moved permanently to Will
Hewer's house in 'paradisical Clapham', as Evelyn called it. William
Nicolson, who had come to London to be consecrated as Bishop of
Carlisle by the new Queen, Anne, wrote an account of the house in his
diary, following a visit in the summer of 1702.[65] Nicolson was particularly
interested in libraries, having earlier borrowed books from Pepys, so he
noted: 'Mr Pepys's Library in 9 Classes [Cases?], finely gilded and sash-
glass'd; so deep as to carry two Rows . . . of Books on each footing . . . The
Books so well order'd that his Footman (after looking the Catalogue)
could lay his finger on any of em blindfold.' The house he described as
being full of objets d'art, paintings and engravings. He particularly singled
out a copy of a study by Antonio Verrio of James II receiving the
Mathematical Scholars of Christ's Hospital that Pepys and Hewer had

commissioned, describing it as 'the blew-coats at Christ-Church Hospital (with the Directors and Governours of the place, Lord Mayor & Aldermen &c) suppos'd to be one of the best Representations of the various Habits of the Times, postures, &c' (Plate 17).[66]

The Clapham house was not as large as Wotton, the family home eventually inherited by John Evelyn following his brother's death in 1699. An inventory drawn up in 1702, together with the memoir that Evelyn wrote for Jack two years later, give a picture of a typical country house, with armour and stags' heads in the hall and paintings throughout the house.[67] Nevertheless, the wide gap that had existed between their childhood homes, Evelyn's 'extravagant old house' and Pepys's narrow city tenement, had now been considerably reduced, and Pepys was spending his last days in considerable material comfort. The relationship between the two men, which had begun on a strictly professional level, had become a close and important one to them both.

PART II

'Even Private Families are ... the Best of Governments'

4

PRIVATE LIVES

S AMUEL PEPYS AND John Evelyn were both blessed with extended families and many friends, though their families could prove mixed blessings at times. Moreover, the Pepys family, as noted earlier, painted a complicated picture. Samuel was the complete Londoner, yet the family up to his father's generation was rooted in the Cambridgeshire country-side, farmers since medieval times. It was his great-grandfather John who lifted the family a rung up the social scale by marrying an heiress and building a manor house at Impington, not far from Cambridge. His six children included the exotically named Apollo; a daughter Paulina who married Sir Sidney Montague and produced a son, Edward, 1st Earl of Sandwich; and Talbot, who became a fashionable lawyer and MP. Thereafter the family tree is filled with lawyers, one of whom became Lord Chief Justice of Ireland during the Commonwealth period, and another who served as Secretary to Sir Edward Coke. There were many connections, too, with Cambridge University, especially the lawyers' college, Trinity Hall.

The notable exception to this upward social mobility was Samuel's father, John, born at Impington in 1601. He was apprenticed to a tailor with premises off Fleet Street, and it was probably his master's business that he took over in Salisbury Court, hard by St Bride's Church. Almost nothing is known of Samuel's mother's family, the Kites, but as her brother was a butcher in Whitechapel, to the east of the City, this may have been the family's trade. Before her marriage, Margaret worked as a laundrymaid, whilst her sister, who later looked after Samuel at times during his childhood, was in service in Hackney. Margaret and John married in 1626 at Newington.[1] The couple had eleven children, seven of whom did not survive infancy, and were buried in St Bride's.

References to his parents in Samuel's diary give the impression of a quarrelsome household. One particular dispute centred on their maid, '(which my father likes and my mother dislikes), I stayed till 10 at night, persuading my mother to understand herself; and that in some high words – which I was sorry for, but she is grown, poor woman, very froward'.[2] One of Margaret's reasons for disliking the maid was that she thought her husband had a fancy for her, though their son described her as 'the most ill-favored slut that ever I saw in my life'.[3] Pepys tended to take his father's part in these quarrels, making his mother sound petty and difficult, but the charge that she is being 'very froward' suggests that he, along with many in seventeenth-century society, assumed that the man should assert his authority in the home.

In 1661, John's eldest brother Robert died, leaving him a property at Brampton. Handing over the tailoring business to Samuel's younger brother Tom, John and Margaret left London for Huntingdonshire. This did not put an end to the quarrelling, which now revolved around their financial affairs, for both seem to have been improvident. In a letter written in 1663, Pepys set out for his father the financial situation concerning the Brampton estate, concluding that his parents had £29 per annum, which he intended to top up to £50 out of his own purse. But in an admonitory tone he advised: 'I would by this oblige my mother and you to the study of thrift and quietnesse, that I may heare noe more of these differences, which to my great griefe I have of late understood doe often arise between you.'[4] In effect, Samuel had become parent to his parents, a responsibility he would maintain until his father's death in 1680.

When Samuel married Elizabeth in December 1655, he added a new area of responsibility, the family of his wife. Elizabeth's father, Alexander St Michel, came from a gentry family in Anjou, and was

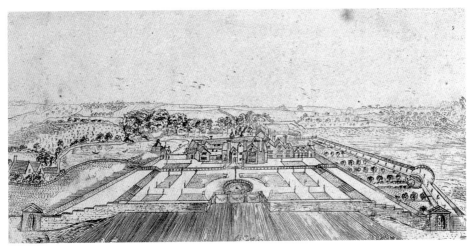

1. Etching made by John Evelyn of his family's home, Wotton House in Surrey, where he was born on 31 October 1620. By the time he made this engraving in 1653 the house had been inherited by his older brother, George, and John had advised him on some changes to the garden, including the levelling of an area for a parterre and fountain, which can be seen in front of the Tudor house.

2. Detail from the map of London published by Newcourt and Faithorne in 1658. This shows Salisbury Court (labelled 'Salsb. Court', to the right of the road running down from the word 'Street' in 'Fleete Street'), where Pepys was born on 23 February 1633 in a house adjoining St Bride's Church. The open space contrasts with the tightly packed houses on either side of the River Fleet. To the east is St Paul's Churchyard, containing the medieval cathedral and St Paul's School, which Pepys attended in the late 1640s.

3. The *pietra dura* cabinet commissioned from craftsmen by Evelyn during his visit to Florence and Rome in 1644. Domenico Benotti created for him the mosaic panels with birds and flowers, and the central panel showing a fountain set in a kind of baldacchino. Vincento Brocchi provided the statuettes that Evelyn had bronzed to match the ormolu decorations.

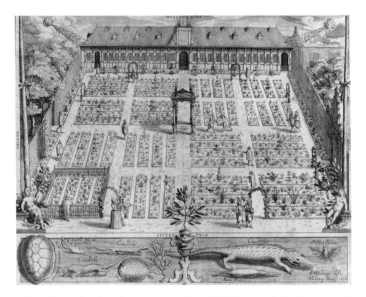

4. The botanical garden at Leiden, from an engraving of 1610, with the beds arranged according to particular families of plants. Evelyn described in his diary how in 1641 he visited the gallery shown at the top of this engraving, 'which is well furnish'd with Naturall curiosities; especially with all sorts of Skeletons, from the Whale & Eliphant, to the Fly, and the Spider … a large Crocodile; The head of the Rynoceros; The Leomarinus, Torpedo, many Indian Weapons, Curiosities out of China, & of the Eastern Countries; so as it were altogether (impossible) to remember all'.

5. Robert Walker's striking portrait of Evelyn, painted in England in 1648 for his young wife in Paris. Originally Walker was going to show Evelyn holding a portrait in miniature of Mary, but Evelyn asked him instead to depict a skull.

6. Charles II dancing with his sister Mary at The Hague in 1660 to celebrate his restoration to the English throne. This painting by Hieronymus Janssens shows the Stuart family and the related dynasties of the Houses of Orange and of Bohemia. The host of the ball is Charles II's cousin,

John Maurice of Nassau, son of Elizabeth of Bohemia. At the back on the far left, James, Duke of York, is shown dining with his brother, Henry, Duke of Gloucester. In the centre of the painting is the future William III, son of Mary Stuart. On the left, portrayed rather dimly, is a consort of viols.

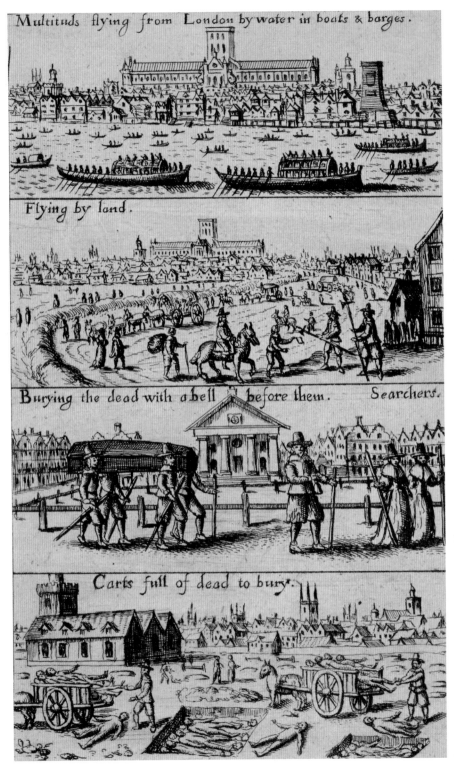

Multituds flying from London by water in boats & barges.

Flying by land.

Burying the dead with a bell before them. Searchers.

Carts full of dead to bury.

7. A broadsheet from Pepys's collection showing scenes in London during the Great Plague of 1665.

8. A map commissioned from the cartographer John Leake by the Lord Mayor and his aldermen to show the extent of the devastation of the Great Fire of London in 1666. Only the north-east portion of the walled city survived the fire, which had spread out westwards beyond the River Fleet and destroyed the area of Pepys's childhood.

9. A print from Pepys's collection entitled 'The New Sukeing Worme Engine'. This fire engine, invented by John Loftyng, carried water through long, reinforced leather pipes. Lofting's engineering works were based in Islington and his presence there is recorded in Lofting Road. One of his engines is shown in front of the Monument designed by Christopher Wren and Robert Hooke as a memorial to the Great Fire. The Doric column, completed in 1671, is 202 feet high, signifying its distance from Pudding Lane where the fire first broke out in a bakery.

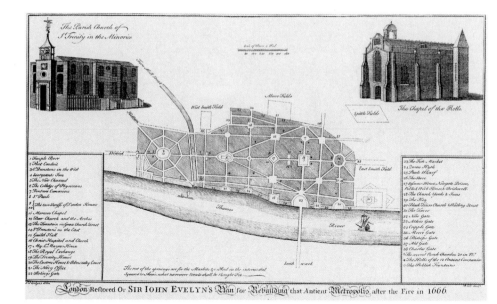

The Parish Church of S.t Trinity in the Minories

Moor Fields

West Smith Field

Spittle Fields

East Smith Field

The Chapel of the Rolls

Thames River

South wark

1 Temple Barr
2 Fleet Conduit
3 S.t Dunstans in the West
4 Sergeants Inn
5 The New Channel
6 The Colledge of Physicians
7 Doctors Commons
8 S.t Pauls
9 The two Offices of London Houses
10
11 Mercers Chapel
12 Bow Church and the Arches
13 The Fountain in great Church Street
14 S.t Dunstans in the East
15 Guild Hall
16 Christ Hospital and Church
17 My L.d Mayors House
18 The Royal Exchange
19 The Serenity House
20 The Custom House & Admiralty Court
21 The Navy Office
22 Billings gate
23 The Fish Market
24 Queen Hyth
25 Pauls Wharf
26 The Stow
27 Sessions House, Newgate Prison, Bridewell Prison, Bridewell
28 The Church Yards & Gates
29 The Key
30 Black Friers Church Watling Street
31 The Tower
32 New Gate
33 Aldters Gate
34 Crypple Gate
35 Moor Gate
36 Bishops Gate
37 Aldt gate
38 Charles Gate
The several Parish Churches 20 in No.
The Halls of the 12 Antient Companies
The Publick Fountains

The rest of the openings are for the Markets &c. And in the interstitial Squares there Arm. what narrower Streets shall be thought Fit.

London Restored Or SIR IOHN EVELYN's Plan for Rebuilding that Antient Metropolis, after the Fire in 1666

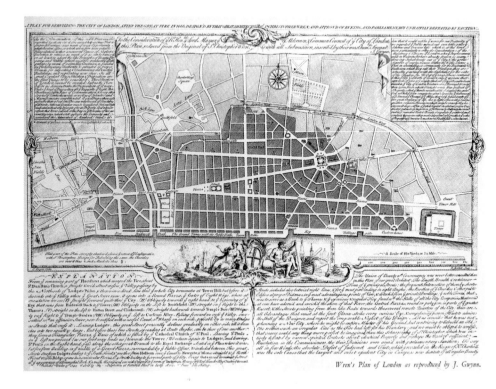

A PLAN FOR REBUILDING THE CITY OF LONDON, AFTER THE GREAT FIRE IN 1666, DESIGN'D BY THAT GREAT ARCHITECT S.t CHRISTOPHER WREN. AND APPROVD OF BY KING, AND PARLIAMENT, BUT UNHAPPILY DEFEATED BY FACTION.

EXPLANATION

Wren's Plan of London as reproduced by J. Gwynn.

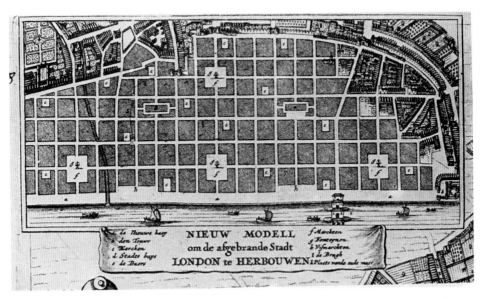

10, 11 & 12. Three plans for the rebuilding of the City of London following the Great Fire. Above left: John Evelyn's 'noblest model' with wide straight streets radiating from central points. Above right: Robert Hooke's strict grid pattern with 'all the churches, public buildings, market-places, and the like in proper and convenient places'. Below left: Christopher Wren's plan, with radiating streets like that of Evelyn, but showing greater sophistication. In the event, none of these plans was adopted.

13. A replica of the bust that Pepys commissioned from the sculptor John Bushnell when his wife Elizabeth died suddenly in 1669, aged only twenty-nine. While studying in Rome, Bushnell took the opportunity to observe Bernini, who believed that the subject of a portrait bust should be depicted in animation. The original bust is still perched high in the Pepyses' parish church of St Olave's, appearing to have been caught in mid-conversation.

14. John Hayls's portrait of Samuel Pepys, painted in 1666. Pepys hired an Indian gown of golden brown silk specially for the occasion, and is shown holding his own composition, a setting of the song 'Beauty Retire' from one of his favourite musical dramas, Sir William Davenant's *Siege of Rhodes*.

1. *The Orb, borne by the Duke of Somerset*.
2. *The Crown, borne by y^e Duke of Ormond*.
3. *The Scepter wth y^e Dove, borne by y^e Duke of Albemarle*.

A P R
LONDON and
Taken at several Sta
By WI L

REFERENCES for WESTMINSTER and part of LONDON

16. Detail from a perspective of London and Westminster by William Morgan, published in 1681. This shows the post-fire skyline that Pepys would have observed as he travelled to the Guildhall in 1699 to become a Freeman of the City of London. However, he would not have seen the dome on St Paul's Cathedral. Morgan must have taken his rendering of this from drawings

KINGS Majestie.
...hop of Durham.
...hop of Bath and Wells.
...arles Eldest Sons.
...ster of the Robes.

F. Sixteen Barons of the Cinqueports.
G. The Earl of Huntingdon Capt. of the Band of G. Pensioners.
H. The Duke of Northumberland Capt. of the Guard in Waiting.
I. The Viscount Grandison Capt. of the Yeomen of the Guard.
K. Gentlemen Pensioners.

15. The coronation procession of James II in April 1685, as depicted by Francis Sandford. Pepys, as one of the Barons of the Cinque Ports, took part in the procession, and is shown holding the front left-hand pole of the canopy. One of his companions from the Tangier expedition, Thomas Ken, who had become Bishop of Bath and Wells, stands on the left of the King.

made by Wren in the course of long discussions about what should crown the new cathedral. Work on building the actual dome began only in 1696, and even then Wren had not decided on the structural form of the upper part.

17. A gouache drawing from the studio of Antonio Verrio, showing James II receiving the Mathematical Scholars of Christ's Hospital. This study, which belonged to Pepys, depicts in miniature a painting by the artist commissioned for the great hall of the school. Pepys borrowed a City alderman's red gown for the King's visit, and can be seen to the right of the throne, gesturing towards some of the kneeling schoolboys.

18. An anti-Catholic engraved broadsheet from Pepys's collection. This was published in 1673, when the conversion of the King's heir presumptive, James, Duke of York, to Roman Catholicism was made public. The print is appealing to the King, as Bethel, to support the English Church, whilst the Pope is shown as Babel.

19. Fireworks celebrating the birth of a son to Mary of Modena and James II in July 1688. Evelyn recorded in his diary how he and his wife watched the fireworks from Pepys's home in York Buildings, and what a spectacular show was presented by the delighted King. *Laetitia Populi* ('joy of the people'), one of the mottoes shown in this engraving, was rather wide of the mark.

20. An engraving of 1695 showing Christopher Wren's St Paul's Cathedral under construction, with the east end almost complete, but with scaffolding and screens keeping the curious well away from the middle part of the building.

21. Chelsea Hospital, from an engraving made in 1744. Evelyn was much involved in the establishment of the hospital for veteran soldiers, which was founded by Charles II and designed by Christopher Wren. The buildings were completed in 1692, housing over 500 men.

disinherited when he converted to Protestantism while fighting in the wars in Germany. (This apostasy evidently continued to cause trouble within his family, for when his daughter Elizabeth went to Paris for her education, there was an attempt to kidnap her and force her into an Ursuline convent.) During a stay in Ireland, Alexander married a widow, Dorothea, originally from Devon. A restless character, he considered joining the imperial army to fight the Turks and paid visits to France to try to regain his inheritance, but for most of the time he lived with his wife and children – Elizabeth and her brother Balthasar – in London. Balthasar, known as Balty, once described to Pepys how his father's head had been 'Full of wheemesis' – schemes to make money through inventions such as a machine for perpetual motion, and taking out patents for the perennial problem of curing smoky chimneys, which 'Soaked his Pockett, and brought all our Famely soe low'.[5]

Pepys tried his best to steer clear of Alexander and his financial problems, but was not able to avoid Balty, a larger-than-life character. Samuel's biographer, Richard Ollard, wrote of him, 'If Balthasar St Michel had not existed, only Dickens could have invented him.'[6] Pepys managed to acquire for him a series of posts in naval administration, in some of which he did well, in others disastrously. Balty's finest and probably happiest hour was when he spent several months in Paris at his brother-in-law's expense, gathering the evidence to discredit Pepys's accusers during the Popish Plot crisis. His home life was disastrous: his first wife found him improvident, secretive and stingy, complaining to Pepys that he kept her 'alwayes in a worse condition then the meanest servant'.[7]

Pepys showed infinite patience, but exasperation overcame him in a letter written in 1686: 'in one of my late letters of general advice to you, I cautioned you against depending upon any support much longer from me'. He then explained that a new stone had lodged in his kidney, and an ulcer developed, causing him constant pain. He ended: 'This satisfaction I have as to your own particular, that I have discharged my part of friendship and care towards you and your family, as far as I have been, or could ever hope to be able, were I to live twenty years longer in the Navy.'[8] Even this plainly expressed letter from an ageing and sick man was not sufficient to deter Balty. The last letter written by Pepys that survives was to the Commander in Chief of the Fleet, requesting relief for Balty who, with his numerous family (he had eight children and two stepchildren), was in a 'known state of want'.[9] Pepys had taken on his wife's family in sickness and in health even forty years after Elizabeth's death.

Evelyn also found himself coping with the affairs of his extended family. He had been able to enjoy youthful financial independence, for at his father's death in 1640 his elder brother George took over the responsibility for running the principal family estate at Wotton, while John inherited some property and money. With marriage, however, his responsibilities began. Sir Richard Browne was an ideal father-in-law in many ways – a civilised and scholarly man, with a wide range of interests – but he combined these with unworldliness, at a time when that quality could prove dangerously expensive. As the English Resident in Paris, Browne was the ambassador in all but name, with the responsibilities that this entailed but not the means to finance them as England was at war with itself.

In 1647, having agreed a marriage contract with Browne for the hand of Mary, Evelyn returned to England to try to untangle problems connected with Sayes Court in Deptford. This 200-acre estate had been leased to the Browne family since the early seventeenth century by the Crown, which meant that, with the outbreak of the Civil War, the whole question of ownership was left hanging. Richard Browne's father died in 1646, and his wife's brother, William Prettyman, was appointed executor, in theory in charge of the estate. When Evelyn arrived at Sayes Court, Prettyman was nowhere to be seen, so he got on with sorting out the library and garden, and looking into the financial situation for Browne. The correspondence between Evelyn and Browne at this time shows how grateful the latter was for the care that Evelyn was taking with his affairs, describing himself in one letter as his 'poore, unfortunate (though truly lovinge) father in law'.[10]

At first, matters seemed to go well, with Prettyman offering to work with Evelyn to make financial arrangements. To enable Browne to fund his establishment in France, in 1651 Evelyn bought the lease and title to the Sayes Court estate from Prettyman through a penal bond worth

£1,500. This, as Gillian Darley points out, was a 'most unusual marriage settlement'.[11] All too soon, however, the relationship between Evelyn and Prettyman deteriorated, when the latter proved incompetent, dishonest and greedy. Although at the Restoration Charles II had promised to reimburse Browne for his expenses as Resident, this was not honoured, while the bond dogged Evelyn for over three decades. Only in 1685, after Richard Browne had been dead for two years, did the Lords of the Treasury admit the justice of Evelyn's claim, which by that time had reached the sum of £11,846. Their lordships also found 'that Mr Pretiman, receiver of first fruits and tenths and indebted to his Majesty in very considerable sums', had maliciously pursued Browne (and now his heirs) for £4,181.17s, with thirty years' interest. Evelyn was later to describe the affair as the 'Tyrannous and unjust persecution' that had taken advantage of his own inexperience and 'Sir Richards Forgetfulnesse, great Age, Impotence Infirmitie to defend himselfe'.[12] It had proved not only an unusual but an extremely costly marriage settlement.

Financial negotiations almost certainly did not feature in the marriage of Samuel Pepys to Elizabeth St Michel. It appears to have been a love match, perhaps made on the spur of the moment, for Pepys, when describing the ecstasy he felt when he heard a certain piece of music, said it made him feel ill, 'as I have formerly been when in love with my wife'.[13] Despite the popularity of romance in books and in drama, love matches were not the norm for anybody with property. Indeed, they were generally frowned upon. One seventeenth-century writer, Daniel Rogers, declared that those who married for love were 'poor greenheads' who, after a few years, would envy the good fortune of those whose union had been built on stronger foundations.[14] Rogers was a Puritan, and could be described as conservative in his opinions. Margaret Cavendish, Duchess of Newcastle, was of a very different ilk, remarkably progressive in her views on a whole range of matters, particularly the education of women, but she too felt that romantic sentiments were not ideal in marriage. She prided herself on never having felt amorous love for her husband: 'I never was infected therewith. It is a disease, or passion, or both.'[15] Pepys's rash step is out of character for a careful man who was beginning to forge his career.

How they met is not known. Clare Tomalin, Pepys's biographer, speculates that it might have been in a bookshop, for Elizabeth loved reading in both English and French. She was of a lively and independent disposition, so the marriage seems to have been stormy from the very start. Having moved into a turret room in his cousin Edward Montague's lodgings in Whitehall Palace, the couple split up and Elizabeth went back to her parents in Charing Cross. Whatever the cause of their quarrel, it was made up and they lived first in Axe Yard and then took up residence in Seething Lane. We probably know more about their domestic life there than we do of any other seventeenth-century couple, or rather the domestic life as seen by Samuel. Just as his diary refers disapprovingly to his mother so it does to his wife. Jealousy and strife stalk the pages, with Samuel smashing a favourite piece of china that he had given her, pulling her nose and slapping her, and Elizabeth retiring to bed in a sulk, or taking out her temper on her servants. According to Pepys, Elizabeth would threaten to turn Catholic, a threat which must have come back to haunt him in the years after her death when he had to cope with the dangers of the Popish Plot.

The very first entry in Pepys's diary records not only the arrival of General Monck and his soldiers in London as a prelude to the restoration of the King, but also the arrival of Elizabeth's menstrual period, which meant their hopes for children were disappointed. These hopes were to be dashed again and again. In another entry Pepys recorded how he consulted 'gossips' about remedies. Ten suggestions were given, ranging from not hugging Elizabeth too hard or too much and wearing drawers made of Holland linen that was thought to be cooling, to drinking sage juice or alternatively mum, a kind of beer, with sugar. It was particularly stressed that in bed they should 'lie with our heads where our heels do, or at least to make the bed high at feet and low at head'.[16] All in vain, for the lack of children may have been the result of the operation that Pepys underwent to remove the stone from his bladder in 1658, or due to a recurring abscess of the labia suffered by Elizabeth which made it difficult to enjoy physical relations. If the latter is the explanation, it also throws some light on Pepys's infidelities.

Pepys's attitude to both his mother and his wife was coloured by the biblical precept that wives should be in subjection to their husbands.[17] This was certainly the belief that John Evelyn pursued to such an extent that it discomfits modern sensibilities. Married to Mary Browne when she was just thirteen years old, John felt he could mould her. In 1648 he drew up *Instructions Oeconomique* for his young bride in which he stressed the importance of a wife being young enough to be formed by her husband and accept his authority, echoing the words in the First Epistle of Peter: 'Woman converts to man, not man to her ... the Woman is the weaker vessel ... whose propertie is to be obedient unto her Husband'.[18] These instructions were exquisitely handwritten into a manual, which Evelyn asked Mary not to show to anybody else. Hating to be mocked, he did not want to be seen as an exacting teacher, an indication that his controlling characteristic was taken to greater extremes than was the norm for the time.

Very fortunately for him, Mary, a shrewd and intelligent woman, was able to cope with this. She had been well educated in the humanist tradition, studying drawing and mathematics, and missing Paris and the female salons when she moved to Deptford. John encouraged her in her studies, hiring a drawing master who also helped her with her flower paintings. Nevertheless, her husband felt that housekeeping should take priority, specifying the equipment for her still-room and keeping a commonplace book with recipes for medicine, preserves, perfumes and cookery.[19] Indeed, Mary became known for her household skills: Samuel Hartlib praised her for 'all manner of sweetmeats most rare', while a friend wrote a letter to her alluding to 'excellent conserves and Wines with which Deptford is so constantly stored'.[20]

Mary and John embarked upon family life in 1652. During her pregnancy, John told Mary that he found himself 'affected with a kind of tendernesse, such as I never perceived in my selfe before'.[21] Their first son, Richard, named after his two grandfathers, became the joy of their lives. When Richard was eighteen months, his thrilled father reported to Sir Richard Browne that he was already 'so forward, & full of prate (for he speakes very many words & goes about daintily), so natural a lover of bookes & pictures, so serious & yet so cheerful & quiet a humour that I hope to present him one day to you as one that may possibly afford you some hopes of his presaging an honest man'.[22]

In all, eight children were born to the Evelyns, with seventeen years of constant pregnancy for Mary because she gave her newborn babies to a wet nurse. In his instructions to his wife, John had likened a family to a political state in miniature:

> for even Private Families, the Husband & Wife, being the first Politiq & Society in the World, are the seminaries both of Church and State, a Compendium of absolute monarchy and the best of Governments . . . Those who have a Family needs no Publiq Calling to redeeme themselves from idlenesse; the Employment of Instituting, and regulating it well is sufficient to take-up our whole time, and to exercise our choicest Talents; especially if there be Children who are to be educated.[23]

This happy anticipation was, however, dashed, first by the death of their second son in 1654, followed in 1658 by those of Richard and his brother George. It has been suggested that parents in seventeenth-century England were inured to the sudden death of their children, but the outpouring of grief from both Mary and John suggest otherwise. Breaking the news of Richard's death to Browne in Paris, Evelyn wrote: 'God, has Sir, taken from us that Deare Child, your Grandson: Your Godsonn; and with him all the joy and satisfaction that could be derived from the greatest hopes . . . indeede his whole life was from the beginning so great a Miracle, that it were hard to exceed in the description of it.' In a letter written three weeks later he described Mary's emotional state: 'still in teares, and in every corner of this house she heares the voyce & sees the face of her deare Companion, that strangly cherfull & beautifull child'.[24]

Denied the chance to educate his son Richard, Evelyn ensured that his four surviving children, John and his three sisters, Mary, Elizabeth and Susanna, were given a good schooling. Whilst he himself taught his daughters Greek and Latin, Evelyn first engaged Milton's nephew, Edward Phillips, as tutor for his son, soon to be replaced by a young

Oxford scholar, Ralph Bohun. Life was not easy for John Evelyn junior, having his dead brother's example to live up to. When he was only two years old, his father described him as 'a goodly child, but not of so ready an apprehension as the other was at his age'.[25] Bohun was prone to moods, and on one occasion his pupil tried to run away, complaining of his tutor's severity. The one person who was able to humour Bohun out of these huffs was Mary Evelyn, and the two became close friends, maintaining a witty correspondence over the years.

John junior was handicapped by a crooked leg, and was to suffer depression throughout his life, possibly a legacy inherited from his paternal grandmother (p. 4). He was not helped by his emotional and demanding father, who constantly wrote to him words of advice and criticism as he grew older. Friends, including Pepys, tried to intervene to support the boy. In one letter to Evelyn, Pepys talked up his son's skills as a linguist.[26] John junior must have been grateful for such help, for he asked Pepys to stand godfather to one of his daughters. His skill enabled him to translate René Rapin's Latin poem *Of Gardens* that was published in 1673, and on this occasion he made his father very proud.

The child who seems to have replaced his son Richard in Evelyn's estimation was his eldest daughter, Mary. She combined high-mindedness with learning, qualities appreciated by Evelyn; indeed, they mirrored his own character. In his diary, Evelyn provides a pen portrait of his daughter. At Christmas 1684 Mary was invited to stay with friends in London for an extended period, but longed to come home to her parents at Sayes Court, 'quite tired, as she confessed, with the vaine & empty Conversation of the Towne, the Theaters, the Court, & trifling visites which consum'd so many precious moments, and made her sometimes (unavoidably) misse of that regular Course of piety, which gave her the greatest satis-faction'.[27] This reference in Evelyn's diary was in fact a kind of elegy to his daughter, for in March 1685 she suddenly contracted smallpox and died. Her mother Mary told Bohun: 'I loved them all yet some distinc-tion might reasonably be allowed the eldest, as first and for many reasons somthing to be preffered.'[28]

Wrapped up in their grief, Mary and John Evelyn did not notice that their daughter Elizabeth had attracted the attentions of the nephew of the naval commissioner in the dockyard, and at the end of July she eloped with the young man, whose name is unknown, and married him. Evelyn turned to Pepys for help in tracking down his daughter and her seducer in 'this clandestine Intrigue'. The editor of the correspondence between Pepys and Evelyn, Guy de la Bédoyère, notes how three letters written by Evelyn to Pepys stand out from the rest.[29] Gone is the polite courtesy, replaced by passionate fury. One of the things that particularly irked him was that some of his neighbours in the dockyard, who may have assisted the eloping couple, were celebrating his humiliation, suggesting that he was not popular, possibly because of his pious airs and graces. He told Pepys that he intended to strike Elizabeth out of his will. This implacable response contrasts with a note in the accounts of John junior, of a payment of £5.7s.6d to his sister; a small sum, but probably helping towards the costs involved in her elopement. Unfortunately, we do not have the response from Pepys during this dramatic period.[30]

The drama all too soon turned to tragedy when, three weeks later, Elizabeth also contracted smallpox. Mary Evelyn went immediately to her bedside, followed eventually by her father when he realised the gravity of her situation, and bringing with him the rector of Deptford to give her a blessing and the sacrament. When Elizabeth died on 29 August 1685, Evelyn noted sadly in his diary, '& thus in lesse than 6 moneths were we depriv'd of two Children for our unworthinesse, & causes best known to God'.[31] Mary and John were left with just two children, John junior and Susanna. John had married in 1680, characteristically well-provided with advice from his father on all aspects of marriage, and two years later a John Evelyn of the new generation was born. This was Jack, who was to fulfil the hopes that his grandfather had demanded constantly from his children through the years.

The Evelyns' youngest daughter, Susanna, who had been described by her mother as rather backward in her accomplishments in comparison with her sisters, now came into her own, showing herself to be skilled with her pencil, paintbrush and needle. This delighted her father, who had cherished from childhood a desire to be an artist, and who translated histories of the techniques of engraving, and of architecture and painting.[32] This delight is clearly to be seen in a poem that he sent to Susanna when she was taking the waters at Tunbridge Wells in 1689. Having listed the temptations that the spa's society might offer her, he finished his letter:

O Wiccked Wells, Good Child, come home,
And fall againe to point & Loome;
If thou forget Cromatique pencil,
And then to words again do wincell,
Far-better Thou hads't learn'd to Spin
Than ever Tunbridge to have seene.[33]

Susanna continued with her art after her marriage to William Draper, recording landscapes with an invention devised by her father, probably a *camera obscura*, as well as portraits, flower studies, and what she intriguingly called 'Indian pictures'. Although some of these works are mentioned in Evelyn's inventory of Wotton in 1702, none can be identified with certainty today, but clearly she was a talented artist, in contact with professional painters of the time.[34] She also produced a large family who, with their cousins Jack and Elizabeth, provided joy and comfort to John and Mary Evelyn.

Pepys, without the joys, and sadnesses, of children, became attached to the members of his household. Just as we have an unusually detailed record of his marriage to Elizabeth, we also know much more about Pepys's household than is the norm through his diary – the written equivalent of the drawings that William Hogarth was to make of his servants in the eighteenth century. When Pepys and his bride set up home together in Montague's lodgings in Whitehall there was no servant, but when they moved into Axe Yard, Jane Birch joined them in 1658 as their maid. The arrival at Seething Lane in 1660 marked a change in lifestyle. Pepys had to have a footboy to attend him in public and underline his increased social status. Will Hewer was also part of the household, combining his role as Pepys's clerk with another as his manservant, before moving out to lodgings and setting off on his own remarkably successful career.

Another member, arriving in January 1661, was Pepys's sister Paulina, known as Pall, who, if her brother is to be believed, was both ill-natured and ill-favoured. Pall was taken into the household not 'as a sister in any respect, but as a servant', and was expected to stand in the presence of her sister-in-law, and not to take her meals with her brother and his wife.[35] As Pepys prospered, so the household grew, as did what the Victorians liked to call 'the servant problem'. Pepys records in his diary in October 1661 coming home 'to find my wife displeased with her maid Doll; whose fault is that she cannot keep her peace, but will always be talking in an angry manner, though it be without any reason and to no purpose, which I am sorry for'. This could well be Doll the cook-maid, a black servant. With the growth of the West Indian trade, slaves were brought to England for domestic service, and Pepys was later to have at least two others, including a boy whose behaviour so upset the household that he was sent back to the West Indies in 1688, to be sold into service in the plantations.

Pepys goes on in his diary to say: '[I] do see the inconvenience that doth attend the increase of a man's fortune, by being forced to keep more servants, which brings trouble.'[36] Just as Pepys required a footboy as a status symbol, so Elizabeth decided that she had to have a waiting woman, thus instituting a drama that runs through the rest of the diary. Elizabeth wanted somebody to sing with her and go to plays, for as Pepys observed, one of her problems was that she had time on her hands. Pall was considered for this role, but rejected. Gosnell arrived in Seething Lane in December 1662 possessed of a good singing voice and handsome face, both of which met with Pepys's approval, and he bought a book of country dances to encourage her. The daughter of a widow with little money but genteel connections, Gosnell was prepared to sing and to attend to Elizabeth's hair, but she did not feel that they went to enough plays, and was displeased not to go to court every week. After she left to become an actress, Pepys went to watch her perform. When she was playing in *The Rivals*, Sir William Davenant's adaptation of Fletcher and Shakespeare's *Two Noble Kinsmen*, he sadly observed that she 'comes and sings and dances finely; but for all that, fell out of Key, so that the Musique could not play to her afterward'.[37]

The problem for Elizabeth's waiting women was one that also beset governesses in households in future centuries: well bred but impecunious, they occupied the middle ground between the family and the servants. After Gosnell's departure, others came and went, not helped by Pepys paying them too much attention. At the same time efforts were made to get Pall a husband after Elizabeth agreed that she should have a dowry of £400. She came to London and began acquiring suitors, often unsuitable, but in 1668 she married John Jackson from Ellington in Huntingdonshire, described by Pepys as a man 'of no education nor discourse'.[38] Although the marriage was apparently not very happy, it produced two sons, one of whom, John Jackson junior, was to become Samuel's heir.

In the same year that Pall was sent back to the country, Deb Willet arrived in Seething Lane. Deb, straight from school in Bow, a model of good deportment, was described by Elizabeth as very handsome. Unfortunately she was too handsome, arousing Elizabeth's suspicions. These turned out to be justified when Elizabeth entered a room one day to find Deb combing her master's hair while he was 'embracing the girl con my hand sub su coats; and endeed, I was with my main in her cunny'. After a violent scene, Deb departed with a warning from Pepys against ever allowing anyone to take those liberties – a breathtaking piece of hypocrisy.[39]

Only months after Deb's departure, Samuel decided to finish his diary and to take Elizabeth on their visit to France, possibly as a gesture of contrition, followed shortly by Elizabeth's sudden death. This changed the complexion of Pepys's household, but it did not stop the dramas, which we learn about through occasional references. In the 1670s, with his increasing wealth and status, Pepys could afford both a housekeeper and a butler. The latter, John James, was dismissed for having an affair with the housekeeper, and took his revenge by giving false testimony in an attempt to implicate Pepys in the Popish Plot (p. 50). While defending himself in the House of Commons, Pepys declared: 'All know that I am unfortunate in my Servants, but I hope that it is no crime to be so'. The person who had found John James in bed with the housekeeper was Pepys's household musician, Cesare Morelli. By the late 1670s, with the alarm about popish plots, it was risky to have a known Catholic in his employ, and Pepys had to go to considerable lengths to ensure Morelli's safe passage out of London, and then out of the country. Pepys's paternalistic interest in his servants is shown by the fact that he finally fell out with Morelli after the latter had married without consulting him.

The servant problems continued. While the nation was recovering from the departure of James II and the accession of William and Mary to the throne, James Houblon, Pepys's merchant friend, was obliged to write to him on behalf of his housekeeper Mrs Fane. Pepys had fallen out with her because of her treatment of the other servants. Pepys responded by declaring that she was a knowing, faithful and vigilant person, but that 'she hath a height of spirit, captiousness of humour, and bitterness of tongue, that, of all womankind I have hitherto had to do withal, do render her conversation and comportment, as a servant, most insupportable'.[40] This was quite a claim considering the uneasy domestic matters of the earlier decades. Nevertheless there is also evidence of fondness within the household. Jane Birch, Samuel and Elizabeth's first servant, left only to marry another member of the household, Tom Edwards, who worked for many years as a clerk in the Navy Office. After Edwards's death in 1681, Jane returned to Pepys and later acted as William Hewer's housekeeper. When Pepys died in 1703, six of his servants were present at his bedside. Jane was given an annuity in his will, and her son, Pepys's godson, received a ring at his funeral. William Hewer, who had started life as Pepys's manservant and office clerk, became one of his closest friends.

Pepys undoubtedly chose to acquaint himself with people who might help him in his career during the 1660s, whilst Evelyn did not have to be so self-serving, given his financial independence. However, the enduring friendships of the two men were numerous and reflected their different fields of interest, numbering among them fellow members of the Royal Society, scholars, and naval and mercantile contacts. These were mostly men, but Evelyn, despite his wariness of the royal court, counted female courtiers among his friends and corresponded with both men and women as a result of his horticultural interests. Pepys's theatrical and musical friends were often women.

Evelyn's correspondence contains letters to several women friends, addressed in elaborate complimentary language. One of the first to receive these was Elizabeth Carey, daughter of a groom of the bedchamber to Charles II in exile in France, and the childhood companion of Mary Evelyn. She was both vivacious and devout, a combination that John Evelyn found particularly attractive. In 1657 he wrote how they 'grew to a Confidence so innocent, so intire that if she had ben my sister, & that sister an Angel I could not have lov'd her more, nor was anything so agreable to me as the progresse of our friendship'.[41] When both returned to England they continued to correspond, with Elizabeth addressing him as 'Dear Master' and 'Dear Governor', while he called her 'Electra'. The convention of using classical pseudonyms was often adopted by circles of platonic friends at this time.

Other recipients of Evelyn's gallantry included Anne, wife of Sir Nicholas Slanning and one of the daughters of Sir George and Lady Carteret. The Carteret family were also well known to Pepys, and in his diary he recorded meeting Anne in Deptford, describing her as 'the best humoured woman in the world, and a devout woman (I having spied her on her knees half an hour this morning in her chamber) . . . and mighty merry'. As with Elizabeth Carey, this proved an irresistible combination to Evelyn, who referred to Anne as 'my Seraphic' in a letter to her mother.[42] The concept of 'seraphic', ardent, angelic devotion had become popular as a result of a book written by the scientist Robert Boyle, *Some Motives and Incentives to the Love of God, better known as Seraphick Love*, published in 1659. His book took the form of a letter to a friend who has been slighted by the woman he loved, urging him to convert his human passion into religious devotion, turning away from the transitory and unsatisfying love of women. When it appeared, John Evelyn wrote to the celibate Boyle arguing the case for the nurturing and saving grace of women. For Evelyn, matrimony provided affection and respect, but he turned to his friendships with women for the platonic ideal.

These high-minded concepts with their religious overtones would have been alien to Pepys at this time. Although he held some women in high esteem, such as Jemima Montague, Lady Sandwich, his relationships with the opposite sex were usually of a much earthier nature, as we learn from his diary. Perhaps due to his wife's character and medical condition, he pursued women who were often vulnerable – servants in his own household, wives of people who worked for him such as Mrs Bagwell, shop assistants such as the linen drapers Betty and Doll Lane in Westminster Hall, and complaisant acquaintances such as the actress Mrs Knepp. Robert Hooke recorded his own sexual relations in his diary, including those with his niece. Pepys certainly did not venture into the realms of incest, but both men reflect an attitude that was all too common at the time.

Yet Pepys was capable of wonderful double standards. Not only did he join John Evelyn in criticising the moral turpitude of the royal court, he also issued a stern reproof to his cousin and patron, Lord Sandwich, when he discovered he was having an affair. In 1663, Montague, recovering from an illness, was lodging at the house of a merchant's wife in Chelsea where he met one of the daughters, Betty Becke. Pepys was shocked that he should 'grossly play the beast and fool', being seen with her in public and 'playing on his lute under her window, and forty other poor sordid things'.[43] Pepys was especially upset because he did not like to witness Lady Sandwich's distress and humiliation. A strong and intelligent woman, she decided to take the bull by the horns and invite the Becke family to visit her in Kensington, with Pepys present at the occasion. He was surprised to find that Betty was 'a fine lady, of a fine Talle [taille, or form] and very well carriage and mighty discreet', and when he engaged her in conversation, found it excellent. His verdict was that she was 'a woman of such an air, as I wonder the less at my Lord's favour to her'.[44]

What is interesting about this incident is that it shows how Pepys made a distinction between women – usually of a lower social status – whom he considered fair game, and those ladies of status as well as intelligence and character, whom he could admire and who might become his friends. Of course we do not know of his sexual adventures after he ended his diary, coinciding as it did with the death of his wife. Did he become less judgemental as he got older and more distant from his emotionally charged marriage? What we do know is that in the 1670s he became part of a close-knit circle of friends through his connection with the Houblon family. The Houblons were a Huguenot family of merchants, a father and nine sons, with trading connections in France, the Iberian Peninsula and the Mediterranean. Pepys's particular friend was Sir James, who lived in state, or 'en Prince' as Evelyn described it, in Great Winchester Street, close to London Wall.[45]

There are hints in Pepys's diary that the Houblons either did not take to Elizabeth or disapproved of her, for when James called at Seething Lane, he left his wife Sarah out in the carriage.[46] However, once Pepys became a widower, he was welcomed into the Houblons' circle, and went to the theatre and on outings with Sarah, as well as singing with her. Two other members of this circle were Pepys's cousins by marriage, Lady Mordaunt and her sister Mrs Steward, both widows who had set up home together in Portugal Row on the south side of Lincoln's Inn Fields. Yet another member was Thomas Hill, who shared Pepys's passion for music. He often acted as the Houblons' agent in Europe and, in a letter written to Pepys in April 1673 from Lisbon, he declared in jest that the two sisters in their correspondence with him betrayed how they

are desperately in Love with you, and sigh out their Passions so charmingly, that I find strange alterations in my self, and tis hard to conclude, whether to envy, or pitty you. Your injoyments in their Conversation, can no where else be found; and theirs is so great, when you entertain them, that they all acknowledge your Humour the best in the whole world.[47]

These friendships endured, and after Pepys had a narrow escape from drowning when the Duke of York's yacht foundered during a visit to Scotland in 1682, the affection in which he was held comes over in a letter from Will Hewer. 'You cann't imagine in what Consternation all your friends in general were upon the Reporte of your being cast away, but more especially those at ... Winchester Street and Portugall Row, to whome I communicated your Letter.'[48] As late as 1695 Pepys wrote a letter 'of compliment and banter' to Mrs Steward about the dearth of muslin in the London shops as a result of the war with France. Like Evelyn, he was now capable of gallant dealings with women.[49]

Both Evelyn and Pepys had friendships with women that stand out as singular. Whereas that between John Evelyn and Margaret Blagge has to be understood in the context of the time, however, the friendship that blossomed between Samuel Pepys and Mary Skinner has a remarkably modern ring to it.

Evelyn first met Margaret Blagge by chance in June 1669. Mrs Howard, the Duke of York's housekeeper at the Treasurer's House in Deptford, invited Mary Evelyn to join a party that included her two daughters, Anne and Dorothy, and their friend Margaret, on a pleasure trip down the Thames to the Kentish coast.[50] The friendship itself, however, began three years later when Margaret approached Evelyn for advice on her financial affairs. Margaret came from a Suffolk gentry family but, unlike the Evelyns, the Blagges lacked the wealth of land and industry as a buttress. When her father died just after the Restoration, the family, in straitened circumstances, lodged with relations. In 1666 Margaret became a maid of honour to Anne Hyde, Duchess of York. This was no sinecure for, despite their high rank, these young girls were expected to fulfil household duties for little money. Margaret, moreover, was entering a world that had declined into sleaziness. The courtier wit Charles Sedley is reputed to have asked one new arrival whether she intended to be 'a Beauty, a Miss [mistress], a Wit or a Politician'.[51] Sedley's own daughter, Catherine, by her own admission was no beauty but she did possess the other qualifications to become the mistress of the Duke of York. Margaret was definitely a beauty and was known for her witty repartee, but she also held strong religious views, so there was no chance that she would succumb.

John Evelyn felt awkward in his dealings with the young ladies of the court, who found him quaint. In a letter to a courtier friend in 1671 he wrote:

> some took me for a schoolmaster, & I believe thought my wife the unhappiest woman in the world ... I was a man of the shade, and one who had conversed more with plants and books than the circle: I had contracted an odd reservedness, which rendered me wholly unfit to converse among the knights of the carpet and the refined things of the antechamber.[52]

But when his friendship with Margaret began the following year, he felt that he had found a kindred spirit, and he met her regularly for prayers and charitable works. The pages of his diary become sprinkled with pentangles, symbol of divinity and of stoicism. He even made a drawing of their seraphic 'altar of friendship', which they both inscribed (Plate 25). Frances Harris, who has written movingly about their relationship, calls this image 'a kind of spiritual betrothal'.[53]

Anne Carey now forgotten, Evelyn bestowed upon Margaret the name Electra, while he was Philaretes, 'lover of virtue'. Margaret's friends, Dorothy and Anne, were Alcidonia and Ornithonia, and Mary Evelyn wryly included herself in the coterie with the countrified name of Hortensia. However, the strains of the intense friendship were beginning to show, for, whether or not he admitted it to himself, Evelyn was falling in love with Margaret. Mary Evelyn, who had early noted how 'never two people were more alike in their way and inclination', intervened in the autumn of 1672 with a finely judged letter in which she reminded her husband of her own claims and suggested he spend more time at Sayes Court and less at the royal court.[54]

Not long into her time as a maid of honour, Margaret had met the rising politician, Sidney Godolphin, and entered a secret understanding with him. When he returned to London from his post in Paris in late 1672, she persuaded him to postpone their marriage and to agree that she should leave the court and go to stay with his cousins at Berkeley House in Piccadilly. She had hoped to dedicate herself to a religious life, but while Robert Boyle as a wealthy man could choose a life of celibacy, Margaret had no such luxury. Although in Catholic France, where she had spent some time, there was the possibility of conventual life, this was not an option in Protestant England. Evelyn, who had originally encouraged Margaret in her desire for celibacy, now urged her to marry Godolphin, causing at one stage a rift between them when she found his manner hectoring. For nearly two years Margaret agonised about her future life when at last the Gordian knot of indecision, which was making all the players in the scenario thoroughly unhappy, was cut by Charles II. He commanded that Margaret should return to court and play a leading role in a masque.

Although his parents had been enthusiastic participants in court masques devised in the 1630s by Inigo Jones and Ben Jonson, Charles II

preferred the public theatre. By 1674, however, there was a new generation of courtiers around him, including his illegitimate son, the Duke of
Monmouth, the two princesses, Mary and Anne, and their young step-
mother, the Duchess of York, who was familiar with masques from her
Italian childhood. It was decided that Christmas should be marked by a
'Celebration of the Splendour and Grandeur of the English Monarchy'.
This would be held in the theatre of Whitehall Palace, with the young
members of the royal family taking various roles, apart from the Duchess,
who was pregnant.

Dryden for some reason was passed over as the librettist, and the text
was written by a young, relatively untried playwright, John Crowne. The
whole thing had to be done in a tremendous hurry, so Crowne made the
decision on the spur of the moment to take the story of Calisto from
Ovid's *Metamorphoses*. He then realised that this would involve a rape
scene, so combined it with another of Ovid's tales, of Diana and Actaeon.
The scenery was to be designed by the King's Serjeant Painter, Robert
Streeter, with music by Nicholas Staggins. Just four months were given
over for the amateur performers to learn their parts, the music to be
composed, dances arranged, costumes made and sets constructed.
Margaret Blagge was drafted in to take the presiding role of Diana, the
goddess of chastity, with the young princesses as her accompanying
nymphs. A most unwilling participant, she was apparently a vital ingredient because she had acted before. As John Evelyn later explained, 'It was
not possible to leave her out who had upon the like Solemnity formerly
... acquitted herselfe with so universal Applause & Admiration'.[55]
Moreover, she and her fiancé Sidney Godolphin recognised that this was
a chance to extract from the King her marriage portion, already eighteen
months overdue.

Calisto was not a great success. The rush meant that the quality of
the text, music and scenery was below par, and only the sumptuous
costumes were regarded as a triumph. Margaret found the experience
deeply humiliating, with her fellow players teasing her about her role as
the epitome of chastity when she was about to marry. As soon as the last
performance was given in April, she fled to Berkeley House, where
Evelyn witnessed her falling on her knees at her oratory, thanking God

that she was delivered from her ordeal. But one good thing did come of the masque, in that the King authorised the payment of her money, and on 16 May 1675 she and Sidney married at a secret ceremony in the Temple Church, a royal peculiar that did not require the publication of banns. The entry in the register recorded that 'Mr Lame married a Cupple ... their names I doe not knowe', and only later did the clerk add their identities on a separate slip.

Evelyn was not let into the secret, finding out about the marriage almost a year later. He must have been hurt, but Margaret cleverly implied that the secrecy was Sidney's idea, so that Evelyn felt that he could accept the authority of a husband. When Margaret asked for his guidance, Evelyn was back in his element, producing a treatise of nearly a hundred pages. Just as he had written his *Instructions Oeconomique* for his young bride in 1648, so he entitled this work *Oeconomics to a Newly Married Friend*. The first nineteen pages were devoted to extended parallels between friendship and marriage. Margaret diplomatically turned to Evelyn's wife for practical help on setting up home and Mary warmly responded with a manual giving details of annual housekeeping expenses for a family of eight, 'as many as were in the Ark'. The couple moved into Sidney Godolphin's lodgings in Scotland Yard which had been renovated for them by Robert Hooke under Evelyn's supervision.

Margaret Godolphin soon became pregnant. One of her last outings was with the Evelyns to The Ark, the collection of curiosities that had been amassed by the gardener John Tradescant and opened to the public in his house in South Lambeth. The 'museum' was now looked after by Elias Ashmole, who had managed to wrest possession from the widow of the younger John Tradescant. Whether Evelyn approved of this legal sleight of hand is not recorded, but he certainly did not approve of Ashmole's astrological interests. When another of the party asked Ashmole to tell them whether Margaret would have a boy, he assured them this would happen, but then stopped Mary Evelyn as she was leaving the room and quietly told her 'something makes me wish, that Lady may have a hapy delivery'.[56] This concern turned out to be all too real, for although Margaret gave birth to a healthy boy, Francis, she died from puerperal fever on 3 September 1678 after days of terrible pain.

Margaret had been fearful of childbirth, and Evelyn had sought to reassure her by telling her that little women suffered little pain. She wrote to Sidney in the last days of her pregnancy to prepare for the possibility that she might die, for the perils were all too evident. Figures for death in childbirth are difficult to ascertain, but lie somewhere between 118 and 147 per 1,000 in the second half of the seventeenth century. Margaret also begged Sidney, should he remarry, to ensure that her son was loved. Sidney never did remarry, and Francis grew up to become a leading statesman under Queen Anne. John Evelyn assuaged his grief by writing a 'Life' of Margaret as a memorial for the widower and circle of devout friends, elevating her to his pantheon of beloved women that his daughter Mary was to join after her death in 1685.

The friendship between Pepys and Mary Skinner is one of the great mysteries of his life. If Elizabeth Pepys was the silent woman, Mary is the woman in the shadows, part of Samuel's life for thirty-three years, as he makes clear in his will, but of whom we know so little. She was probably born around 1653, the daughter of Daniel and Frances Skinner. Her father was a merchant from Braintree in Essex who had a London house in Mark Lane, close to Pepys's home in Seething Lane. The couple most likely met at St Olave's Church in 1670, the year after Elizabeth's death. It would seem that they began a secret affair that caused a breach between Pepys and her parents when it was discovered. The evidence for this comes from a letter that her brother, also called Daniel, wrote to Pepys in July 1676. By the time that letter was written, the Skinners were reconciled to the relationship between Samuel and Mary, and she probably had moved into his lodgings in Derby House in Westminster. Later that year, Robert Hooke recorded in his diary giving a recipe for varnish to Mrs Pepys.

Why did the couple not marry? The answer could lie with Pepys's stormy first marriage: he had had enough of matrimony. His double standards as far as his relationships with women was concerned is well attested, and he had the best of both worlds with Mary, a sexual partner who still allowed him the freedom to enjoy friendships with other women, such as Lady Mordaunt and Mrs Steward. But the answer could equally lie in Mary's character. Society in seventeenth-century England was strongly patriarchal, as reflected in common law, meaning that a woman was the property of her father until marriage and of her husband thereafter. Through family bequests Mary had money of her own and from the glimpses we get of her, she was an independent and resourceful person. For instance, in September 1693 Pepys was celebrating Michaelmas by driving out of London to Chelsea with his nephew John Jackson and a party of ladies when his coach was held up by highwaymen, who stole his purse and some possessions. When Pepys asked if he could have back a single item, a mathematical instrument, one of the high-waymen, as a gentleman, agreed to return it to him at a tavern in Charing Cross the following day. This was a fatal mistake, for the highwayman, Thomas Hoyle, was taken at the tavern and tried at the Old Bailey. According to the law report, the ladies were frightened, apart from one: 'My Lady Pepys saved a Bag of Money that she had about her.' Lady Pepys was surely Mary Skinner, hiding her money under her skirts.[57]

Mary was clearly the mistress of Pepys's household. When the housekeeper, Mrs Fane, fell out with Pepys over her sharp tongue (p. 88), Mary stood up for her and saved her from being dismissed. She was seen as a threat by John Jackson, determined to inherit Pepys's money, and by Balty St Michel, ever ready to enjoy Pepys's charity. The latter called at Buckingham Street one day in May 1689 to find that Pepys was absent, imprisoned as a Jacobite suspect. Instead he encoun-tered Mary and as a result wrote a furious letter to the prisoner: 'I understand that by the malicious inventive ill Offices of a female Beast, which you keepe, I am like allsoe to lye under your Anger and disgrace'. Having just married for the second time, Balty was in pursuit of favours, so went on, 'I hope, and humbly pray (though she told me impudently, and arrogantly, you Scorned to see me) that with your Generous Usuall goodness, wisdom, manhood and former kindness you will not damn him Unheard whoe Shoold Joy to hazard . . . his dearest Bludd for your Service.'[58] Not surprisingly, Pepys was shocked by the rude tone, which could scarcely have helped Balty's case.

Ironically, Pepys was soon after being importuned by one of Mary's brothers, Peter Skinner, whom he had helped to a job and who was now in trouble. In terms of abject extravagance, Peter began a letter in 1689,

'If Tears and Sighs and the un-feigned sorrows of a perplexed and uneasie Mind can make any Impression upon your Honor's good Nature to pardon my offending you'. He had evidently been forbidden to approach his sister, whom he described as 'ye Darling of my Repose, the Center of all my Happiness and all my Earthly Felicity'.[59]

On a more positive note, Pepys's friends seem to have accepted Mary as his partner, sending their wives' compliments along with their own. Even the high-minded Evelyn overlooked the fact that their relationship had not been blessed by matrimony, referring to Mary delicately as 'Mr Pepps inclination'.[60] In a letter written in January 1699, he first wished Pepys a happy and prosperous new year, before wishing 'the Lady, all the satisfaction of a Versailles in the Cabinet she is adorning', pointing out in his ornate manner that it was not worth going to France 'so long as it is more perfection in York Street'.[61] This reference is ambiguous. Mary Skinner was an artist and a decorator, and could have been working on the room, armed with the varnish recipe supplied years earlier by Robert Hooke. Or it could signify that her portrait was hanging there, perhaps the picture now in the Pepys Library in Magdalene College, Cambridge, thought to be of Mary in a fashionably low-cut dress of teal-coloured satin (Plate 27).

Pepys developed his library as a record of his life, both in the collection of the books, as will be explored in Chapter 9, and in his furnishing of the room. The paintings hanging on the walls are shown in drawings made by Sutton Nicholls around the year 1693. Kneller's portrait of James II can be seen in one of them – a brave gesture, for at the time James was in exile in France and still a potential threat to the rule of William and Mary (Plate 28). Other portraits were of Pepys's great friends, including that of John Evelyn, also commissioned from Godfrey Kneller in 1689. For this, Evelyn was depicted against an exotic background, holding a copy of his most famous book, *Sylva*.

Pepys also had an engraving made from Evelyn's portrait, which he included in his collection 'of Heads in Taille-Douce & Drawings' (Plate 26). It appears on a page with four other of Pepys's closest friends: Sir Anthony Deane, Sir James Houblon, Dr Thomas Gale and William Hewer. In the 1660s Deane had been a shipwright at Woolwich and shared naval and scientific interests with Pepys, as well as being arrested alongside him on suspicion of plots in 1679 and 1689. James Houblon shared his love of music, 'good discourse' and commercial interests. Thomas Gale, married to a distant cousin of Pepys, was a fellow member of the Royal Society. William Hewer, one of Pepys's first servants, had risen up through the navy, and repaid his former master's patronage by looking after him in his old age with 'all the Care, kindness and faithfulness of a Son'.[62] Pepys placed his own portrait in the centre of this select group of closest friends who had shared the ups and downs of his life.

Shortly before he died, Evelyn wrote a memoir for his grandson Jack in which he recommended him to choose as a friend someone to whom he could freely open his mind. 'Such a one is indeede to be esteem'd an inestimable Treasure & hard to be found.'[63] Samuel Pepys had become just such a treasure to John Evelyn.

PART III

'I Do Indulge Myself a Little the More in Pleasure'

5

TAKE NOBODY'S WORD FOR IT

F OR MEN LIKE John Evelyn and Samuel Pepys, with an unquench-
able desire for knowledge, the ideal institution was the Royal
Society. In 1662 the Society received its first charter from Charles II,
with a second the following year, increasing its privileges and ampli-
fying its name to the Royal Society of London for the Promotion of
Natural Knowledge. Its chosen motto was *Nullius in Verba* ('Take
nobody's word for it'), from the Epistles of Horace, particularly appropriate for a society whose primary motive was knowledge through practical experimentation. Evelyn was instrumental in getting the royal
connection, whilst Pepys was elected a fellow in 1665.

Evelyn's interests in both the arts and the sciences started early
in his life, as can be seen in his travels in Europe during the 1640s
(pp. 13–17). A virtuoso in the making, he regarded mainland Europe as
a terrestrial cabinet. Even when he was living with the Brownes
in Paris in 1651, he attended chemistry lessons given by Nicaise Le
Fèvre, a Huguenot recently arrived in the city. Le Fèvre identified
three strands in chemistry: philosophy, medicine and pharmacology.
Evelyn appreciated this wide range, writing 'the End is to perfect,
and prepare medicines for the benefit of mans body also mettals, beesids
the discovering of many secrets of Nature both delightful & profitable'.[1]
On his return to England he installed a laboratory at Sayes Court

and began to connect with like-minded men in person and through correspondence.

Back in 1644 the first weekly meetings of an 'invisible college' were held at Gresham College in Bishopsgate. The Elizabethan financier Sir Thomas Gresham had bequeathed his London house and an endowment for seven professors to lecture successively on each day of the week, and the college began to function following the death of his widow in November 1596. According to Gresham's will, the lectures in English and Latin were to be 'for the gratuitous instruction of all who chose to attend'. In addition to the traditional arts subjects of divinity, music, law and rhetoric, there were to be professors of astronomy, geometry and physic.

By adding the last three posts in what we would describe as the sciences, Gresham was recognising that Oxford and Cambridge were stuck in a groove, debating ancient texts rather than developing these disciplines. It was in London in the last years of the sixteenth and early part of the seventeenth centuries that informal scientific activities were taking place. In *The Jewel House*, Deborah Harkness describes how practitioners, men and women, were testing new medicines and challenging traditional authorities; Dutch immigrants living in Lime Street in the heart of the City were cultivating plants imported from the Middle East and studying their characteristics; and instrument makers were constructing ingenious mechanical devices, such as the astronomical staff and the astrolabe. In sum, London 'provided later scientists with its foundations: the skilled labor, tools, techniques and empirical insights that were necessary to shift the study of nature out of the library and into the laboratory'.[2]

As well as these groups, there were individuals who at the time worked towards this scientific revolution. Hugh Platt, for instance, was fascinated by a wide range of topics from medical remedies to the properties of soil, and from cloth dyeing to sprinkler systems for cultivating indoor plants. By profession he was a lawyer, but he was also heir to a brewing fortune that enabled him to spend time exploring his manifold interests in discussions with experts, to carry out practical experiments and to make copious notes, some of which were turned into publications. In 1605 he was knighted by James I for his services as an inventor.

Although Platt represents a striking example of the inductive approach to natural knowledge, it is his fellow lawyer, Francis Bacon, who has been hailed as the man who set the stage for what is described as the Scientific Revolution. Despite his close connections with the courts of Elizabeth and James I, Bacon was not a man of great wealth, and was a very busy lawyer. So, although in his writings he advocated the pursuit of knowledge through inquiry and experiment, he was a thinker rather than a doer. He also belonged to a higher social order than many of the 'scientists' of the City. Bearing in mind one of his most famous sayings – knowledge is power – it is not surprising that he sought 'to transform London's doubtlessly energetic – but to his mind inchoate and purposeless – inquiries into nature into a tool of state that could benefit the commonwealth'.[3] He did this by conceiving an ideal institution, Salomon's House. This was included in a book published in English in 1626, the year of his death, allegedly from a chill caught after experimenting with preserving a chicken with snow: the ultimate in practical experimentation.

Salomon's House was the concept that inspired the men of the 'invisible college' in London in the 1640s. When politics took a dangerous turn with the outbreak of the Civil War, the group divided in 1648, some staying in London while others went to Oxford. Charles I had used Oxford as his headquarters during the Civil War, resulting in repercussions once the Parliamentarian troops led by Sir Thomas Fairfax took over the city. More than 300 university members were expelled along with all but three heads of colleges during 'visitations', to be replaced by men more sympathetic to Puritanism and the Parliamentarian cause. John Fell, son of the expelled Dean of Christ Church, complained: 'Within the compass of a few weeks an almost general riddance was made of the loyal University of Oxford, in whose rooms succeeded an illiterate rabble, swept up from the plough-tail, from shops and grammar schools, and the dregs of the neighbour university.'[4] The 'neighbour university' was, of course, Cambridge, and the arrival of their fellows meant that Oxford became a crucible for the development of knowledge in the various sciences. Three colleges in particular were centres for exploration into this field: Christ Church through Fell's replacement, John Owen; Magdalen under the presidency of Thomas Goodwin; and Wadham where the warden was Dr John Wilkins. Wilkins became the brother-in-law of Oliver Cromwell, and all three men served on a select committee when Cromwell was appointed Chancellor of the university. A club for experimental philosophy was formed in Oxford by the Parliamentarian physician William Petty and Thomas Willis, a Royalist soldier who stayed after the fall of the city to Fairfax and began to study medicine. The club met at Petty's lodgings in the High Street, conveniently over an apothecary's shop where materials could be acquired.

When Petty left Oxford to be physician to Cromwell's army in Ireland, the group moved to the Wadham lodgings of Dr Wilkins. In the Bodleian Library are the rules drawn up in October 1651, stipulating weekly meetings to be held every Thursday.[5] The astronomer Seth Ward set out the ambitious aims of the club: to equip a laboratory and observatory, to carry out chemical experiments, and to examine and index all the scientific books in 'our public library', the Bodleian. Three years later Robert Boyle was persuaded by Wilkins to leave his Dorset home and begin work on his famous experiments on the nature of air, in his lodgings, in the High Street. Here he was joined by Robert Hooke. From a comparatively modest background, Hooke had gone up to Christ Church in 1653, possibly as an organ scholar, possibly as a 'servitor' attending one of the wealthier students. According to John Aubrey, even at Westminster School Hooke had shown himself to be 'very mechanicall'.[6] His relationship to the university is rather mysterious: he apparently did not attend lectures, never matriculated, nor took a degree. Instead he worked as assistant first to Thomas Willis and then Boyle, building for the latter his air-pump. The conventional academic system did not provide an adequate scientific training, so Boyle had studied abroad and with private tutors, and Christopher Wren had assisted the anatomist Dr Charles Scarborough before going up to Oxford.

Clearly, it was exciting to be part of this Oxford group. Henry Oldenburg, an itinerant German scholar who was taken on as tutor to Boyle's nephew, called them the 'Oxonian sparkles'.[7] Initially Boyle had been wary of 'the prattling of our book-philosophers', but in a letter he expressed his delight at finding instead 'a knot of such ingenious & free philosophers, who I can assure you do not only admit & entertain real learning but cherish & improve it, & have done & are likely to do more toward the advancement of it than many of those pretenders that busy the press'.[8]

John Evelyn must have been infected with this excitement when in 1654 he paid a visit to his old university as part of a tour undertaken with his wife Mary. Visiting Wadham, he was taken into the college gardens by John Wilkins to see the beehives constructed by one of his students, Christopher Wren. Evelyn recorded in his diary how Wren showed him 'the Transparant Apiaries, which he had built like Castles & Palaces & so ordered them one upon another, as to take the Hony without destroying the Bees; These were adorn'd with variety of dials, little statues, Vanes, &c.' He was also shown a hollow statue that could be made to speak through a 'long & conceald pipe' and a gallery full of

Magical curiosities: a Way-Wiser [an instrument for measuring distance travelled by road], a Thermometer, a monstrous Magnes, Conic and other Sections, a Balance on a demie Circle, most of them of his [Wilkins's] owne & that prodigious young scholar, Mr. Chr:Wren, who presented me with a piece of White Marble he had stained with a lively red very deepe as beautifull as if it had ben naturall.[9]

Oxford may have sparkled, but London also had its attractions for those in search of scientific knowledge. When Wren became Gresham Professor of Astronomy in 1657, he found that the capital had 'so general a Relish of Mathematick and the *libera philosophia* in such a Measure, as is hardly to be found in the Academies [Oxford and Cambridge] themselves'.[10] In London Evelyn made the acquaintance of Samuel Hartlib. Born at the turn of the century in Elbing, a Baltic town that was then part of Poland, Hartlib had made his way to London in 1628 following the unwelcome arrival of the Habsburg armies. He became an unofficial agent for the Parliamentary cause, and at the end of the Civil War turned himself into what he called a conduit pipe, employing scribes and translators to copy portions of letters and treatises for circulating to others on a diverse range of practical scientific matters that included medicine, horticulture and land improvement.

In his diary Evelyn described Hartlib as 'A Publique Spirited, and ingenious person, who had propagated many Usefull things & Arts'.[11] Evelyn remembered at their first meeting talking of smoking chimneys and an ink that could provide a dozen copies if moist paper was pressed on it. Hartlib's account, on the other hand, described how Evelyn was 'desirous to see my Bee-hive' and to talk of 'a great Apparatus for a Universal Mechanical Work'.[12] This 'great Apparatus' was Evelyn's ambitious project to write a comprehensive history of trades, but he was finding it too much, and was eventually to abandon it.

At this time Evelyn was also working on a translation of *De Rerum Natura*, 'The Nature of Things', written in the first century BC by the Roman poet and philosopher Lucretius. In his poem Lucretius had provided an explanation of the philosophy of Epicurus, including the principles of atomism, the nature of the mind and soul, consideration of celestial and terrestrial phenomena, and how the universe operates according to physical principles rather than divine intervention: all areas that were occupying the minds of seventeenth-century natural philosophers. Evelyn only published one out of the six books of Lucretius before, again, abandoning the project. In his collection are a series of other unpublished documents on a range of scientific subjects, including mathematics, physics, natural history and a translation of an anonymous alchemical work, 'Coelum sanitas'.[13]

Following the unexpected death of Oliver Cromwell in September 1658, the possibility of a restoration of the monarchy gradually became a reality. Evelyn rather contrarily reacted to the approaching end of the 'long winter' by considering withdrawal from the world to a small community of natural philosophers. As noted earlier, this was an idea that Francis Bacon had propounded with Salomon's House in his *New Atlantis*, a fictional vision of the future of human discovery. The concept could be described as being like a modern research university for applied and pure science. In a letter to Robert Boyle, John Evelyn asked 'why might not some Gentlemen, whose Genius's are greately suitable, and, who desire nothing more than to give a good example, preserve science,

and cultivate themselves, joyne in Society together'. With his characteristic eye for detail, he proposed purchasing

> of 30, or 40 akers of Land, in some healthy place, not above 25 miles
> from London, of which a good part should be tall wood, and the rest
> upland-pastures or Downes, sweetely irrigated. We would erect upon
> the most convenient site of this, neere the wood, our Building; viz.
> one handsome Pavillion, containing a Refectory, Library, with-
> drawing roome, and a Closset.

This house would be a communal centre, with lodgings for guests
and, for the fellows, apartments or cells 'somewhat after the manner
of the Carthusians'. 'There should likewise be an Elaboratory, with a
Repository for rarities and things of nature, an Aviarie, Dove-house,
Physicall-Garden, Olitory Garden and a Plantation of Orchard fruits
etc.' Servants were to be kept at a 'convenient distance', and he expressed
the wish to bring his wife, but apparently not offering this luxury to
others. Boyle, who had declared himself celibate, may not have found
this a problem, but others may have thought differently. Evelyn even
made a drawing to show how his college might be laid out.[14]

By the time Evelyn had written this interesting letter in the autumn of
1659, the move towards a restoration of the monarchy was gaining
momentum, and by the new year General Monck was in London with his
troops. Less than a year later, with Charles back on the throne, a meeting
was held in rooms at Gresham College. This inaugural meeting of what was
to become the Royal Society was attended by twelve people from a variety
of backgrounds. There were former members of the Oxford group, such as
Wren, Boyle, Petty and Wilkins, who was soon to depart northwards to
become Dean of Ripon. Prominent members of the royal court also
attended, including William, Lord Brouncker, who became the society's
first president, and the Scottish politician Sir Robert Moray. Finally, there
were London physicians and intellectuals, such as the physician Jonathan
Goddard and Laurence Rooke, the Gresham Professor of Geometry.

This original twelve drew up a list of forty people they should invite
to join. Again, these men came from a variety of backgrounds. Those

connected with the court included Pepys's kinsman Lord Sandwich, John Evelyn and Sir Kenelm Digby, who had retired to Gresham College where he lived as a recluse following the sudden death of his wife, the beautiful Venetia Stanley. They were joined by Oxbridge academics such as the astronomer Seth Ward and London medical men. In the following years the membership rose, so that by May 1663, 135 elections had occurred: this group is known as the original fellows. The royal seal of approval was given by the election of Charles II, his brother the Duke of York, and his cousin Prince Rupert of the Rhine. The first overseas members were the Dutch natural philosopher Christiaan Huygens and the French physician Samuel Sorbière. Just as John Wilkins, Cromwell's brother-in-law, had encouraged those with Royalist sympathies to be part of the club for experimental philosophy in Oxford, so the Royal Society from its outset refused to exclude membership on doctrinaire or religious grounds. For example, John Evelyn was a staunch Anglican, the botanist and physician Nehemiah Grew a Nonconformist, and Sir Kenelm Digby a Roman Catholic.

In his diary for 21 January 1661, Samuel Pepys noted how he went with the instrument maker and inventor Ralph Greatorex 'to Gresham College (where I never was before) and saw the manner of the house, and find great company of persons of Honour there'.[15] This was one of the early meetings of the Society, not yet Royal, and although Greatorex attended these, he never became a fellow. The 'great company of persons of Honour there' included Lord Brouncker and Sir William Petty, with whom Pepys was later to work at the Navy Office, and John Evelyn. Therefore this may have been the first time that the diarists were together. As a student at Magdalene College, Pepys had received rudimentary instruction in the four subjects of the quadrivium: mathematics, geometry, astronomy and music. His tutor Samuel Morland, moreover, was a scientist and inventor whose experiments in the nature of flight attracted the attention of Hartlib and his circle in the 1650s, and who invented a calculating machine and a kind of photocopier. It is doubtful, however, that Morland was a source of inspiration to Pepys, who wrote of him in disparaging terms, particularly with regard to his political opportunism.

Pepys's interest in science probably arose from his natural curiosity, nourished by his naval work. Although he stated in his diary that he had never been to Gresham College before, he may have been referring to the Society rather than the building, for as a London schoolboy he could have attended the 'gratuitous' lectures there. In a letter in 1656 to his cousin Montague he referred to them both attending experiments in magnetism with 'Sir W.P.', who might have been the founding fellow, Sir William Pearsall, a gentleman from Staffordshire.[16] Pepys haunted the shops of instrument makers, purchasing microscopes, thermometers and devices for drawing in perspective. Following his visit to the Society with Greatorex he attended private experiments performed by friends such as Dr Clarke, who administered opium to dogs and then dissected the animals.[17]

As a convivial man, Pepys enjoyed conversing in coffee-houses with men with original minds. One man with a truly remarkable originality of mind was William Petty, who had been knighted in 1661. Self-educated, he had become Professor of Anatomy at Oxford in 1651 before going to Ireland as Cromwell's physician-general, where he undertook an ambitious survey of Irish landholding. He combined a flair for mechanical invention with an ability to consider what we would think of as modern concepts, such as proposals for a decimal coinage and a proto-National Health Service. Unsurprisingly he was a member of Harrington's Rota Club (p. 21), where he may well have first made Pepys's acquaintance, and his interest in ship design brought them together. Pepys often marvelled at his conversational powers, on one occasion discussing with him the consciousness of dreams, noting how his companion was 'one of the most rational men that ever I heard speak with a tongue, having all his notions the most distinct and clear'.[18] Once he was elected a fellow, Pepys enjoyed not only the meetings at Gresham College, but also the suppers and conversations held afterwards at the nearby Crown tavern.

Samuel Hartlib, such an influential figure in the 1650s, was very ill by the time the Society began to form itself, and died in 1662. Pepys's former tutor, Morland, despite his scientific interests, never became a fellow. An even more surprising absence from the list of members is

Thomas Browne, one of the leading and most respected thinkers of the time whose *Religio Medici*, setting out his struggle to reconcile his Christian faith with his profession as a physician and natural philosopher, had wielded a strong influence following its first appearance in print in 1642. Browne corresponded with many of the fellows, including John Evelyn, but the Royal Society was London-centric and his priority was the care of his patients in Norwich. The cost of membership could also exclude: fellows at first paid a 10 shilling admission fee which rose to £1 in early 1661, and £2 in autumn 1662. On top of this, they paid a subscription of one shilling a week, or £2.12s per annum. This would have been beyond the means of many craftsmen professionally concerned with the results of some of the practical experiments, such as apothecaries and instrument makers. This, together with a lack of education as opposed to technical knowledge, was the likely reason why Greatorex, Pepys's companion in 1661, never became a member.

A good description of what it was like to attend a Royal Society meeting at Gresham College is provided by the overseas fellow Samuel Sorbière on his visit to London in 1663:

> There is a large Table before the chimney, with Seven or Eight Chairs covered with Green-cloth about it, and Two Rows of Wooden and Naked Benches to lean on, the First being higher than the other, in form like an Amphitheatre. The President . . . sits at the middle of the Table in an Elbow Chair, with his back to the Chimney. The Secretary sits at the end of the Table on his left Hand, and they have each of them Pen, Ink and Paper before them. I saw nobody sit on the Chairs . . . All the other Members take their Places as they think fit, and without any Ceremony; and if any one comes in after the Society is fixed, no Body stirs but he takes a Place presently where he can find it, that no Interruption may be given to him that speaks. The President has a little Wooden Mace in his Hand, with which he strikes the Table when he would command Silence; They address their Discourse to him bare-headed, till he makes a Sign for them to put on their Hats; and there is a Relation given in few Words of what is thought proper to be said concerning the Experiments

proposed by the Secretary. There is no body here eager to speak, that makes a long Harangue, or intent upon saying all he knows: He is never interrupted that speaks, and Differences of Opinion cause no manner of Resentment, nor as much as a disobliging Way of Speech: There is nothing seemed to me more civil, respectful, and better managed than this Meeting.[19]

Sorbière here paints a picture of a genteel civility which would not always appear to have been the case, for there were many disputes within the Royal Society. Ironically, one involved Sorbière himself, who, on his return to France, wrote an account that Thomas Sprat, the Society's historian, adjudged insulting, resulting in an international incident with Charles II and Louis XIV having to intervene. The calm waters were certainly stirred up in May 1667 when Margaret Cavendish, Duchess of Newcastle, was permitted to attend. Women were specifically excluded from becoming fellows by the founding statutes, but despite protests from many fellows, Margaret took advantage of being the wife of William Cavendish FRS, a member of one of the great aristocratic dynasties of seventeenth-century England, to secure an invitation. Pepys ensured that he was at the meeting, and recorded how he found her dress 'so antic [crazy] and her deportment so unordinary, that I do not like her at all, nor did I hear her say anything that was worth hearing but that she was full of admiration, all admiration'.[20] It was probably unfortunate for the feminist cause that the break with convention should involve the Duchess. As Margaret Lucas, a rather awkward maid of honour, she had married the Duke from the house of Sir Richard Browne in Paris when the English court was in exile, so Mary Evelyn knew her well. In an uncharacteristically sharp letter Mary described her as 'a woman so full of herself, so amazingly vain and ambitious'.[21] The Royal Society did not repeat this particular experiment for another two centuries.

The experiments performed during the Duchess's visit were, according to Pepys, 'of Colours, Loadstones, Microscope, and of liquors: among others, of one that did while she was there turn a piece of roasted mutton into pure blood – which was very rare'.[22] A week had been spent preparing these, and the roasted mutton set-piece, supervised by Boyle, consisted of dissolving the meat in oil of vitriol, which made it look like blood. This was a selection contrived for the occasion, but demonstrates the breadth of the subject range covered by the Society.

Sometimes the experiments were held elsewhere, using the range of facilities offered by the capital. Tests to see whether materials became heavier when burnt were conducted in the furnaces of the Mint in the Minories. A diving bell holding a man was lowered by cable to spend half an hour underwater in the wet dock at Deptford. An experiment with an 'arched viall' to sound strings with a keyboard was held at the Post Office (see p. 139). A group of fellows, including Evelyn, went off to a private garden near St James's Park to satisfy the King's curiosity about *mimosa pudica*. The sensitive plant was tested not only by being touched, but also with the application of nitric acid and the use of a glass to intensify the sun's rays. Even the Monument, built to Wren and Hooke's design to preserve the memory of the Great Fire, was used for some experiments until the vibrations caused by the traffic proved too much of an interference. In addition, some fellows had their own laboratories where they were able to expand upon the experiments they had seen at Gresham. Prince Rupert, for instance, had laboratories in Chelsea and at Windsor Castle, while Boyle had a room at the London residence of his sister, Lady Ranelagh, and Evelyn could work away in his at Sayes Court. Even the King had his own laboratory until he grew bored with it.

Alongside practical experiments, fellows also devoted time to the receipt, reading and distribution of written discourses, in recognition of the importance of disseminating the results of experiments in a credible manner throughout Europe. Members were obliged to submit any work they planned to publish; this would be presented at the meetings, with one or two fellows taking the text away and reporting back a week or two later, the work then being duly registered in a manuscript volume. This was the one way that an author's work could be protected from usurpation. The Royal Society's Secretary, Henry Oldenburg, launched in 1665 the periodical *Philosophical Transactions*, circulating the institution's work in English throughout Europe. It is still going today.

Again, the range of subjects tackled was very wide. The first formal publication authorised by the Society was read on 23 January 1661 by Sir Kenelm Digby. *A Discourse Concerning the Vegetation of Plants* drew on his detailed observation but developed wider conclusions, such as a nitrous salt that he referred to as a hidden food of life: his interests often betrayed a touch of alchemy. In the autumn of that year, Jasper Needham presented the Society with papers on china varnish, japanning or lacquering, and gilding, techniques that he had investigated in Paris on behalf of his friend John Evelyn, for his project on trades. In February 1665 Evelyn himself read a paper entitled 'Paneficium; or the several manners of making bread in France, & where by general consent the best bread is eaten'.[23]

The Society also interested itself in the field of archaeology. There was at this time a growing consciousness of the nation's prehistory. In 1658, Thomas Browne published *Hydriotaphia, or Urn Burial*, his investigation of the discovery of burial urns at Walsingham in Norfolk, which has been credited as being the first archaeological treatise in English. Ten years earlier, John Aubrey had come upon the prehistoric site of Avebury in Wiltshire while out hunting at Christmas. As a Wiltshire-born man and an antiquarian, he was familiar with Stonehenge, but the stones and huge earth bank at Avebury astounded him. If Stonehenge was likened to a parish church, to Aubrey, Avebury was a cathedral, and he began to observe and draw the site. In 1662 he became an FRS at the suggestion of his friend Walter Charleton, physician to Charles II, and at a meeting the following summer the two men presented their drawings of the stone circles. Charleton concluded that both Stonehenge and Avebury dated back to Danish times, while Aubrey thought, correctly, that Avebury was a prehistoric monument, and his reading of Roman writers led him to suggest it was a Druid temple.

One intriguing project put forward in 1664 was the improvement of the English language. In his history of the Society, Thomas Sprat records the proposal for 'erecting an English Academy', explaining, 'I know, indeed that the English Genius is not so airy and discoursive, as that of some of our neighbors [i.e. the French], but that we generally love to have Reason set out in plain, undeceiving expressions.' Sprat was dismayed by the effect that the Civil War had had upon words, 'fantastical terms, which were introduced by our Religious Sects'.[24] Sir Peter Wyche, a diplomat and early member of the Royal Society, was asked to chair a committee. The dramatist John Dryden was invited to be a member, for he had strong views on the subject, later writing, 'A man should be learned in several sciences, and should have a reasonable, philosophical, and in some measure a mathematical head, to be a complete and excellent poet.'[25]

Evelyn was also invited, but declined because the meetings clashed with those of the Commission for Sick and Wounded Seamen. Nevertheless he furnished Wyche with a long letter, introducing his thoughts on the matter by blaming the corruption of the English tongue 'from Victories, Plantations, Frontieres, Staples of Commerce, Pedantry of Scholes, Affectation of Travellers, Translations, Fancy and Style of Court, Vernility and mincing of Cittizens, Pulpits, Politique Remonstrations, Theaters, Shopps, etc'.[26] Whether this comprehensive condemnation influenced the committee is not known, but Sprat reported that their recommendation was that writers should aim to achieve 'a close, naked, natural way of speaking: positive expression; clear senses; a native easinesse bringing all things as near the Mathematical plain-nesse, as they can; and preferring the language of Artizans, Countrymen, and Merchants, before those of Wits or Scholars'.[27] It would have been much more useful to have invited Pepys, with his clear style of writing, on the committee rather than the prolix Evelyn. Like many of the other committees set up by the Society, there was a general falling away of activity and the project was abandoned, so that England did not get the attempted control imposed on the French language by the Académie française.

Pepys was lucky in his inaugural meeting of the Society in February 1665, for Robert Hooke conducted an experiment involving an air-pump or 'pneumatic engine' as it was often called. Pepys recorded in his diary that the theme was 'the nature of fire, and how it goes out in a place where the ayre is not free, and sooner out where the ayre is exhausted; which they showed by an engine on purpose'. He went on to note: 'Above all, Mr. Boyle today was at the meeting, and above him, Mr. Hooke, who is the most, and promises the least, of any man in the world that ever I saw.'[28] This was a very perceptive observation. Boyle was a wealthy aristocrat, assured of his status, who did not have to concern himself with making his way in the world. Hooke, on the other hand, was from a humbler background, the son of an Anglican curate. This was not as humble as Pepys's own origins, and, like Pepys, Hooke had benefited from an excellent education; but while Pepys grew in confidence as he gained status, Hooke could be thin-skinned and difficult. He also cut a rather unprepossessing figure: small, crooked in body, careless of dress, constantly in poor health.

He was also overcommitted. When he was appointed Curator of Experiments to the Royal Society in 1662, he offered to conduct two or three experiments on the days that the fellows met, an immense source of pressure. The following year, after being given an honorary MA by Oxford University, he was elected a fellow of the Society, which complicated his relationship with the other fellows, as he was also their servant. Another year on, and he moved from his lodgings in Boyle's residence to Gresham College, began to lecture on the history of nature and art under an endowment provided by a City financier, Sir John Cutler, and in 1665 he became Professor of Geometry.

After the City of London was largely destroyed by the Great Fire, Hooke became part of the team under Christopher Wren with responsibility for the rebuilding. As Surveyor, Hooke's immense task was to deal with compensations resulting from the widening of the streets, and settling property disputes. The post-fire City churches are now often described as 'Wren churches', but Hooke played a role in their design and is thought to have been the principal architect of several of them.[29] In addition, he undertook the design of the halls of livery companies and public institutions such as the Navy Office and the Royal College of Physicians. His first biographer observed: 'The Rebuilding of the City . . . requiring an able Person to set out the Ground to the several Proprietors, Mr. Hooke was pitch'd upon, and appointed City-Surveyor for that difficult Work, which being very great, took up a large proportion of his Time, to the no small hindrance of Philosophical Disquisitions.' No wonder one of Hooke's modern biographers chose the title *The Man Who Knew Too Much*.[30]

The Royal Society not only produced its journal, but was also permitted by the terms of the royal charter to license books, a way of freeing the work of fellows from potential censorship by the Church. The first of these, published in 1664, was *Sylva, or a Discourse of Forest-Trees and the Propagation of Timber*, by John Evelyn. The book arose from a report that he had written and read to the Society two years earlier, to answer questions posed by the principal officers and commissioners of the navy concerned about the shortage of timber for His Majesty's ships (Plate 30). Always tending to the discursive, in *Sylva* Evelyn expanded beyond the economic boundaries to look at the aesthetic considerations of the cultivation of trees – impeccable timing as far as the fashion in gardening was concerned. This was the very moment when the King was organising the planting of avenues of trees in the park of St James's Palace in London, inspired by those that he had seen during his exile in France.[31] Where the King led, his wealthier subjects followed, and the planting of trees became the height of horticultural fashion, so that Evelyn's book became an important volume to have in a propertied gentleman's library.

The following year saw the publication by the Royal Society of Robert Hooke's *Micrographia*. This caused great excitement for, as the subtitle explained, it provided 'some physiological descriptions of minute bodies made by magnifying glasses with observations and inquiries thereupon'. For the first time, readers could see images of the tiniest creatures, such as the flea, gnat and bug, and details of their structures such as the face of the large grey drone-fly. These were shown in the beautiful drawings made by Hooke, a skilled draughtsman, who also oversaw their etching for the book (Plate 32). The accompanying text provided clear descriptions of observations and captions to the illustrations. Of the louse Hooke wrote:

> This is a Creature so officious, that 'twill be known to every one at one time or other, so busie, and so impudent, that it will be intruding it self in every one's company, and so proud and aspiring withall, that it fears not to trample on the best, and affects nothing so much as a Crown; feeds and lives very high, and that makes it so saucy, as to

pull anyone by the ears that comes in its way, and will never be quiet till it has drawn blood.[32]

The book introduced readers not only to the world of minute animals, but also to the snowflake, the sting of the nettle, and mould on blue cheese that resembled ranunculi flowers (Plate 33).

Just before attending his inaugural meeting at Gresham College, Pepys had seen Hooke's new book at the shop of his bookseller, Joshua Kirton, in St Paul's Churchyard, 'which is so pretty that I presently bespoke it'. Three weeks later, having had it bound, he collected it, declaring it 'a most excellent piece, and of which I am very proud'.[33] So excited was he by his new acquisition that he sat up reading it until two in the morning. The previous August he had bought a microscope from the optical instrument maker Richard Reeve, who had a shop in Long Acre. It cost him £5.10s, which he noted was 'a great price, but a most curious bauble', and Reeve threw in a scotoscope, a portable *camera obscura*. With the help of the first English book on the microscope, Henry Power's *Experimental Philosophy*, Samuel and Elizabeth together struggled to see anything through the lens.[34] The problem was that they could only see darkness. Hooke had increased the light for his viewings with the help of a bowl of water and an oil lamp, or possibly a mirror. The solution for Pepys came in the summer of 1666 when Reeve and another instrument maker, John Spong, spent the afternoon in the dark room in the Navy Office, giving him detailed instructions on how to use his microscopes and telescope. He wrote in triumph, 'and most excellently things appeared indeed, beyond imagination'.[35] No wonder he was enthralled by Hooke's masterpiece.

As the Royal Society entered its second decade, so it lost some of its initial sparkle. The momentum had been interrupted first by the plague, when those who could afford to left London, and then by the Great Fire. Although Gresham College survived the flames, the building was commandeered to serve as the Royal Exchange because Gresham's other great foundation had been destroyed. The Society was temporarily accommodated by Lord Howard at Arundel House, returning to Gresham College in 1673. It was also beset by financial problems: the very strength of the diversity of the background of the fellows also proved a weakness when courtiers and others initially fascinated by the experiments got bored. Right from the start finances had been difficult. It had been hoped that the King would provide funding, but this did not materialise, so that schemes such as for a purpose-built college, mooted in 1667, remained pipe dreams. In the 1670s reform became imperative. The deaths of John Wilkins in 1672, of Sir Robert Moray in 1673 and Jonathan Goddard in 1675 came as serious blows, and Robert Boyle was hardly active after 1674. Attendance was declining and so too were the payments of subscriptions.

Moreover, some aspects of the Society's activities had become a source of amusement. The King himself led this particular charge. Pepys recorded in his diary for 1 February 1664 how he went to the Duke of York's lodgings in Whitehall to hear Sir William Petty telling Charles of trials he had undertaken on a double-bottomed boat:

> The King came and stayed an hour or two, laughing at Sir W Petty ... and at Gresham College in general. At which poor Petty was I perceive at some loss, but did argue discreetly and bear the unreasonable follies of the King's objections and other bystanders with great discretion – and offered to take oddes against the King's best boats; but the King would not lay, but cried him down with words only. Gresham College he mightily laughed at for spending time only in weighing of ayre, and doing nothing else since they sat.[36]

In his first comedy, the playwright Thomas Shadwell included a dig at the Royal Society. Set in London in March 1668, *The Sullen Lovers* contains the observation: 'Others after twenty or thirty years study in Philosophy arrive no further than at the Weighing of Carps, the Invention of a travailling Wheel, or the poisoning of a Cat with the oyle of Tobacco; these are your Wits and Virtuoso's.'[37] Eight years later, in 1676, Shadwell devoted an entire play, *The Virtuoso*, to satirising the Society's activities. He was the leading advocate of Ben Jonson's style of comedy, where each character represents a humour, displaying one unique and excessive folly. The principal character in *The Virtuoso* is Sir

Nicholas Gimcrack, a 'rare mechanic philosopher', who opens the second act by learning to swim like a frog on a table with the help of a Swimming Master. Sir Nicholas explains:

> I doubt not, Sir, in a very little time to become amphibious; a man, by Art, may appropriate any Element to himself; You know a great many Virtuoso's that can fly; but I am so much advanc'd in the Art of Flying, that I can already out-fly that pond'rous Animal call'd a Bustard; nor should any Greyhound in England catch me in the calmest day, before I get upon wing: Nay, I doubt not, but in a little time to improve the Art so far, 'twill be as common to buy a pair of Wings to fly to the World in the Moon, as to buy a pair of Wax Boots to ride into Sussex with.[38]

Shadwell then goes on to poke fun at a series of Royal Society experiments. One such was the transfusion of blood, with the playwright suggesting that if that of an ass was transfused to a virtuoso, you wouldn't be able to tell the difference. Sir Nicholas apologises for not performing the dissection of a lobster through the failure of his fishmonger to deliver, but promises a lecture after dinner 'concerning the Nature of Insects, and will survey my Microscopes, Telescopes, Thermometers, Barometers, Pneumatick Engines, Stentrophonical Tubes and the like'.[39] He has got his friends to bottle air in all parts of England, and keeps them like fine wine in his cellar. An experiment with mercury in a barometer had actually been conducted years earlier to test how the air pressure might work on the summit of the 12,000-foot Pico de Tenerife, so Gimcrack's lightest bottle of air comes from Tenerife; the heaviest proves to be from Sheerness and the Isle of Dogs. Instead of a lamp, he reads the Geneva Bible by the light of a putrid leg of pork.

Shadwell could have read of the experiments in the *Philosophical Transactions* but is far more likely to have been given descriptions by attendees at meetings. Although Pepys was a friend of Shadwell, and stood godfather to his son John, he would seem an unlikely source, for he enjoyed his Royal Society connections and would not have wanted to jeopardise them. There is added piquancy to the whole scenario in the fact that John Dryden was a fellow of the Society. Shadwell was maintaining a long-running feud with him, and used the dedication to *The Virtuoso* to attack his fellow playwright for 'feminine understanding', as displayed by his fondness for repartee and alleged dislike of Jonson.

The person who was most upset by the play was Robert Hooke. He wrote in his diary after attending a performance by the Duke of York's Company at the Dorset Garden Theatre, 'Damned Dogs, *Vindica me Deus*. People almost pointed.'[40] Although he thought that the satire was all directed at him, others were also being teased. It was Robert Boyle who had published an account of being able to make out printed letters by the light of rotting meat. He wrote about how his servant girl had been 'frightened by something of luminous that, notwithstanding the darkness of the place [larder] she saw where meat had been hung before'. He took the putrid piece of veal and applied a printed paper to 'some of the more resplendent spots' and found he could read 'several succeeding letters of the title'.[41]

The elaborate and abstruse language used by Sir Formal Trifle, described in the cast list as 'a florid coxcomb', was probably a hit at John Evelyn. An example of Trifle's conversation –

Upon my integrity he has advanc'd transfusion to the Achme of perfection, and has the Ascendent over all the Virtuosi in point of that Operation. I saw him do the most admirable effects in the World upon Two Animals; the one a Domestick Animal commonly call'd a Mangy Spaniel; and a less Famellick Creature, commonly call'd a Sound Bull Dog

– strikes a chord with Evelyn's style.[42] Evelyn would seem to have suspected this, for when Margaret Godolphin questioned him about the play, he responded sharply. At this time, the summer of 1676, Robert Hooke was refurbishing Godolphin's lodgings in Scotland Yard for the married couple, so her curiosity was roused. In a long letter Evelyn told her how 'I have learned more profitable and useful things from some hours conversation in that Meeting [of the Royal Society] than ever I have done from the quintessence and sublimest rapture of those empty casks whose noise you so admire at court'. He went on to explain that the Society's only purpose was 'the investigation of Truths & discovery of Errors & Impostures ... without any Offence or provocation to anybody'. The fellows were not aiming to produce a new philosophical theory, but rather to 'collect a plenty of Materials by new & joint Attempts for the Work', and had in fact produced many useful inventions such as watches, cranes, pumps and mathematical instruments.[43]

In fact, although he was not going to confess it openly, Evelyn's attendance at meetings had been falling off, partly because he was so busy, but also because he recognised that the Society was failing to fulfil its ambitious early programme. In December 1675 an attempt was made by a close-knit group to re-establish the Royal Society as a club conforming to its original intellectual intentions. As Hooke noted in his diary: 'Agreed upon a new clubb to meet at Joes [coffee-house], Mr. Hill, Mr. Lodowick, Mr. Aubery and I to joyn to us Sir Jo[nas]: More, Mr. Wild, Mr. Hoskins.' By the new year regular meetings were being held at Christopher Wren's home of a New Philosophical Club, 'Ingaging ourselves not to speak of any thing that was then revealed *sub sigillo* to any one nor to declare that we had such a meeting at all'.[44]

One of the problems was the character of the Society's first President. Lord Brouncker, Pepys's music-loving naval associate, was a difficult man who had roused enmity within certain quarters. Not the least of the problems was his mistress, Abigail Williams. As Walter Charleton explained in the bluntest of terms to his friend John Aubrey: 'If you would make him [Brouncker] your Patron & raiser, you have no other way to doe it, but by bribing his mercenary [Abigail] – who by that means alone became his, after she had passed through almost as many hands, as the R.S. has members, & many more than she has teeth in her gumms of Natures setting.'[45] The breakaway group mentioned by Hooke was short-lived, for two obstacles to a new future for the Royal Society were removed when Brouncker was persuaded to stand down as President and the Secretary, Henry Oldenburg, died in September 1677.

Oldenburg and Hooke had been in dispute with each other over various matters, but in particular over the development of the balance-spring regulator watch mechanism. In January 1675 Oldenburg read out two letters from Christiaan Huygens giving notice of 'new invention of watches by himself'. Hooke reacted angrily, declaring that if the Society's journals were consulted, along with Thomas Sprat's *History*, it could be seen that he had invented just such a mechanism some ten years earlier. The Society was not convinced, but Hooke took his case, and a watch of his design made for him by Thomas Tompion, to the King, who granted patents in his favour. The fear of losing what we would now call intellectual property was a constant among the 'professional' scientists of the Royal Society. The particular problem as far as Hooke was concerned was that because he was so busy he left inventions unfinished until a rival threatened.

Following Oldenburg's death, Hooke became Secretary for a time. Taking the opportunity to look through the records, he realised that Oldenburg had refused to record his discoveries. Hooke clearly was able to rouse intense antipathy in others. Thomas Molyneux and his brother William were both natural philosophers, and William was the first Secretary and Treasurer of the Dublin Philosophical Society which exchanged papers and correspondence with the Royal Society. In 1683, Thomas wrote to William in Dublin, calling Hooke 'The most ill-natured man in the world, hated and despised by most of the Royal Society, pretending to have had all the other inventions when once discovered by their authors to the world.'[46] Hooke was by this time locked in a long-running feud with Isaac Newton, who became a fellow in 1672. In *Micrographia* Hooke had set out his red and blue or wave corpuscular theory, in which he maintained that a prism was a refracting medium producing the colours. When Newton came up with his theory of light, which held that the colour was in the white light before hitting the prism, Hooke felt he should have been credited, albeit they had come to different conclusions. In 1677 Hooke had written to Newton about the source of gravity, but Newton, away looking after his sick mother, did not reply for many months, and then came up with his famous phrase about standing on the shoulders of giants. He had learned about the orbit of planets from Galileo and could see no reason why he should credit Hooke.

Hooke was replaced as Secretary in 1682 for, although he was gifted in so many fields, he was not up to all the languages involved with the

Philosophical Transactions. His character, always difficult, was becoming more erratic with his constant drug-taking to alleviate pain and melancholia. Nevertheless, he was able to maintain warm friendships, with John Aubrey for instance, and with the two people with whom he worked most closely, Robert Boyle and Christopher Wren. His relationship with Pepys was likewise warm. In his diary Hooke refers to his civility and kindness, and he knew of Pepys's domestic arrangements, for he gave him the recipe for white varnish for 'Mrs Pepys', Mary Skinner (p. 96).[47]

The Royal Society was clearly in need of an overhaul. John Evelyn in his preface to the third edition of *Sylva*, published in 1679, made an impassioned plea for the Society to be taken seriously and supported. Still smarting from the jokes made at the Society's expense by Thomas Shadwell, he wrote: 'it may not perhaps seem unreasonable to Disabuse some (otherwise) well-meaning People, who led-away and perverted by the noise of a few Ignorant, and Comical Bouffoons, (whose Malevolence, or Impertinences intitle them to nothing that is truly Great and Venerable) are with an Insolence suitable to their Understanding, still crying out and asking, What have the Society done?' As in his letter to Margaret Godolphin, he went on to list some of the achievements made by the fellows, including 'the improving pocket watches by springs applied to the balance' first invented and demonstrated by Hooke.[48]

The Society had also got into trouble over publishing. Subscription schemes were used to persuade reluctant publishers to undertake production. When Martin Lister, for instance, wanted to publish his translation of a book on insects by Johannes Goedaert in 1682, the Society helped to pay for the impression by buying fifty copies for its fellows, and a further hundred copies for other recipients. As with Evelyn's *Sylva* and Hooke's *Micrographia*, the Society was usually able to use its imprimatur along with guaranteed subscription to get stationers to take the financial risks, which could sometimes be considerable because the titles often involved illustrations. On one occasion, however, the entire publication was funded by the Society. When Francis Willughby died, his *Historia Piscium* was completed by the naturalist John Ray and published in 1686. Unfortunately this project turned out to be a financial disaster, and the book has been uncompromisingly described as 'expensive to produce, aesthetically unimpressive, slow to sell and of imperceptible scholarly impact'.[49]

Shortly before Willughby's book was published, Pepys became President of the Royal Society. He was well aware of his lack of scientific knowledge, but knew that he could contribute by paying his subscription regularly, giving money when asked, and raising funds. Although he never gave papers at the Society's meetings, he had served on the council from 1672 and spoke regularly. Now his administrative skills were required to pull the institution together. The problem of subscription arrears was tackled by ordering the names of all miscreants to be omitted from the next list unless they paid up. Sixty were scratched, including the Duke of Buckingham: Pepys was not going to show favour to those of high status. He insisted on a written statement of the cash position, and prepared orders for the Society's clerks, based on his experience of training clerks in the Navy Office. The clerks had to be unmarried and childless – though an exception was made for the astronomer Edmond Halley – and have a good knowledge of English, French and Latin together with some mathematics. They must keep the minutes, not on loose papers, but in books with proper indices. They were to be paid at least £50 per annum.

Pepys presented the substantial sum of £63 to the Society to pay for the plates in Willughby's unfortunate book, and ordered the printing of Isaac Newton's *Principia Mathematica*. Although he was absent from subsequent meetings concerning its production, his name therefore appears on the title page of this groundbreaking book (Plate 31). The summer of 1685 was an extremely busy one for Pepys, for the new King, James II, demanded his entire attention dealing with naval matters. The Royal Society failed to pay for the printing, but Newton's wealthy friend Edmond Halley generously did so in his role as Secretary. *Principia Mathematica* appeared after Pepys had finished being President, but he was very proud to be associated with Isaac Newton and his work that laid out laws of motion and universal gravitation based on mathematical principle rather than philosophical arguments. The person who was conspicuously missing from the book was Robert Hooke: Newton ungraciously omitted any acknowledgement of his contribution to the theories contained therein. He was underlining the fact that, despite his many skills, Hooke was not a mathematician.

During his presidency, Samuel Pepys held some meetings of the Royal Society at his own home in York Buildings. John Evelyn describes in his diary for 15 December 1685 an experiment performed at one of these meetings by Frederick Slare. In the 1670s Slare had acted as laboratory assistant to Robert Boyle, and was particularly interested in white phosphorus. Evelyn was fascinated by the experiment, describing it in lyrical terms: 'it first produced a white clowd, then boiling, divers Corruscations & actual flames of fire mingled with the liquor, which being a little shaken together fixed divers suns & stars of real fire perfectly globular upon the walls of the Glass . . . It seem'd to exhibit a Theorie of the eduction of light out of the Chaos'.[50]

In December 1690 Evelyn was in turn offered the presidency but, recognising that it might prove a political nightmare 'in this ill Conjuncture of publique affairs', refused the honour, cleverly devolving it upon Sir Robert Southwell, who as Secretary of State for Ireland had the ear of King William.[51] When, however, Robert Boyle died on the last day of 1691, Evelyn did agree to act as a trustee of the bequest included in Boyle's will for an annual lecture to defend Christianity from atheism. He had long admired Boyle for his promotion of the compatibility between religion and the new science. Pepys, not well enough to attend Boyle's funeral, instead invited Evelyn, along with Isaac Newton and Thomas Gale, to a memorial dinner at his house.

More dinners at York Buildings followed, for Pepys's health was deteriorating, and rendering him virtually housebound. The meetings were held on a Saturday, so were known as 'Saturday's Table', the 'Round Table' and 'Tripe Day', as tripe, a favourite dish for Pepys, was often served. 'Saturday Academists' were invited, along with book lovers and scholars, for conversation in his library and occasional music parties. Mary Skinner was sometimes present, for Evelyn mentioned her to his grandson as one of the 'deipnosophists'. This term was derived from the title of the Greek work by Athenaeus, in which a group of learned men discussed cultural subjects over dinner. The importance that Pepys attached to these dinners with Royal Society associates can be judged from a letter to Evelyn in October 1691: 'You may easily imagine what a summer I have had, that have not stirred one Mile out of Towne since I saw you, nor had the pleasure of one hour's Conversation worth owneing since you left it.' Thomas Gale had recently resumed 'his Saturday-visitts, in which Mr Evelin's Name and Excellencys have ever contributed to the best part of our Entertainment, and his Absence to the Worst'.[52] But these occasions inevitably came to an end when Pepys moved out to Clapham. In a letter to him in December 1701, Evelyn wrote: 'In good earnest, Sir, I passe not by Yorke-Buildings without serious regret. Saturday, which was wont to be a Jubily, and the most advantagious and gainefull, as well as the most diverting to me of the Weekly Circles, is from a real Sabbath and day of repose now become wholy saturnine, lugubrous, and solitary.'[53]

Evelyn was still able to attend the formal meetings of the Royal Society, and in February 1702 heard a paper about his remarkable anatomical tables, read by the surgeon William Cowper. Purchased decades earlier in Padua during his European tour, these had been given to the Society by Evelyn in 1667. He must have been delighted that at the meeting in 1702 the fellows confirmed that the tables were more accurate than even those of Vesalius, the founder of modern human anatomy. When the paper was printed in the *Philosophical Transactions*, it was prefaced by a letter from Evelyn explaining how he had acquired the tables, their perilous journey to England, and his recollection that they cost him 150 scudi (p. 16).[54]

When Robert Hooke died alone in his rooms in Gresham College the following March, two surprises met those who discovered his body. Firstly, although he had often talked of leaving a bequest to the Royal Society so that a library, a laboratory and a lecture might be endowed in his name, there was no will to be found among the profusion of papers. Instead, his property passed to a cousin. Secondly, although Hooke had the reputation of being a miser, they discovered a chest holding the huge sum of £8,000, which would equate to almost £1 million in today's money. It was a sad end for an extraordinary man. Samuel Pepys followed him to the grave just two months later but, in his case, surrounded by family and household. His nephew John Jackson asked that there should be an autopsy (p. 248), possibly at the request of Pepys himself, in the hope that his chequered medical history might provide significant evidence for physicians. The findings were dramatic – and, by a twist of fate, one of the doctors who performed the autopsy was John Shadwell, son of the dramatist who had poked so much fun at the Royal Society in his plays.

Evelyn continued to attend Royal Society meetings, in 1703 witnessing Isaac Newton's assumption of the presidency, a post that he held for twenty years. The financial crises that had beset the Society in the 1670s and early 1680s were now past, although jokes at the Society's expense continued. In 1700 the poet and lawyer William King in a satire called *The Transactioneer* took a swipe at *Philosophical Transactions* by means of an index with sample entries such as 'Hoggs that sh-te Soap, p. 66; Cows that sh-te Fire, p. 67', and 'Mr Ray's Definition of a Dil-oe, p. 11'.[55] Quarrels among the fellows also continued unabated, aptly described as 'the rough world of jealousy and ambition beneath the superficial politeness of seventeenth-century philosophical correspondence'.[56] The future of the Society in the new century had, however, been assured, and John Evelyn and Samuel Pepys, loyal and long-serving fellows, had contributed in no small measure to this survival.

6

PLEASURE ABOVE ALL THINGS

S AMUEL PEPYS CONFIDED to his diary that he had two great pleasures: women and music. After spending an evening in March 1666 with friends, where he sang with Elizabeth Knepp, an actress in the King's Company, he wrote: 'and God forgive me, I do still see that my nature is not to be quite conquered, but will esteem pleasure above all things; though, yet in the middle of it, it hath reluctancy after my business, which is neglected by my fallowing my pleasure. However, music and women I cannot but give way to, whatever my business is.'[1] He loved performing music, was an enthusiastic and perceptive audience, and was fascinated by its science and theory. When Evelyn learnt of the death of his friend, the one characteristic he particularly noted was that Pepys was 'skill'd in Musick'.[2]

Evelyn would have said of himself that he lacked this skill. The playing of an instrument was an accomplishment considered appropriate for cultured men and women, but Evelyn makes clear in his diary that he was not of this persuasion. Of his time in Oxford as an undergraduate he wrote, 'now I began to looke upon the rudiments of Musick, in which I afterwards arriv'd to some formal knowledge: though to small perfection in hand because I was so frequently diverted, with inclinations to newer trifles'.[3] While on his travels in Italy he took lessons in Rome and Venice on the theorbo, a large lute, and later in

Orleans on the lute itself, but again noted ruefully, 'to small perfection'.[4] Yet his diary also shows that he enjoyed listening to a wide range of music.

Although Pepys's parents' home in Salisbury Court was modest, the inventory of its contents records a pair of virginals in one of the upper chambers, and his father played the bass viol. By the time Pepys's diary opens, despite a lack of formal training, he was already proficient on the lute, viol and flageolet, a kind of miniature recorder. The period is an intriguing one as far as music in England is concerned. During the Interregnum the principal establishments for commissioning composition and performance were in trouble: the court was in exile, the Church of England and the theatres proscribed. Puritans, however, did not object to secular music. Indeed, Oliver Cromwell seems to have held little objection even to church music, having the organ that had been removed from Magdalen College Oxford set up at his lodgings in Hampton Court Palace, and listening for relaxation to the Latin motets of Richard Deering, a Catholic composer of the previous generation. Domestic music-making was able to flourish, or as Roger North put it, 'many chose rather to fidle at home, than goe out, and be knockt on the head abroad'.[5] Consorts of viols became fashionable, with music written by John Jenkins and Matthew Locke.

With the absence of the king, the monopoly for music printing disappeared, enabling John Playford in particular to concentrate on producing publications, such as his hugely popular *English Dancing Master*, first issued in 1651, *Music's Recreation on the Lyra Viol* in 1652, and three years later his *Brief Introduction to the Skill of Music*. In 1653 Henry Lawes, the major composer of the period, published his *Ayres and Dialogues* designed for the voice and lute or bass viol.

These reflected and inspired the passion for performance of music by amateurs which is so strongly conveyed in Pepys's diary. Day after day he records taking music lessons and his regular practice on his collection of instruments, which grew to include the harpsichord, bass viol, violin and theorbo. Impromptu concerts were held at his home, but he also seized any opportunity to play. He performed on his flageolet while being rowed down the Thames, and on a hot night in June took the instrument up onto the leads of his home in Seething Lane, where he was joined by his neighbour Sir William Penn, 'talking and singing and drinking of great draughts of Claret and eating of botargo [dried mullet roe] and bread and butter' until midnight, by the light of the moon.[6]

London seems to have been suffused with the sound of music alongside the more prosaic hubbub of the city. On board the *Naseby*, the ship of Pepys's kinsman Edward Montague, a spontaneous concert was held while awaiting the return of Charles II to his kingdom: 'After supper my Lord [Montague] called for the Lieutenant's Gitterne, and with two Candlesticks with money in them for Symballs we made some barber's Musique.'[7] The gittern, a kind of guitar or cither, as well as other simple instruments were kept in barbers' shops for waiting customers to play. Later, Pepys described having his hair cut while a boy played on the violin.[8] On a visit to Epsom in 1663, he came upon a group on the common:

a company got together that sung; I at that distance, and so all the rest, being a quarter of a mile off, took them for the waytes [musicians employed by the town to play on ceremonial occasions]; so I rid up to them and find them only voices – some Citizens, met by chance, that sing four or five parts excellently. I have not been more pleased with a snapp of Musique, considering the circumstances of the time and place, in all my life anything so pleasant.[9]

With the Restoration there was a return to the past. The King's Musick was re-established, with a string orchestra of twenty-four violins in emulation of the '*grande bande des vingt-quatre violons du roy*' that Charles II had admired at the court of his cousin, Louis XIV. This group of musicians was called upon to play when the King dined in state and at court balls. Pepys, viewing the coronation banquet on 23 April 1661, described walking up and down Westminster Hall to 'look upon the ladies – and to hear the Musique of all sorts; but above all, the 24 viollins'.[10] The full complement of players was rarely used, but divided into two groups of twelve. By September 1662 they were being deployed in the services of the re-established Chapel Royal. This establishment was under the formidable authority of Captain Henry Cooke. He had been a chorister there in the reign of Charles I, and now reappointed a number of his contemporaries as Gentlemen, but had to start the boys' section from scratch, incurring displeasure by removing choristers from provincial cathedrals. So effective were his activities that the Children of the Chapel Royal trained up many of the outstanding musicians of the later seventeenth century, including John Blow, Pelham Humfrey and Henry Purcell.

The return of the King and his courtiers with a taste for French music inevitably caused ripples. An early incident occurred in the autumn of 1660, at a play performed in the Cockpit, the private royal theatre in Whitehall. Edward Montague, now Lord Sandwich, reported to Pepys how the King had upset one of the English musicians by asking a Frenchman to play.[11] Charles paid for Pelham Humfrey from the Chapel Royal to go to France to study the style of Jean-Baptiste Lully, Louis XIV's music master. When Humfrey returned, Pepys was appalled by the affectations that he had picked up during his travels, describing him as 'an absolute Monsieur, as full of form and confidence and vanity, and disparages everything and everybody's skill but his own. The truth is, everybody says he is very able; but to hear how he laughs at all the King's music here ... that they cannot keep time, nor tune nor understand anything.'[12]

The King himself liked music to which he could beat time, a trait disdainfully described by Roger North as 'yet a mode among the *Monseurs*, always to act the musick, which habit the King had got, and never in his life could endure any that he could not act by keeping the time'.[13] In more tactful mode, Pepys also noted this when he attended a service at the chapel in Whitehall Palace in 1663: 'here I first perceived that the King is a little Musicall, and kept good time with his hand all along the Anthem'.[14]

But the King could also be fickle in his tastes, and grew bored with his chamber group, in 1666 breaking up his 'French Musick'. Instead, he turned to Italy. The discarded French musicians were obliged to return to France, their salaries in arrears, a fate also meted out to some of their English counterparts. Pepys described how the harpist had died of want through receiving no salary for five years, and would have been carried to his grave in the dark had not his friend, the organist John Hingston, given a shilling to hire the service of link boys.[15] The canny Italian musicians insisted on special methods of payment to ensure that they would receive money regularly, so Charles sold four gondolas that had been presented to him by the Venetian Republic to fund the enterprise. The 'Italian Musick' provided musical entertainments for the King and Queen Catherine in their chambers, and the music for the Queen's Catholic chapel.

There had been a long tradition of interest in, and taste for, Italian music. The madrigal form had been very important in Elizabethan times, whilst Italian monodies, compositions in which one part or voice carried the melody, the others accompanying, were available through publications from the early seventeenth century. Giacomo Carissimi was one of the most popular Italian composers, and his works were widely disseminated in England. Evelyn acquired a manuscript transcription of one of his motets while visiting Rome in April 1645.[16] Ten years later, back in England, he noted in his diary hearing the redoubtable Henry Cooke performing, declaring him 'the best singer after the Italian manner of any in England; he entertain'd us with his voice & Theorba'.[17] Pepys shared Evelyn's enthusiasm for the work of Carissimi, writing of an evening spent 'singing the best piece of musique, counted of all hands in the world, made by Seignor Charrissimi the famous master in Rome'.[18]

National pride and prejudice played their part in musical taste at this time, and not all were fans of the new Italian and French music. The English composer Matthew Locke wrote of

those Mountebanks of wit, who think it is necessary to disparage all they meet with of their own Countrye-mews, because there have been and are some excellent things done by Strangers, I shall make bold to tell them (and I hope my known experience in this Science will inforce them to confess me a competent Judge) that I never yet saw any Forain Instrumental Composition (a few French Corants excepted) worthy an Englishmans transcribing.[19]

Some of Pepys's observations appear at first sight to be similarly preju-
diced. For example, when he went to hear Luis Grabu directing the
Royal Violins, he noted 'the manner of setting the words and repeating
them out of order, and that with a number of voices, makes me sick'.[20]
This, however, does not accord with his enthusiastic comments elsewhere about French and Italian music. What was concerning him was
the concordance of music and words in different languages. After
hearing an Italian musician singing at the house of Lord Brouncker, he
concluded that 'there is a proper accent in every country's discourse; and
that doth read in that setting of notes to words, which therefore cannot
be natural to anybody else but them; so that I am not so much smitten
with it as it may be I should if I were acquainted with their accent'.[21]

One of the friends with whom Pepys sang and discussed music was
the merchant Thomas Hill. Pepys first met him in 1664, noting in his
diary that he recognised immediately how he was 'a master in most sorts
of Musique and other things . . . to my great content, having not been in
so good a company a great while'. Hill spent much of his working life in
Italy and later in Lisbon as agent to the Houblon family, who also
became close friends of the diarist. Pepys was able to have 'the rarest
discourse' with Hill about the musical scene in Rome.[22]

In addition to Thomas Hill, Pepys built up a coterie of musical friends,
and also encouraged members of his household if they showed musical
promise. He recorded in his diary for 1664 that 'I have got a new boy that
understands Musique well, as coming to me from the King's Chappell, and
I hope will prove a good boy'. This was Will Hewer, who did indeed prove
'a good boy', becoming one of Pepys's closest friends and looking after him
in old age. Pepys hired a composer, William Smegergill, to teach Will the
lute.[23] However, the hiring of a musical companion for Elizabeth Pepys
did not go so smoothly, with jealousy developing 'because that girl doth
take music mighty readily, and she [Elizabeth] doth not; and music is the
thing of the world that I love most'.[24] Like many comments about his wife,
this has to be taken with a pinch of salt, for Elizabeth clearly did have
musical ability, achieving difficult technical effects in singing, and learning
to play a wind instrument so that she and her husband might play duets.
Problems in the other direction had already occurred over the hiring of a

dancing master for Elizabeth. In 1662 Pepys bought for his wife a copy of John Playford's very successful *Dancing Master*, but grew jealous of the master hired to teach Elizabeth, 'a pretty neat black man' called Pemberton, and quarrels over dancing fill the diary for months thereafter.[25]

Despite these domestic disputes, musical soirées held at Pepys's house in Seething Lane seem to have been jolly affairs. One diary entry records Thomas Hill fetching the composer and singer Edward Coleman and Nicholas Lanier, Master of the King's Musick, to one of these gatherings, 'with whom with their Lute we had excellent company and good singing till midnight, and a good supper I did give them'.[26] On another occasion he returned from his office at 9 pm to find a large party dancing. A recital was then given by Edward Coleman's wife, Catherine, a professional actress and singer.

Once Pepys stopped keeping his diary, we no longer have this level of detail about his music, but he undoubtedly continued to hold concerts at his home. Evelyn attended one in April 1687 when the castrato Giovanni Francesco Grassi sang and played:

> I heard the famous Singer the Eunuch Cifacca [his stage name] esteemed the best in Europe & indeede his holding out & delicatenesse in extending & loosing a note with that incomparable softnesse, & sweetness was admirable: Fore the rest, I found him a mere wantone, effeminate child; very Coy, & prowdly conceited to my apprehension: He touch'd the Harpsichord to his Voice rarely well.

Getting Cifacca to give this performance was a coup effected by Mary Evelyn's kinswoman, Lady Tuke, who had earlier written explaining how she had told the singer that Pepys had the best harpsichord in England and was a great lover of music, so that 'you may have the pleasure to heare him sing without putting your self at charge in other places'.[27] Evelyn proudly goes on in his diary to note how the concert had been 'before a select number of some particular persons whom Mr Pepys . . . invited to his house, where the meeting was, and this obtained by peculiar favour & much difficulty of the Singer, who much disdained to shew his talent to any but Princes'.[28]

The reference to Cifacca 'putting himself at charge' is interesting. Richard Luckett, in his analysis of the music-making of the period, marks a significant development just after the end of Pepys's diary. In 1672, he suggests, public concerts began. This development he attributes to the fortunes, or rather misfortunes, of John Banister, who was deposed from the directorship of the King's Musick in favour of the French composer Luis Grabu. Pepys had noted in his diary how Banister had made his feelings on the subject loudly vocal, and with his difficult character lost several other posts. In need of money, he introduced concerts where the performers received formal payment from their listeners.[29]

Such public concerts were held in the 1680s and 1690s in York Buildings, the residential complex where Pepys had his home. They were promoted by newspapers like the *London Gazette* and from 1692 the *Gentleman's Journal* edited by Peter Motteux. A Huguenot refugee from Rouen, Motteux modelled his magazine on the French *Mercure Gallant*, including in it poetry, literary and theatrical criticism, songs, and essays on the fashions and scientific discoveries of the time. He was also a librettist, a friend of playwrights such as John Dryden and William Congreve, and of composers and musicians including Henry Purcell and John Blow. York Buildings became one of the principal music venues in London, attended by royalty and aristocrats – the Duke of Northumberland was obliged to offer a reward in the *London Gazette* in 1690 for the return of a sable muff lost at a musical evening. In May 1693 Motteux devised an entertainment based on Thomas Shadwell's masque for *Timon of Athens*, including songs set by Henry Purcell. Four years later, in January 1697 the *Post Boy* announced 'Mr Purcel's Farewel', a concert held in York Buildings in tribute to his death, at the tragically early age of thirty-four.[30]

Pepys had known one of the Purcells of the previous generation, either Henry's father, also called Henry, or Thomas, his uncle; in his diary for 1660 Pepys recorded singing Italian and Spanish songs with one of them in a room at the Turk's Head coffee-house in Westminster, looking out over the river.[31] It would be inconceivable that Pepys did not follow the fortunes of the prodigiously talented Henry Purcell of the next generation. He certainly heard his anthem 'My heart is inditing' at the coronation of James II in 1685. John Evelyn describes attending a concert at Pepys's house in the summer of 1698 where he heard 'Mr Pate, who was lately come from Italy, reputed the most excellent singer, ever England had'. Included in the repertoire were 'severall compositions of the last Mr Pursal, esteemed the best composer of any Englishman hitherto'.[32] Pepys had in his library a copy of Purcell's *Sonnata's of III Parts*, published in 1683, with a dedication to the King, probably engraved from the composer's own handwriting (Plate 35). Did Charles give the books to Pepys, knowing his great love of music, or did James do so, after his brother's death? A third possibility is that the King's library was in such a chaotic state in the mid-1680s, as was noted by Evelyn, that Pepys himself may simply have bought the books. The sadness is that we do not have his response to Purcell's music.

Although Pepys played a variety of instruments, he was very conscious of his lack of formal training. He could read a single line, but did not know 'the scale of Musique' and refers in his diary to trying to 'con his gamut'. The traditional notation of music at the time was hexachordal, a pattern of six tones, rather than the octave system where each octave is considered identical, beginning with the note C. While the hexa-chordal system was suited for singers, it required what Richard Luckett describes as 'mental gymnastics' when playing instruments, with pieces involving frequent mutation.[33] Pepys must have been helped in coping with this by the arrival in his household of Cesare Morelli on the recom-mendation of Thomas Hill. In a letter to Pepys written from Lisbon in April 1673, Hill explains:

> here is a Young Man, borne in Flanders, but breed in Rome, who has a most admirable Voyce, and sings rarely to his Theorba, and with great skill. This young man Lives with a nobleman, upon a very mean Sallary, and having been formerly in England, most passion-ately desires to return thither againe . . . I know none more deserving than hee. He speaks Latin, Italian, French and Spanish, and tis ten thousand pittyes to Let him live here among People who will see no Virtue but their owne.[34]

Morelli was Pepys's household musician until forced as a Catholic to leave at the time of the Popish Plot (p. 49). He transposed songs into the bass voice, and among the books in Pepys's library is his 'Table to the Ghittar' (Plate 36). As the lute gave way to the guitar as the fashionable instrument of the period, so guides like this were provided to show what Morelli described as 'the relation of each fret upon every string to the common scale of musick'.

Pepys's music books in his library at Magdalene consist of about seventy volumes, less than one-fortieth of his whole collection, although his favourite 'practical music' was probably kept in loose sheets or flimsily bound, so has not survived. Not surprisingly, Evelyn had far fewer music books. According to the catalogue that he compiled in 1687, they consisted of just twenty-nine works, the majority of which would seem to have been acquired during his travels in Europe. Thereafter, he bought mostly books of songs for his family: his eldest daughter, Mary, was a keen singer. Pepys, on the other hand, continued to add the latest books on music to his collection right up to the end of his life. Among these is a substantial collection of treatises, including two by fellow members of the Royal Society: Lord Brouncker, who was particularly interested in harmonic theory, in 1653 translated Descartes's *De Musica*, while Pepys's friend John Wallis, Professor of Geometry at Oxford, published his *Opera Mathematica* in 1699.

Both Pepys and Evelyn considered the association between music and mathematics to be close, and Evelyn catalogued the two subjects together. Towards the end of his life, Pepys wrote to a friend that music was a 'science peculiarly productive of a pleasure that no state of life public or private, secular or sacred; no difference of age or season; no temper of mind ... nor ... distinction of quality, renders either improper, untimely or unentertaining'.[35] On 5 October 1664, the two diarists, along with other Royal Society virtuosi, attended a musical experiment in the garden of the Post Office in the City. In his diary John Evelyn recorded: 'To Lond: at our Society Experiments ... also was brought a new invented Instrument of Musique, being an harpsichord with gut-Strings, sounding like a Consort of Viols with an Organ, made vocal by a Wheele, & a Zone of parchment that rubb'd horizontaly against the Strings.' Pepys called this curiosity an Arched Viall, 'where, being tuned with Lutestrings and played on Kees like an organ – a piece of Parchment is always kept moving; and the strings, which by the keys are pressed down upon it, are grated, in imitation of a bow, by the parchment; and so is intended to resemble several vyalls played on one bow'. With his musical ear, Pepys found this uncomfortable and unsatisfactory, producing a sound 'so basely and harshly that it will never do. But after three hours' stay, it could not be Fixt in tune; and so they were fain to go to some other Musique of instruments, which I am grown quite out of love with'.[36]

Automata were very fashionable at this time, and John Evelyn duly noted examples that he saw and heard in gardens in Europe during his travels in the 1640s. In Amsterdam, for instance, he saw 'many quaint devices, fountaines, artificiall musique, noyses of beasts and chirping &c'. He was also shown 'a rarity, a Chime of Purselan [porcelain] dishes, which fitted to clock-work, ring many changes, and tunes without breaking'.[37] The wonders of automata intrigued Pepys too. In June 1661, he went to hear music at the Globe tavern in Greenwich, 'and saw the simple motion that is there, of a woman with a rod in her hand, keeping time to the music while it plays – which is simple methinks'.[38] The woman was a mannequin, and the music was provided by an organ. During the Commonwealth period, the playing of organs in churches was forbidden, so many were removed to taverns.

Robert Hooke had looked at the musical potential of insects when researching his great work, *Micrographia*. He recorded the structure of their wings under the microscope, but had also determined the pitch of their flight sound by tuning a 'musical string' in unison with it, thus deducing the frequency of the wing stroke. Flies, he had concluded, made many hundreds, if not thousands, of vibrations per second, while the motions of the bee were even quicker, and might be 'the quickest vibrating *spontaneous* motions of any in the world'.[39] Pepys was naturally fascinated by Hooke's work and, meeting him in the street, had a discussion with him

about the nature of Sounds, and he did make me understand the nature of Musicall sounds made by Strings, mighty prettily; and told

22 & 23. Portraits of Mary
Browne and John Evelyn
made in pencil by Robert
Nanteuil in Paris in 1650.
The artist also depicted
Mary's parents, Sir Richard
and Lady Browne, to
celebrate the marriage of
Mary and John.

24. The artist Matthew Dixon painted a portrait of Margaret Blagge in 1673 for John Evelyn. This is an engraving after that painting by W. Humphreys.

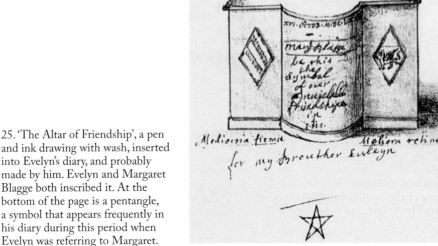

25. 'The Altar of Friendship', a pen and ink drawing with wash, inserted into Evelyn's diary, and probably made by him. Evelyn and Margaret Blagge both inscribed it. At the bottom of the page is a pentangle, a symbol that appears frequently in his diary during this period when Evelyn was referring to Margaret.

Mr. Evelyn.

Sr. Anth. Deane.

Sr. James Houblon.

Mr. Pepys.

Dr. Gale — Dean of York.

Mr. Hewer.

26. Pepys with his friends, from his collection 'of Heads in Taille-Douce & Drawings'. He has gathered around him five of his friends of long standing. At the top is John Evelyn, from a portrait by Godfrey Kneller commissioned by Pepys, in which he is holding a copy of *Sylva*. Flanking Pepys is Anthony Deane, a shipwright from Woolwich who many years earlier had educated Pepys in navy practices, and James Houblon, the City merchant who shared his love of music and 'good discourse'. Below are Thomas Gale, Secretary of the Royal Society when Pepys was President, and William Hewer, who had joined Pepys's household in 1660 and was to look after him in his old age.

27. Portrait by an unknown English artist, now thought to be of Mary Skinner, Pepys's partner for the last thirty years of his life. It hangs in the Pepys Library at Magdalene College, Cambridge.

28. Around the year 1693 Pepys commissioned the artist Sutton Nicholls to portray his library in York Buildings from different perspectives. This drawing shows the view out to the Thames, with five of the glazed bookcases made for Pepys by the naval joiner, Thomas Simpson. Pepys's large folios were probably kept under the draped table, whilst a map and portraits of his friends hang on the walls. Among the portraits was one of his patron, James II, then in exile in France.

29. The frontispiece to Thomas Sprat's *History of the Royal Society*, published in 1667. Evelyn provided the idea for the image, which was executed by Wenceslaus Hollar. It shows the bust of Charles II being crowned by Fame, with the Society's first President (and Pepys's naval superior) Viscount Brouncker on the left, and Francis Bacon on the right. Behind are a whole range of scientific and mathematical instruments, clocks and books by Copernicus, Bacon and William Harvey.

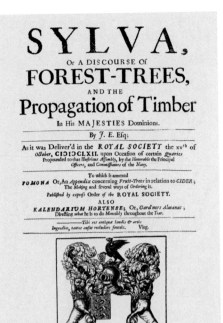

SYLVA,
Or A DISCOURSE of
FOREST-TREES,
AND THE
Propagation of Timber
In His MAJESTIES Dominions.

By J. E. Esq;

As it was Deliver'd in the *ROYAL SOCIETY* the xvᵗʰ of
October, CIƆIƆCLXII. upon Occasion of certain *Quæries*
Propounded to that *Illustrious Assembly*, by the *Honorable* the Principal
Officers, and *Commissioners* of the Navy.

To which is annexed
POMONA Or, An *Appendix* concerning *Fruit-Trees* in relation to *CIDER*;
The *Making* and several ways of *Ordering* it.
Published by express Order of the ROYAL SOCIETY.
ALSO
KALENDARIUM HORTENSE; Or, *Gard'ners Almanac*;
Directing what he is to do Monethly throughout the Year.

————*Tibi res antiquæ laudis & artis*
Ingredior, sanctos ausus recludere fonteis. Virg.

LONDON, Printed by *Jo. Martyn*, and *Ja. Allestry*, Printers to the *Royal
Society*, and are to be sold at their Shop at the *Bell* in S. *Paul's* Church-yard,
MDCLXIV.

30. The title page of Evelyn's *Sylva, or a Discourse of Forest-Trees*, published by the Royal Society in 1664. It was the first book to be so published, and Evelyn was also involved in the design of the coat of arms, providing a series of sketches, and the choice of the motto, taken from the Epistles of Horace.

PHILOSOPHIÆ
NATURALIS
PRINCIPIA
MATHEMATICA.

Autore *JS. NEWTON*, *Trin. Coll. Cantab. Soc.* Matheseos
Professore *Lucasiano*, & Societatis Regalis Sodali.

IMPRIMATUR·
S. PEPYS, *Reg. Soc.* PRÆSES.
Julii 5. 1686i

LONDINI,
Jussu *Societatis Regiæ* ac Typis *Josephi Streater*. Prostant Vena-
les apud *Sam. Smith* ad insignia *Principis Walliæ* in Cœmiterio
D. *Pauli*, aliosq; nonnullos Bibliopolas. *Anno* MDCLXXXVII.

31. The title page of Isaac Newton's *Philosophiae Naturalis Principia Mathematica*, published in 1687. The Royal Society gave the work its imprimatur, so Pepys, as President the previous year, appears on the title page.

Schem. XXXV.

32 & 33. Illustrations from Robert Hooke's groundbreaking *Micrographia*, published by the Royal Society in 1665. Right: Hooke explained in his text that the louse, a busy and impudent creature, was no respecter of persons, afflicting the King as much as his subjects. Below: The graceful flowers are in fact a spot of blue cheese mould taken from a sheepskin book binding, which Hooke described as 'a very pretty shap'd Vegetative body'.

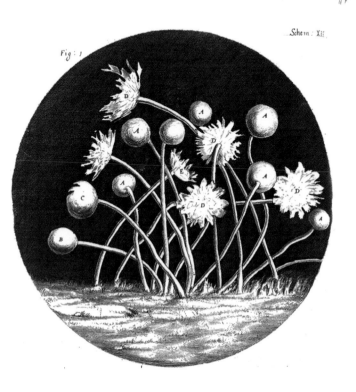

Schem : XII

Fig : 1

34. An illustration by Francis Barlow facing the title page of John Playford's *Musick's Delight on the Cithren*, published in 1666. The young musician, in fashionable courtier's dress, studies his book to learn new tunes for the 'cithren', a guitar with wire strings. Less fashionable stringed instruments, such as the mandolin and bass viol, hang neglected on the wall.

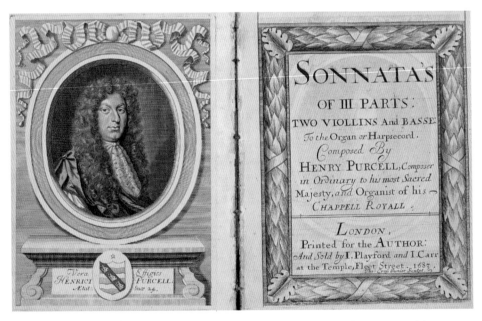

35. The title page of Purcell's *Sonnata's of III Parts*, published in 1683, with a portrait of the composer. In fact, it contains four parts, for Purcell added a *basso continuo* part for an organist or harpsichordist. This copy, which came into Pepys's collection, contains a dedication to the King, possibly written by Purcell himself.

36. A page from Cesare Morelli's manuscript, 'A Table to the Ghitarr', which he prepared for Pepys to show 'the relation of each fret upon every string to the common scale of musick'.

37. An *arca musarithmica*, a device invented by Athanasius Kircher to assist musical composition. His idea was that even a non-musical person could set a chosen text, following the combinations of notes, rhythmic shapes, harmonies and keys inscribed on little wooden sliders or *tariffa*, arranged in columns in the box. Kircher's intended customers were Jesuit missionaries, but Pepys acquired a box, though it is not known whether he was able to make use of it. Nevertheless, he recorded in his diary how he paid the substantial sum of 35s for Kircher's book, *Musargia*, in February 1668, expressing the hope 'to find great satisfaction in it'.

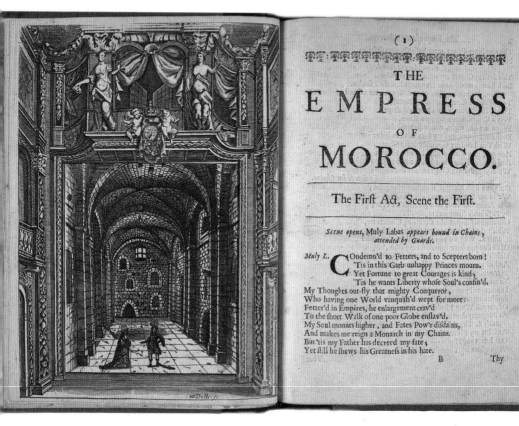

38. The opening scene of *The Empress of Morocco* by Elkanah Settle, first performed at the Duke's Theatre, Dorset Garden, in July 1673. The illustration offers a rare glimpse of how plays were staged at the time. Musicians would be housed in the box above the proscenium arch. The lantern hanging midway back on the stage would have offered some illumination of the drama unfolding below.

39. The Duke's Theatre, Dorset Garden, from an eighteenth-century engraving. After the Great Fire destroyed the Salisbury Court Theatre, a magnificent new building was built a short distance along the Thames to house the Duke of York's Men under Sir William Davenant, although he died before it was completed. Its design has traditionally been attributed to Christopher Wren, but this is now disputed. The theatre opened in 1671 with a performance of Dryden's *Sir Martin Mar-All*.

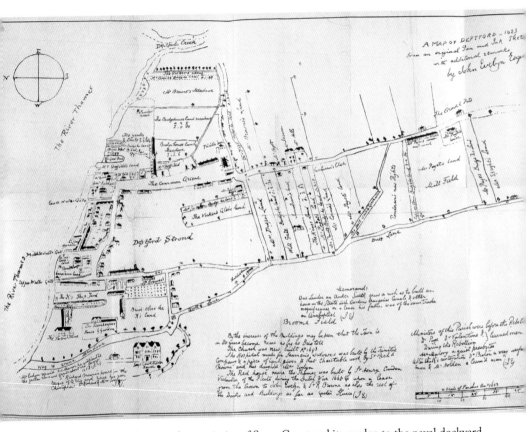

40. A sketch map showing the proximity of Sayes Court and its garden to the naval dockyard at Deptford. Evelyn added notes to an original pen and ink drawing of 1623, now damaged by damp and among his papers in the British Library, but the map was reproduced in Nathan Dews's *History of Deptford*, published in 1884.

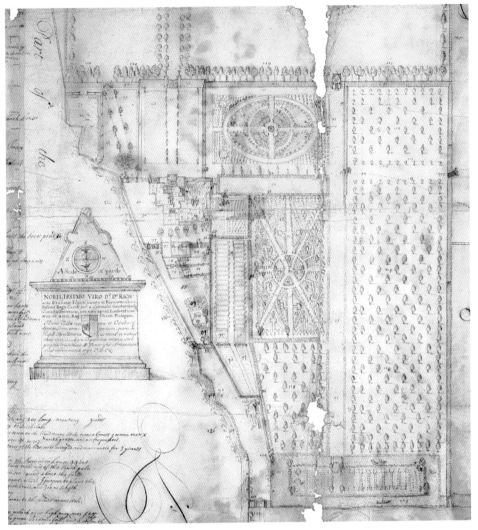

41. Evelyn's drawing of the layout of his garden at Sayes Court. At the top he shows the oval parterre, based on the one that he had seen in Paris in the garden of Pierre Morin. Below this is the kitchen garden and the grove, and below again, the great orchard. At the bottom are rectangular beds built on an island in the Thames.

42. Evelyn acquired glass beehives from John Wilkins in Oxford and kept them in his walled garden at Sayes Court. But in *Elysium Britannicum* he adopted a more whimsical approach, with drawings of beehives in the form of Gothic church fonts.

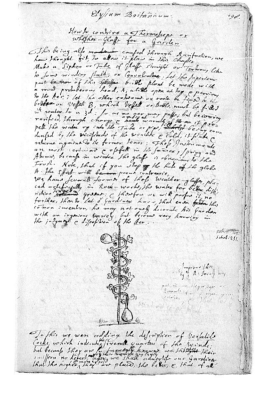

43. Evelyn's pen and ink drawing, 'How to contrive a Thermoscope or Weather-Glass for a Garden', from his *Elysium Britannicum*. Like all good gardeners, he was keen to be able to predict weather conditions, especially as his garden at Sayes Court seemed particularly susceptible to extremes. In *Elysium Britannicum*, he explained that the instrument was 'a Siphon or Tube of Glasse straight or Tortuous like to some winding Stalke or Convulvulus'.

44. An 'advent calendar' of garden tools and equipment from Evelyn's *Elysium Britannicum*. These include basic tools such as pruning knives and watering pots, but also a knife-grinder and a book in which to write the names of plants. Perhaps the most unusual object is no. 53, 'a Bed-stead furnished with a tester and Curtaines of Green' to protect tender flowers from 'the parching beames of the Sunn'.

45 & 46. Engravings from Evelyn's translation of *Le Jardinier François*, published in 1658. Left: In his diary in December of that year he noted, 'Now was published my French gardiner the first and best of that kind that introduced the olitorie [kitchen garden]'. In the foreground of the engraving is the kitchen garden with raised beds for melons and cucumbers, and in the background the broderie parterre that was fashionable at this time. Below: The still room from *The French Gardiner*. At Sayes Court Evelyn had what he described as his elaboratory. This was equipped with furnaces and distilling equipment for the extraction of essences from plants, such as Hungary water from rosemary flowers, which he recommended to apply to the hair. Mary Evelyn, meanwhile, had her own still room in the main part of the house, and became known for her household skills. Some of her recipes were reproduced by Evelyn in *Acetaria*.

me that having come to a certain Number of Vibracions proper to make any tone, he is able to tell how many strokes a fly makes with her wings (those flies that hum in their flying) by the note that it answers to in Musique during their flying.

Later he pressed Hooke further on the subject after a meeting of the Royal Society, and was told that the harmonies and discords in music came as a result of the equality of the vibrations. He confessed to his diary that he was not satisfied by this explanation, 'but will at my leisure think of it more, and see how far that doth go to explain it'.[40]

While on his European tour, Evelyn had visited Athanasius Kircher, the Professor of Mathematics at the Collegio Romano, and observed some of the mechanical models he had made in support of his theory of music (p. 15). Such was Pepys's interest in theoretical works that in 1668 he paid the substantial sum of £1.15s for Kircher's *Musurgia Universalis*, published in 1650. Also in the library at Magdalene is an *arca musarithmica*, a device invented by Kircher to help in musical composition (Plate 37). Kircher's idea was that even a non-musical person could set a chosen text with the help of combinations of notes, rhythmic shapes, harmonies and keys indicated on small wooden sliders – *tariffa* – arranged in columns in a box. In his book Kircher explained, 'It is apparent from that which is put forward here the infinite number of possible combinations which are given by the different ordering of the five columns. Assuredly these are so many that had an angel begun with the combinations at the dawning of the World, it would not be finished today'.[41] It is not known whether Pepys had his *arca* specially made or whether he was given it.

Nor is it known whether Pepys managed to produce any compositions using this device. Just as he strove to 'con his gamut', he also worked at his compositions, and chose to be depicted holding the music for the song 'Beauty Retire' when he had his portrait painted by John Hayls in 1666 (Plate 14). Four years earlier, his diary is filled with references to 'Mr Berchenshaw'. This was John Birchensha, a music theorist and teacher, who in a letter to the Royal Society claimed that by following his rules, 'not only those, who skilfully can sing or play on some Instrument, may learn to compose but also those, who can neither sing nor play'.[42] John Evelyn remarked in his diary that the rules represented 'a mathematical way of composure very extraordinary: True as to the exact rules of art, but without much harmonie'.[43] Pepys's experience of the theory began happily enough in January: 'at home, and Mr Berchenshaw . . . who stayed with me a great while talking of Musique; and I am resolved to begin to learne of him to compose and to begin tomorrow, he giving me so great hopes that I shall soon do it'.[44] The course of lessons cost him a substantial £5, which he confessed to his diary troubled him to part with.

The two men worked on composing songs, but by the end of February disillusion had crept in:

> I finding that he cries up his rules for most perfect (though I do grant them to be very good, and the best I believe that ever yet were made) and that I could not persuade him to grant wherein they were somewhat lame, we fell to angry words, so that in a pet he flung out of my chamber and I never stopped him, being entended to have put him off today whether this had happened or no, because I think I have all the rules that he hath to give, and so there remains nothing but practice now to do me good – and it is not for me to continue with him at 5*l* per mensem. So I settled to put all his rules all in fair order in a book.[45]

Although Pepys gave Birchensha the benefit of the doubt, there is a suspicion of charlatanism, reinforced by the fact that he was later caricatured by the dramatist Thomas Shadwell in *The Humorists*, written in 1670. Shadwell, a sharply satirical observer of contemporary manners and amusements, described Birchensha as 'a rare fellow, give him his due, fa la la, for he can teach men to compose that are deaf, dumb, and blind'.[46] We do not know whether Pepys attended a performance of *The Humorists* as he ceased his diary two years earlier. It is very likely, however, that he did go to see the play, for he was an inveterate theatregoer: it has been estimated that in the first eight months of 1668 he saw at least seventy-three performances. Shadwell was a personal friend, so he may have given him the background for the gibe.

It should come as no surprise that Pepys was so keen on the theatre, for he was born in the midst of the drama that was enacted daily on the streets of London, and in particular in Salisbury Court. On the south side of the court, as it sloped down to the River Thames, a theatre was constructed out of an old barn and opened in 1629. The public play-houses built in Elizabeth I's reign, such as the Globe at Bankside, had taken their concept from the galleried courtyards of inns, with an open central area, and it has been suggested that their layout was also influenced by arenas for animal baiting.[47] This style of theatre had become outmoded by the 1620s, although the Red Bull in Clerkenwell, the Cockpit in Drury Lane and the Fortune in Golden Lane retained the configuration. The future lay instead with indoor theatres, where plays could also be performed in winter months, and special effects and lighting employed. Shakespeare's later plays, for example, were performed at a playhouse within the former monastery of Blackfriars. The plot of land on which the Salisbury Court Theatre was built was long and narrow, and this suited the way plays were being staged, with an apron jutting into the auditorium, and graduated tiers of seats. Real tennis courts proved suitable for this with their unencumbered halls and ranges of windows in the upper part. Gibbons's Tennis Court, built in 1633 in Clement's Inn Fields, offered the additional attractions of a bowling alley and a French cook, but the Civil War intervened to stop both sport and food, so plays were occasionally performed there.

Although Parliament had officially banned professional performances in London from September 1642, the acting companies defiantly continued to put on plays. In 1649, following the execution of Charles I, the ordinances were revived and imposed more effectively, with soldiers dispatched to dismantle the furnishings of the theatres. Even this did not deter the battered Red Bull, with the actors and sometimes the audience fighting the soldiers during the raids. Some actors turned instead to giving private performances in houses and tennis courts in London and in the mansions of gentry in the suburbs.

Sir William Davenant chose a subtler course of action. His first plays had been for the public theatre, but in the 1630s he became a servant of the Queen, Henrietta Maria, and produced a series of masques. On Ben

Jonson's death in 1637, he was appointed unofficial Poet Laureate. Imprisoned briefly in the Tower by Parliament as 'an active enemy of the commonwealth', on his release he devised a plan to create a form of theatre which he termed 'moral representations' in a bid to circumvent the ordinances. Knowing that the Lord Protector, Oliver Cromwell, loved ceremony and music, Davenant combined declamation, music and dancing in *The First Day's Entertainment*, held at Rutland House in Charterhouse Yard in May 1656. A prologue made apology for the narrow chamber in which it was performed, inviting those present to regard it as a way 'to our Elyzian field, the *Opera*': the first appearance of that word in an English context. At one stage in the performance a Parisian and a Londoner debated the merits of their respective capitals, and Davenant took the opportunity to flatter the government by condemning the French for harbouring the exiled Charles II and his court. An anonymous observer also reported that at the end of the performance there were 'songs relating to the Victor' – in other words, the Lord Protector.[48]

Perhaps unsurprisingly, no official criticism followed, so in the autumn of that year Davenant put on *The Siege of Rhodes*, again at Rutland House. This he described on the title page of the printed version as 'A Representation by the Art of Prospective in Scenes, And the Story sung in *Recitative Musick*', carefully avoiding any terms that might associate it with the theatre. An advance copy was sent to Bulstrode Whitelocke, Lord Commissioner of the Treasury, who had during the reign of Charles I put on a masque at Whitehall. Davenant followed this up with the dispatch of a memorandum to Cromwell's Secretary of State, arguing that such entertainments provided diversion from 'Melancholy that breeds Sedition; which made our Ancestors intertaine them with publique meetings for prizes in Archery, Horse-Races, matches at Foot-ball, Wakes, May-poles and sports of Christmas, Theaters and other publique Spectacles'.[49]

Further emboldened, Davenant transferred *The Siege of Rhodes* to the Cockpit Theatre, increasing the musical element, with 'Recitative Musick' by Henry Lawes, Captain Henry Cooke and Matthew Locke, and instrumental music by Charles Coleman and George Hudson, all of which have been lost. This version has been described as the first English opera, but it is more accurate to describe it as a music drama, with the speeches given in recitative, and to reserve the term opera for a performance that was entirely sung. However, the future of all types of theatre seemed to be getting more perilous with the hardening of attitudes by the Council of State following the Lord Protector's death in the autumn of 1658. This turned out to be a temporary problem, for on 29 May 1660 Charles II returned to his kingdom, and the whole theatrical scene in London was about to change fundamentally.

Davenant, along with the dramatist Thomas Killigrew, moved quickly, using their friendship with the King to establish a monopoly over what promised to be a very lucrative activity. Under patents they secured considerable powers: to build theatres whenever they chose; to hold the exclusive right to present 'tragedies, comedies, plays, operas, music scenes and all other entertainments of the stage whatsoever'; to charge what they thought reasonable; and to present actresses for the first time on the public stage. The company at the Red Bull, having endured years of persecution by the authorities, was not going to go lightly, and continued performing until Killigrew had its manager, Michael Mohun, committed to prison. The quarrel was resolved when Mohun and his actors became the nucleus of the troupe now formed by Killigrew as the King's Company, playing at the former Gibbons's Tennis Court in Vere Street. Sir William Davenant, meanwhile, took charge of the Duke of York's Company, initially at the Salisbury Court Theatre while he converted another tennis court, Lisle's, in Lincoln's Inn Fields.

Killigrew enjoyed significant advantages over his rival in having secured the most experienced of the actors and managing to assert exclusive rights to the performance of almost all the well-known plays on the grounds that the King's Company could claim descent from the King's Men. He thereby had the whole range of Elizabethan and Jacobean drama to call upon, but lacked the incentive to commission new plays. His plays did not require scenery, which was just as well, because the Vere Street theatre had no such provision. In time the latter problem was overcome when he moved into the Theatre Royal in Bridges Street, Covent Garden, and was able to commission elaborate sets for his plays.

Davenant, meanwhile, had to train up a comparatively inexperienced company, but did have one of the greatest acting talents of the age, Thomas Betterton. He overcame the disadvantage of the limited repertory by gaining exclusive rights to nine of Shakespeare's plays as well as his own early works, and by making the most of every new production. Davenant enjoyed the rumour that he was the son of a liaison between his handsome mother, who kept an inn in Oxford, and William Shakespeare, but this did not stop him treating his 'father's' plays in a cavalier manner, adapting and rewriting them to suit contemporary taste. He was a much better manager than Killigrew, both financially and in his dealings with his players, and he quickly established that his was going to be the better of the companies. In early March 1661 Samuel Pepys noted in his diary how he went to Killigrew's Theatre Royal, but finding so few people there, went instead to Davenant's Salisbury Court, which he found 'as full as could be'. He watched *Love's Mistress, or The Queen's Masque*, an allegorical drama by Thomas Heywood, revived from the 1630s, 'wherein there is some good humours'. A week later he saw the same play put on by the King's Company, but did not enjoy it as much.[50]

Pepys provides in his diary a vivid and invaluable picture of what it was like to go the theatre in the 1660s. The principal London season was from September through to June, the months when Parliament and the law courts were in session. The pace was relentless, with the playhouses open six days a week and the actors rehearsing in the morning, playing in the afternoon, and sometimes going to the royal court in the evening to put on further performances. The public plays usually commenced at 3.30 pm, so that in Richard Flecknoe's comedy of 1667, *The Demoiselles à La Mode*, comes the summons: 'Hark you, hark you, whither away so fast? Why to the Theatre, 'tis past three o'th Clock and the Play's ready to begin.' As the century proceeded, plays came to start slightly later, no doubt reflecting the change in the fashionable time for dining.

Handbills announcing the forthcoming performance were distributed around the streets. Once when Pepys was going out after his dinner he found *The Bondman* advertised 'upon the posts'. He was in a dilemma, as in his effort to eschew pleasurable things he had sworn not to go to plays more often than once a month. On this occasion, however, he resolved his conscience because he had only seen a part of one the week before.[51] It was also the custom to print the prologues and epilogues as broadsides and sell these in the street as a taster. Word of mouth was very important, and Pepys was provided with all kinds of theatrical gossip by Wotton, his shoemaker in Fleet Street. People kept their friends abreast of the latest plays by letter. Mary Evelyn, who enjoyed her visits to the theatre, wrote to her friend Mr Tyrrell in Ireland in 1669 bringing him up to date about the plays being performed and gossip about the players. An account of the plays available in the early part of 1662 is a rhyme apparently written by a London man to his friend in the country. He begins with those on offer with the King's Company:

> First then to speake of his Majesty's Theatre
> Where one would imagine Playes should be better
> Love att the first sight did lead the dance
> But att second sight it had the mischance
> To be dash't out of Countenance as
> It never after durst shew itts face.

This was Thomas Killigrew's *Princess; or, Love at First Sight*. Pepys had seen it the previous November, pronouncing it a poor thing, as did everybody else, for it lasted only two days.[52] The versifier was equally critical of Sir William Davenant's eccentric idea of combining two of Shakespeare's plays, *Measure for Measure* and *Much Ado About Nothing* as *The Law against Lovers*:

> Then came the Knight agen with his Lawe
> Against Lovers the worst that ever you sawe
> In dressing of which he playnely did shew it
> Hee was a far better Cooke than a Poet
> And only he the Art of it had
> Of two good Playes to make one bad.

He ends by glumly saying that all the new plays are indifferent in quality, and cannot say whether this is going to change in the future.[53]

Although the play might commence at 3.30 pm, the theatres were opened earlier to allow in the audience, probably from noon. Pepys describes being let in early: 'I having sat here a while and eat nothing, did slip out, getting a boy to keep my place; and the Rose tavern and there got half a breast o mutton off of the spit . . . and so the play again'.[54] The interior of a playhouse and its audience are well described by François Misson, a Frenchman who came to London at the end of the century. The particular house he is talking of is a second manifestation of the Theatre Royal, following a disastrous fire in 1672, but it holds true of the earlier venues:

> an Amphitheater fill'd with Benches without Backboards, and adorn'd and cover'd with green Cloth. Men of Quality, particularly the younger Sort, some Ladies of Reputation and Vertue, and abundance of Damsels that hunt for Prey, sit all together in this Place, Higgledy-piggledy, chatter, toy, play, hear, hear not. Farther up, against the Wall, under the first Gallery, and just opposite the Stage, rises another Amphitheater, which is taken up by Persons of the best Quality, among whom are generally very few Men. The Galleries, whereof there are only two Rows, are fill'd with none but ordinary People, particularly the Upper one.[55]

The cost of boxes was 4s per seat, and single seats might be purchased; the pit cost 2s.6d; the middle gallery 1s.6d; and the upper gallery 1s. A brass disc was issued indicating the part of the theatre, but there were no numbered seats. When he went to the theatre on New Year's Day 1668, Pepys remarked in his diary of the changing clientele: 'I do not remember that I saw so many by half of the ordinary prentices and mean people in the pit, at 2s 6d apiece as now; I going for several years no higher than the 12d, and then the 18d places'.[56] The audience capacity varied from theatre to theatre, but averaged around 700.

The Lord Chamberlain closed the theatres with the arrival of the plague and in the following year London was struck by the Great Fire.

After the Salisbury Court Theatre was burned to the ground, along with neighbouring Dorset House, a new theatre for the Duke of York's Company was built in the classical style on the site of the gardens with its entrance facing the Thames (Plate 39). Although Covent Garden had been well away from the fire, Thomas Killigrew told Pepys that house attendance had dropped by at least a half. Nevertheless, he went on to assure him that business was recovering, and that the behaviour of theatre audiences was much more sophisticated than in the past: 'now all things civil, no rudeness anywhere; then, as in a bear-garden'.[57] This claim, however, is not supported by contemporary accounts, which make clear that the theatre could be a rowdy place, especially in the pit, with many a brawl and even an occasional stabbing. Thomas Shadwell referred in one of his plays to the young bloods 'at Sixteen forsooth, set up for Men of Town. Such as come Drunk and Screaming into a Playhouse, and stand upon the Benches, and toss their full Periwigs and empty Heads, and with their shrill unbroken Pipes cry *"Dam-me, this is a Damn'd Play: Prithee let's to a Whore, Jack"*.'[58]

Shadwell's great rival, John Dryden, paints a similar scene:

But as when Vizard Masque appears in Pit,
Straight, every Man who thinks himself a Wit
Perks up; and, managing his Comb, with grace,
With his white Wigg setts off his Nut-brown Face:
That done, bears up to th' prize, and views each Limb
To know her by her Rigging and her Trimm.[59]

A 'Vizard Masque' was slang for a whore, referring to the face mask that was worn by many prostitutes. But such masks were also donned by respectable ladies; Pepys records buying one for his wife.[60] One of the striking aspects of the Restoration theatre is that men and women mixed freely on both the sides of the footlights. Pepys records taking his wife and women friends, and Evelyn often accompanied his wife, although she also refers in letters light-heartedly to taking along 'a gallant'.

One of the features of the Theatre Royal were the orange sellers. They were organised by Mrs Mary Meggs, known familiarly as Orange

Moll, who in 1662 was granted on payment of £100 'full, free & sole liberty, licence, power, & authority to vend, utter, & sell oranges, Lemons, fruit, sweetmeats, & all manner of fruiters and Confectioners wares & Commodities'.[61] Two people were to sell in the pit, and one 'in & about the boxes & lower rooms'. The galleries were not, apparently, to enjoy the wares or charms of the orange girls. Mrs Meggs was clearly a formidable lady: Pepys witnessed how she saved the life of a member of the audience who was choking, 'but with much ado Orange Mall did thrust her finger down his throat and brought him to life again'.[62] Orange Moll hired a young Nell Gwyn along with her older sister Rose as orange sellers, and they plied their trade selling fruit at sixpence each. They also would have taken messages from the men in the audience to actresses backstage. It was not an easy life, as two of the maids of honour from the royal court found out when they decided as a jape to disguise themselves as orange girls. They were accosted at the playhouse, and ambushed in their coach on their way home by Henry Brouncker, brother of Pepys's musical Lord. Described by Pepys as 'a pestilent rogue, an Atheist, that would have sold his King and country for 6d almost', Henry Brouncker kept a 'little country-house ... always stocked with several working girls'.[63]

Nell famously made her escape from the life of an orange girl to become one of the leading actresses of Thomas Killigrew's company, and after affairs with the actor Charles Hart and the courtier playwright Charles Sackville, became mistress of the King.[64] The appearance of women on the stage at the Restoration revolutionised the appeal of the theatre, especially when they were given cross-dressing roles. Pepys, connoisseur of the female form, observed in 1661 the leading lady coming onto the stage in men's clothes and revealing 'the best legs that I ever saw'.[65]

The atmosphere backstage was as febrile as in the pit. After performances, gallants went to the green room and the tiring rooms to see the actresses. Pepys describes going to visit his friend, the singer Elizabeth Knepp, and watching Rebecca Marshall 'come dressed off of the stage, and looks mighty fine and pretty, and noble – and also Nell [Gwyn] in her boy's clothes, mighty pretty; but Lord, their confidence, and how many men do hover about'. He kissed a woman called Peg, who was mistress of the playwright courtier, Sir Charles Sedley – 'a mighty pretty woman, and seems, but is not, modest'.[66] Peg was probably Margaret Hughes, who subsequently became mistress of the King's cousin, Prince Rupert.

The connection between the royal court and the theatres was a close one, with the King a frequent attender of plays. After going to see a performance of *The Siege of Rhodes* in 1662, John Evelyn noted in his diary: 'In this acted the faire and famous Comedian call'd Roxalana for that part she acted, & I think it was the last; then taken to be the E. of Oxford's Misse (as at this time they began to call lew'd women)'. If this was indeed one of the first uses of miss or mistress in the English language, it was to be used increasingly, rousing Evelyn to a tirade about how the appearance of the actresses inflamed 'severall young noble-men & gallants' who took them as 'their whores, & to some their Wives'. In his scandalous list were Charles Sackville, Earl of Dorset, and Nell Gwyn, Prince Rupert and Margaret Hughes, and 'another greater person than any of these' – the King, 'to the reproch of their noble families, & ruine both of body & Soule'.[67] The ever-practical William Davenant had his actresses lodged in his own house adjoining the theatre, so that the Duke's Company was far less bothered by unwanted pregnancies and sudden departures than was the King's Company.

At the Restoration, both Killigrew and Davenant, but particularly the latter, were calling out for new plays. The call was answered by two groups: courtiers and professional writers. The sense that emerges is that every man of leisure who considered himself cultured thought he had a play in him. Even John Evelyn tried his hand, as noted by Pepys. On 5 November 1665 he went down to Sayes Court, where Evelyn showed him his etchings and read to him selections of his writings, including 'part of a play or two of his making, very good, but not as he conceits them, I think to be'. Pepys was a shrewd appraiser of plays, so it is not surprising that Evelyn's efforts were never printed. One of them was likely to have been *Thersander*, a tragi-comedy in verse.[68]

With the 1660s had come an appetite for tragi-comedies, usually with an ending that was happy or where it transpired that the tragic male lead was a victim rather than a flawed hero. In parallel was the growing taste for the French romances of Madeleine de Scudéry, enjoyed by readers such as Elizabeth Pepys, with their complex plots featuring princes and princesses with exotic histories (p. 228). Charles II, having spent some of his exile in Paris, had acquired a taste for the French fashion in plays. According to Roger Boyle, Earl of Orrery and older brother of the scientist Robert, the King commanded him to write a play for him, and he responded by producing *The General* in 1661. Orrery had enjoyed an interesting career during the Interregnum: a personal friend of Oliver Cromwell with a marked antagonism towards the Irish Catholics and their political aspirations, he proposed a union by marriage between Cromwell's daughter Frances and Charles II. In the troubled period after Cromwell's death, he retired to Ireland, and invited the King to land at Cork, thus anticipating General Monck's overtures to Charles that led to his restoration. The general in the title of the play was a soldier who revolts against a usurper to restore the true king, with much discussion about concepts of love and honour.

Another courtier who produced tragi-comedies was Sir Charles Sedley, a hard drinker who earned notoriety in 1663 by appearing on the balcony of a tavern in Bow Street where he stripped naked and performed a pantomime of lust and buggery, ending his performance by urinating on the crowd and thereby provoking a riot. His next appearance was in court where he was bound over to good behaviour on a bond of £500 and borrowed the huge sum to pay the fine from the King – raising many eyebrows as to what this presaged for the future. Pepys, however, could appreciate his wit. Once, when he overheard Sedley chattering in the audience, Pepys quipped that he was more entertaining than what was taking place on the stage. The following year Pepys was able to hear Sedley's wit on that stage when he went to see his *Mulberry Garden*, a tragi-comedy based partly on Molière's *L'École des Maris*. He was not, however, impressed, noting his disappointment with the language and design of the play, and disapproving of the musical setting.[69]

Just as with music of the period, there was debate about the comparative merits of English and French drama. In an essay published in 1668 entitled 'Of Dramatick Poesie', John Dryden conjured a dialogue among four friends taking a boat along the River Thames on the day of the battle between the English and Dutch navies in June 1665. The names of the four were aliases: Lisedeius for Sedley; Crites for Sir Robert Howard, Dryden's brother-in-law; Eugenius for Charles Sackville – all three courtier playwrights – while the fourth, Neander, was Dryden himself, the 'new man' obliged to earn his living through his writing. Dryden had Lisedeius pronounce, 'There is no Theatre in the World has any thing so absurd as the English Tragic-comedie, 'tis a Drama of our own invention ... here a course of mirth, there another of Sadness and Passion, and a third of Honour, and a Duel: Thus in two hours and a half we run through all the fits of Bedlam.'[70]

Another genre developed at the behest of Charles II was comedy in the Spanish style. Samuel Tuke, a cousin of John Evelyn's wife Mary, was asked by the King to adapt a Spanish play for the English stage, and duly obliged with *The Adventures of 5 Hours* based on *Los empeños de seis horas*, probably written by Don Antonio Coello y Ochoa. Pepys went to see the first public performance with his wife in January 1663 at the Duke's Theatre in Lincoln's Inn Fields. His reaction was delight: 'And the play, in one word, is the best, for the variety and most excellent continuance of the plot to the very end, that ever I saw or think ever shall ... And the house, by its frequent plaudits, did show their sufficient approbation.'[71] Pepys's enjoyment must have been enhanced by the appearance of his favourite actor, Thomas Betterton, as Don Henriq. John Evelyn was also present, but not so enthusiastic. Despite having helped with the translation, he found the language stiff and formal, although he did concede that Tuke had produced an incomparable plot.[72]

Tuke's play proved a great commercial success, so the style was taken up by a new dramatist, George Etherege, just twenty-seven when his *Comical Revenge, or, Love in a Tub* was first performed at the same theatre in March 1664. The serious portions of the play were in rhymed verse, while the comic underplot was written in prose, a style that was to prove the foundation of the future English comedy of manners. The audiences loved it, enjoying the way that Etherege evoked the stifling manners of England under Cromwell in contrast to the freedom of the present. However, neither Evelyn nor Pepys was impressed: Evelyn dismissed it as facetious, and although Pepys professed it to be very merry, he felt it unworthy of the theatre.[73] Perhaps they both sensed that the present was becoming rather too free.

John Dryden chose to widen the range with his dramas: as well as comedies and tragi-comedies, he wrote rhymed heroic plays. His first was *The Wild Gallant*, a comedy that may have been first performed at court in 1663 before moving to the Theatre Royal. When Pepys went to see it, he was not impressed: 'it was ill acted and the play so poor a thing as I never saw in my life almost, and so little answering the name, that from beginning to end I could not, nor can at this time, tell certainly which was the wild gallant'.[74] Dryden went on to assist Sir Robert Howard with a heroic play, *Indian Queene*, first performed the following year. Both Pepys and Evelyn remarked on its spectacular nature. John Evelyn, so often disapproving, praised 'a Tragedie well written, but so beautiful with rich Scenes as the like had never ben seene here as happly . . . on a mercenarie Theatre'. The disapproval returned in full measure, however, when in 1668 he went to see Dryden's *An Evening's Love, or the Mock-Astrologer*: 'a foolish plot, & very prophane so as it afflicted me to see how the stage was degenerated & poluted by the licentious times'.[75]

Dryden's great rival was Thomas Shadwell, who revered above all playwrights Ben Jonson and his sharp observations of ordinary life. Shadwell was particularly upset by what he interpreted as criticism of Jonson in Dryden's essay, *Of Dramatick Poesie*; and Dryden's appointment as Poet Laureate on Davenant's death in 1668 must have rubbed salt in the wound, for Jonson had been the previous incumbent. In his preface to *The Sullen Lovers*, Shadwell proclaimed himself a follower of Jonson's comedies of humours and inveighed against Dryden, the opening salvo in what was to become a long-running debate that moved on to charges of plagiarism and the question of what was the primary purpose of comedy, to instruct or to please. Somehow Pepys managed to maintain friendships with both playwrights.

The Sullen Lovers, or The Impertinents opened at the Duke's Theatre on 2 May 1668, with the King and the Duke of York in the audience, along with Pepys, who admitted it had 'many good humours in it; but the play tedious and no designs to it'.[76] In the play, Shadwell poked fun at Dryden's brother-in-law, Sir Robert Howard, as Sir Positive at-all, 'a foolish Knight that pretends to understand everything in the world, and will suffer no man to understand any thing in his Company; so foolishly Positive, that he will never be convinced of an Error, though never so grosse'.[77] This habit of satirising identifiable individuals was a weapon that Shadwell continued to wield: in *The Virtuosi* in 1676, his target was the members of the Royal Society, infuriating John Evelyn, who suspected that he was one of the victims (pp. 122–3).

The Virtuosi particularly roused Evelyn's ire, but he was not enthusiastic about the theatre in general, especially the performances in public as opposed to those at court. The 'mercenary theatre' he considered to give rise to all kinds of profanity and depravity. In this he differed from his wife Mary, who no doubt enjoyed her theatre visits with her 'gallants' more when they were free from her husband's disapproving presence. Evelyn was by no means alone in his disapproval, but he was certainly in the minority, for the Restoration theatre proved very popular with all levels of London society. Although he could be critical, Pepys loved his visits, imposing limits to his attendances upon himself which he all too often exceeded. He was able to enter into the drama and to enjoy the wit, clever plots and writing. He also, of course, enjoyed the music that played such an important role in all dramatic performances.

When the two companies of players were appointed in 1660, King Charles gave each twelve musicians from his King's Violins. They would play while the audience assembled, beginning with 'Curtain Music' or overture, followed by 'Tunes for Four Acts' and the 'Conclusion'. Some idea of the variety on offer can be seen from Matthew Locke's music for Thomas Shadwell's version of *The Tempest*, performed in 1674: for the Curtain, storm music; First Act, rustic air; Second, minuet; Third, corant; Fourth, martial music; Conclusion, as the audience left, canon. The musicians were usually housed in a loft within the proscenium arch, but if one of the actors or actresses performed a dance, the musician appeared on the stage.

The spoken performance would commence with a Prologue as the curtain rose. Dryden excelled in delivering these with wit and topicality. Thereafter, the curtain remained raised, and scenes were changed by drawing together two portions of flats as the audience looked on. Scenery had been sumptuous for the early seventeenth-century court masques, with designs by Inigo Jones. The Restoration court did not partake in masques, partly because the King did not like them. Only one masque was held at court, *Calisto, or The Chaste Nimph* by John Crowne with Margaret Blagge a reluctant participant; it was not deemed a success and was not repeated (p. 94). Magnificent stage effects were instead to be enjoyed on the public stage. Inigo Jones's nephew, John Webb, designed the first scenery for Davenant's *Siege of Rhodes*, and Robert Streeter, the King's Serjeant Painter, provided the scenery for Dryden's *Conquest of Granada by the Spaniards* in 1670. John Evelyn, who had seen ornate scenery in theatres in Italy and France during his travels, affirmed that Streeter had produced 'very glorious scenes & perspectives'.[78] A lawsuit gives us an idea of the time taken to produce such scenery, and the costs: Isaac Fuller claimed the huge fee of £335 for the six weeks it took him to paint a scene of Elysium for Dryden's *Tyrannic Love*, during which he said that he never had time to undress, and slept in his studio. It is hardly surprising that scenery was constantly reused.

Theatres were illuminated by wax candles in pendant chandeliers hanging from the proscenium arch, well in front of the curtain and thus lighting up the apron. These were lit before the Prologue was spoken, but had to be regularly snuffed as the play proceeded. When Pepys went to a performance of Shadwell's *The Impertinents* in 1669, he noted that the candles hurt his eyes as he sat in a box that was level with them.[79] Footlights were provided first by oil lamps, and later by 'floats', cotton wicks running through cork and floating in oil in a tin box at the front of the stage with a tin reflector. When darkness was required for the dramatic action, the floats were lowered and any candles on the stage were removed.

For special effects, trap doors were often used, and flying machines. Attending a performance of Ben Jonson's *Bartholomew Fair* at the

Theatre Royal in 1664, Pepys got into conversation with Thomas Killigrew who told him of his plans for the future. These included four 'operas' in one year, 'where we shall have the best Scenes and Machinery, and the best Musique, and everything as Magnificent as is in Christendome, and to that end hath sent for voices and painters and other persons from Italy'.[80] The Italians, along with the French, were considered the masters of theatrical effects, and three members of the Duke's Company, the actors Thomas Betterton and Joseph Haines, and the chief machinist, Thomas Wright, were duly dispatched to Paris to study the latest developments.

In 1668 Pepys went to *The Virgin Martyr* by Dekker and Messinger. He was not too keen on the play, which had been written nearly half a century earlier, but was entranced by the music and the stage effects. In his diary he wrote, 'but that which did please me beyond anything in the whole world was the wind-musique when the Angell comes down, which is so sweet that it ravished me; and endeed in a word, did wrap up my soul so that it made me really sick, just as I have formerly been when in love with my wife'.[81] The wind music was provided by a type of recorder that had been developed in France, whilst the angel was almost certainly Nell Gwyn, lowered by ropes and pulleys. It would seem that Nell was associated with spectacular descents. A year earlier Mary Evelyn had been to see a new play based on the plot of *Artamène, ou le Grand Cyrus* by Madeleine de Scudéry. In a letter to Ralph Bohun she described how an extra part had been added 'as it fits Ayery Nell who is the life of the play'.[82]

The range of stage effects on offer to audiences is described in a verse by an anonymous author dating from 1673:

Now empty shows must want of sense supply,
Angels shall dance, and Macbeths Witches fly:
You shall have storms, thunder and lightning too
And Conjurers raise spirits to your view:
The upper Gall'rie shall have their desire,
Who love a Fool, a Devil and a Friar:
Damn'd Plays shall be adorn'd with mighty Scenes,

And Fustian shall be spoke in Huge Machines:
And we wil purling streams and fire-works show,
And you may live to see it rain and snow.[83]

The most sumptuous and expensive scenery and costumes were reserved for the musical dramas and, from the mid-1680s, for all-sung operas. The first opera in English that has survived is *Albion and Albanius*, with music by Luis Grabu and a libretto by John Dryden, first performed in 1685 at the Dorset Garden Theatre at a prodigious cost, in excess of £4,000.

Whether Samuel Pepys went to see this milestone in the history of English music and drama is impossible to say, for he had long given up keeping his diary. However, from a journal that he kept for a few weeks at the beginning of 1680 we do know that he was assiduously attending the theatre into that decade. This manuscript, entitled 'Journall of Mr Pepys's Proceedings with James and Harris', is part of his 'Book of Mornamont' in which he put the evidence that proved he was not implicated in the Popish Plot (p. 50). Most of the journal is made up of evidence being gathered in his defence, but every so often he includes notes of his social activities, probably as an aide-mémoire to corroborate the other details.

In the two and half months covered in the journal, Pepys went four times to the theatre in the company of Lady Mordaunt and her sister Mrs Steward, who lived in Portugal Row, and members of the Houblon family at Great Winchester Street. Two of the plays are not identified, but on 27 January he notes 'coming home at night after I had carried my cousin Wyn Houblon home from a play, She would if she could'.[84] Pepys had first seen this comedy by George Etherege twelve years earlier, noting in his diary 'how silly the play, there being nothing in the world good in it and few people pleased in it'.[85] His negative response may have been exacerbated by the fact that he lost his wife in the scrum of people resisting going out in the rain, and ended up wandering around the pit for over an hour. Hopefully, *She Would if She Could* had improved with age. The second named play is Thomas Otway's *The Orphan*, which Pepys went to see on 6 March. It was probably the

premiere of this anti-pastoral drama, which evoked elements of inno-
cence, simplicity and closeness to nature played out in a country estate
in Bohemia, only for the action to end in tragedy.

What Pepys thought of this conceit is not recorded. As with the
music of Purcell, we can only imagine his reaction to the works of dram-
atists such as Otway, Wycherley and, later, Congreve, and appreciate the
perceptive and vivid remarks that he shone on the first exciting decade
of Restoration drama and music.

7

HORTULAN AFFAIRS

JOHN EVELYN DECLARED in a letter of 1652 how 'A Friend, a Booke and a Garden shall for the future perfectly circumscribe my utmost designes', a sentiment that he had taken from Cicero. He sounds here like a man resignedly approaching his old age, but in fact Evelyn was just thirty-two and recently returned to England.[1] Setting aside his characteristically elaborate verbosity, this does suggest the importance that gardens and gardening – 'hortulan affairs', as he put it in another flourish – were to have upon Evelyn's life. It was his long-lasting passion, expressed in a wide area of activities. In addition, it related to his strong religious faith: he defined the garden as 'a place of all terrestrial enjoyments the most resembling Heaven, and the best representation of our lost felicitie'. Referring to the Fall of Man and the expulsion of Adam and Eve from the Garden of Eden, he talked of 'the pit from whenc[e] we were dug' and evoked the memorable horticultural image that 'we all came out of this parsly bed'.[2]

Music and the theatre were the great passions of Samuel Pepys, whilst Evelyn was an interested looker-on; but with gardening, the opposite pertained. Pepys did not have the opportunity to grow up with gardens. There would have been a minimal backyard in Salisbury Court, and the one 'gardening activity' that his diary records him as having indulged in was famously burying his Parmesan cheese and his wine in the garden of the navy lodgings in Seething Lane to protect them from the encroaching flames of the Great Fire.[3] Although Pepys owned a house with a substantial garden at Brampton in Huntingdonshire, he never lived there for any length of time, and warded off the complaints from his relatives that they were obliged to cultivate the vegetable plots to furnish the kitchen. Late in life, Pepys wrote to Dr Charlett, Master of University College, turning down the opportunity to subscribe to a comprehensive plant catalogue that had been initiated by Robert Morison, the Professor of Botany at Oxford. His explanation of his decision was that

> I am not wholly unfurnished of Books of Plants, and 2 or 3 not common Ones; but it being a Study that my Manner and the Scene of my Life have kept mee altogether a Stranger to (I speake it with regrett) . . . and thinke it too late in the Day to bee now setting out upon a Journy of that Length.[4]

He could have said the same about gardening. Nevertheless, as a curious man, Pepys was interested in observing gardens and certainly talked to Evelyn about them.

Sometimes with adversity come positive benefits, and for Royalists like Evelyn the English Civil War provided an opportunity to observe at first hand the famous gardens of Continental Europe that were regarded as the leaders in style. In his diary descriptions of the gardens he visited in the Low Countries, France and Italy, Evelyn recorded his own experiences and responses rather than drawing on guidebooks and other publications, as he did with some other aspects of his travels. In the Low Countries in 1641 he noted the use of trees in avenues in cities such as Amsterdam and Antwerp. When he visited the garden of Cardinal Richelieu at Rueil to the west of Paris in early 1644, he excitedly described its magnificence, asking 'whither [as I much doubt] Italy have any exceeding it for all varietyes of Pleasure' with its parterres and walks, and its cascades terminating in a grotto resembling the yawning mouth of Hell.[5] In Paris itself he particularly noted the gardens of the Luxembourg, likening them to Paradise, but one open to the public. He observed 'the infinite numbers of Persons of quality, & Citizens, & strangers who frequent it, and to whom all accesse is freely permitted':

> so as you shall meete some walkes & retirements full of Gallants & Ladys, in others melancholy Fryers, in others studious Scholars, in others jolly Citizens; some sitting & lying on the Grasse, others, running, & jumpi[n]g, some playing at bowles, & ball, others dancing & singing; and all this without the least disturbance, by reason of the amplitude of the place; & what is most admirable, you see no Gardners or people at Worke in it, and yet all kept in such exquisite order.[6]

From the magnificence of the Luxembourg, Evelyn moved on to a much smaller garden, but one that was to have particular significance for him. This was the garden in the Faubourg Saint-Germain of Pierre Morin, 'a person who from an ordinary Gardener, is arriv'd to be one of the most skillfull & Curious Persons of France for his rare collection of Shells, Flowers & Insects: His Garden is of an exact Oval figure planted with Cypresse, cut flat & set as even as a Wall could have form'd it'. Morin was a florist, a gardener who specialised in the cultivation of certain types of flowers, in his case tulips, anemones, ranunculi and crocuses, which Evelyn noted 'were held for the rarest in the World, which constantly drew all the Virtuosi of that kind to his house during the season'. He lived in a kind of hermitage to the side of the garden where he kept his collections, including one of butterflies, which 'he spreads, & so medicates, that no corruption invading them he keeps in drawer, so plac'd that they present you with a most surprizing & delight-full tapissry'.[7]

Evelyn's suggestion that Italy would not have anything to compare with the magnificence of Rueil turned out to be quite wrong, and he was astounded by the gardens he encountered as he made his way down to Rome. Just outside the city, at Frascati, he visited the Villa Aldobrandini and found many of the garden features that he had come most to admire: 'for its elegance, situation & accommodation of plentifull water, Groves, Ascents & prospect, surpassing in my opinion the most delicious places that my eyes ever beheld'. From the hillside's summit he described seeing a horrid Cascade seeming rather a greate River than a streame, precipitating into a large Theater of Water representing an exact & perfect Raine-bow when the sun shines out: Under this is made an artifice(i)all Grott, where in are curious rocks, hydraulic Organs & all sorts of singing birds moving, & chirping by force of the water, with severall other pageants and surprizing inventions ... To this is a Garden of incomparable walkes & shady groves, aboundance of rare Fruit, Orangs, Lemons, &c.[8]

After visiting Venice, Evelyn arrived in Padua in the summer of 1645, and met up with his mentor, Lord Arundel, and the Earl's grandson, Henry Howard. Arundel took the two young men around the city, showing them some of its artistic treasures and fine classical architecture. Another English exile who arrived in Padua that winter was the poet Edmund Waller. Unlike most poets, Waller was a very wealthy man, with large estates in Buckinghamshire, but in 1643 he had been implicated in a political fiasco known as Waller's Plot which had called for an armed rising against Parliament. After a spell in prison, he was fortunate to be released, heavily fined and permitted to go into exile. Like Evelyn, he was interested in gardens, and they were to become friends.

Evelyn stayed in Padua for several months, matriculating at the university and attending lessons in human physiology with the distinguished Professor of Anatomy, Johann Vesling (p. 16). He also took the opportunity to explore the botanical garden, one of the first of its kind in Europe, founded in 1545 with the support of the Venetian Senate in a shrewd move, for the Republic dominated the lucrative Mediterranean trade in spices from the east. The planting had been organised by Vesling's predecessor, with plants for medicine, or simples. Like the botanical garden at Leiden that Evelyn had visited in 1641 during his tour of the Low Countries, Padua was laid out in four quadrants, but with a much more complex design. A circular earthen rampart had been thrown up around the garden, penetrated by four tunnels. From the ramparts visitors might look down on the design of enclosed parterres, with each quadrant representing a continent, and an attempt made to plant according to the orientation, with cedar and cypress trees to the east. With permission from Vesling, Evelyn was allowed to take a representative sample of medicinal plants to dry and paste into an album, a *hortus hyemalis* or winter garden that was to become one of his most treasured possessions. On an early visit to Sayes Court, Pepys was shown the book by Evelyn and noted how the colour of the plants was preserved, making it much more useful than a printed herbal.[9] Shortly after getting his *hortus hyemalis*, Evelyn visited Lord Arundel and obtained from him a detailed itinerary for his journey back through northern Italy. It was to be their last meeting, for the Earl died the following year.

Evelyn must surely have made the notes on European gardens in his diary to inspire his future horticultural activities. He may have had in mind the development of the gardens of his family home in Surrey, Wotton; indeed, in a letter to his brother George from Paris in January 1651 he sent advice concerning the removal of part of a hillside to form a mount, filling up the moat and levelling an area for a parterre and fountain. He may also have assumed that he would be able to buy a property of his own with a garden that he could develop. In 1652 he tried to purchase Henry Howard's Albury estate that neighboured Wotton, but Howard changed his mind about the sale. Instead, Evelyn took on the estate of Sayes Court in Deptford, the English home of his wife's family who had been naval administrators since the reign of Elizabeth, leasing the property from the Crown. While Sir Richard was Resident in Paris, his father, Christopher Browne, had been looking after the garden as best he could, but it was ripe for improvement when the Evelyns took up residence in 1652.

The site of Sayes Court was by no means ideal. It was no bucolic rural retreat, for it bordered on the naval dockyard, with the homes of the ship-builders and other workers reaching right up to the gates (Plate 40). The 200-acre estate was a bleak, flat site, triangular in shape and tapering towards the north to the river, yet stopping short of it, thus missing out on a dramatic Thames frontage. Water on the site lay in sluggish channels and ponds, and the soil was poor. Evelyn was later to describe it as 'being rather on the Gravell and Sand, without any Marish Earth', requiring the substantial addition of lime, loam and cattle dung to make it fertile.[10] He wrote in his diary how 'it was my fortune to pitch here, more out of necessity and for the benefit of others than choice',[11] but he was determined to create a garden drawing on all the experiences he had enjoyed during his travels in Europe. 'My poor villa' was how he described it, a countryside residence all too adjacent to London. Richard Browne suggested that he might pull down the architecturally insignificant Tudor house and rebuild on a better site overlooking the river, but Evelyn resisted this, arguing that 'the Convenience of such trees & shelter which it now hath & must then have wanted must have bin parted with: which could never have donne well: so naked & defenceless, in a place so low and empty of variety as this is without them'.[12] Despite the drawbacks of the site, Sayes Court actually suited Evelyn, for it gave him easy access to the City and to the royal court, yet enabled him to withdraw when he wanted. Much later, when he retired to his family home in Surrey, he would write to Pepys complaining of the dullness of country life.

In addition to a small walled garden at Sayes Court, there was an orchard and a field of 100 acres which had been used as pasture for the cattle supplying the royal household at Greenwich. To Evelyn it represented a *tabula rasa* on which he might create a new plan, and one that avoided 'those painted and formall projections of our Cockney Gardens and little plotts, which appeare like Gardens of Past-board and March-pane, and which smell more of paynt then of flowers and Verdure'.[13] He began with the walled garden, planting up the beds with flowers and herbs that he could cultivate himself, treating it as a refuge from the more public space of what was to be the 'great garden' beyond. In this little garden he installed the glass-fronted beehives that he was given by John Wilkins during his visit to Oxford in 1654 (p. 107). Opposite the parlour windows he also erected an aviary. Evelyn was later to recommend the construction of vivaries where wild animals might be kept, though he admitted that the British should realistically confine themselves to more modest creatures, such as squirrels and tortoises.[14] He himself had a pet tortoise.

On the west side of this garden Evelyn had a building with a pillared portico in which he accommodated his 'elaboratory'. In a speech delivered as part of Christmas festivities at Gray's Inn in 1594–5, Francis Bacon had pleaded the cause of philosophy, urging the creation of a 'most perfect and general library' and a cabinet of curiosities, to be accompanied by 'a spacious wonderful garden wherein whatsoever the sun of diverse climates, out of the earth of divers moulds, either wild or by the culture of man brought forth', and a still-house or laboratory 'so furnished with mills, instruments, furnaces, and vessels, as may be a palace fit for a philosopher's stone'.[15] Evelyn's laboratory was kitted out with furnaces and distilling equipment to extract essences from plants, such as Hungary water from rosemary flowers and spirit of roses or violets. It was to be quite distinct from Mary's domestic still-room in the main part of the house. Over the outer door of his laboratory Evelyn set a sign reading 'Purgatorium', the prelude to entering the great garden, or Paradise.

To separate the main sections of the great garden, Evelyn used hedges of various kinds: espaliered fruit trees, cypress, and above all holly and alaternus, an evergreen from Provence that was particularly favoured by bees. Immediately to the west of the private garden was the nursery where he raised the large number of plants needed for his ambitious plans. The kitchen garden lay to the north of the nursery, with its beds of vegetables and herbs, including hotbeds, that would have resembled the engraving in his edition of *The French Gardiner* (Plate 45). Further to the west was the garden proper with its parterre. This he modelled on the formal garden of Pierre Morin that he had visited in Paris in 1644. Like Morin, he set an oval of cypress within a rectangle lined with alaternus, filling the quadrants with evergreen thickets and private walks that led into secluded arbours. Mary Evelyn, who would have been familiar with Morin's garden, was allowed to embellish these arbours with 'emblems' of particular women friends. The outer oval was occupied by grass and flower pots, the inner circle by a parterre of flower beds, twelve in all, surrounding an artificial mount set about with cypress and topped by a sundial. The pattern of the parterre could be best appreciated from the vantage point of the mount. Beyond the parterre, separated by a raised terrace, lay a grove of deciduous trees mixed with thickets of 'thorne, wild fruites, greenes, &c'. All the elements of the garden can be seen in a detailed plan that Evelyn drew, so detailed that the centre of the Oval Garden is laid out like a daisy, each petal edged in box (Plate 41).

Within a few years, however, Evelyn became tired of the elaborate creation of the parterre, adjudging it fussy and flat, and attributing to it female qualities in contrast to his slower, but more lasting designs; once the planting of the groves and trees had been completed they would, he thought, present 'a prospect of a noble & masculine majestie far surpassing those trifling bankes and busy knotts'.[16] Changing fashions probably played a part, with grass becoming a favoured ingredient for English gardeners. In his diary for July 1666, Pepys recorded having conversed with the architect Hugh May as they walked to and fro in Whitehall. May had spent the Civil War in Holland, so was familiar with European gardens. They discussed 'of the present fashion of gardens to make them plain – that we have the best walks of gravel in the world – France having none, nor Italy; and our green of our bowling-alleys is better than they have'.[17] Pepys may well have been told this by Evelyn, who by 1663 had taken out the box and cypress of his Morin-style garden and in the place of parterres of flowers had created smooth grass plots. Mary, with her wry sense of humour, observed 'that there is no end of improvement and that the various fancies of men have the reward of praise, when poore women are condemned for altering their dresse, or changing the patron [pattern] of a gorget, and for this esteemed vain creatures'.[18]

Raised amid the trees on his father's estate at Wotton, Evelyn described himself as 'wood born', celebrating the mystery by which a tiny grain 'which lately a single Ant would easily have born to his little Cavern' would, with its 'insensible rudiment, or rather habituous spirit', ascend 'by little and little ... into an hard erect stem of comely dimensions, into a solid Tower as it were'.[19] As Evelyn had explained to Sir Richard Browne soon after his arrival at Sayes Court, trees were vital to provide interest to the flat nature of the site. He liked a combination of evergreen and deciduous to maintain interest and provide shelter all the year round.

Evelyn was not only busy gardening, but also conversing and corresponding with other gardeners. He came to know Sir Thomas Hanmer through his father-in-law. Both men were part of Charles I's court circle and in France during the English Civil War. It would seem that Browne, in Paris, sent seeds and bulbs to Hanmer who was based in Angers. In December 1648, for instance, Browne obtained for him anemones and ranunculi, probably from the nearby garden of Pierre Morin, for Hanmer was a florist. With the end of the war Hanmer returned to England, settling in Lewisham, but it took Evelyn some years to realise that such a knowledgeable gardener was living near him, remarking in 1657 how 'I never knew it till the other day but we are since very Civill & often converse in matter of flowers wherein he excels'.[20] Hanmer was, however, preparing to move up to his family home at Bettesfield in Flintshire, so that Evelyn regretfully added, 'but he being now leaving us & returning into Wales that sweete Conversation will fade'. In fact, the 'sweet conversation' continued by correspondence, and Hanmer provided him with detailed information on tulips and daffodils for his writings.[21]

Another correspondent was Thomas Browne, the physician based in Norwich whose writings Evelyn much admired. Browne had received a thorough training as a physician, studying at Montpellier and Padua and receiving a doctorate at Leiden. In 1658 he published *The Garden of Cyrus* as a companion to *Hydriotaphia, or Urn Burial* (p. 115). Dedicated to the 'ardent horticulturalist' and declaring that 'Paradise succeeds the Grave', the book looked at the occurrence of the number five and, in particular, the quincunx or lozenge shape formed by the planting of groups of five trees in ancient Persian orchards. Browne had both a garden and a wildflower meadow in Norwich, and this interest is reflected in his book, which includes an account of the plants of Norfolk. John Evelyn began to correspond with Browne in 1660, sending him his plan for a form of Salomon's House that reflected the ideas he had put to Robert Boyle (pp. 108–9). In October 1671, shortly after Browne was knighted, Evelyn visited him in Norwich, recording in his diary: 'I went to see Sir Tho: Browne (with whom I had sometimes corresponded by Letters tho never saw before) whose whole house & Garden being a Paradise & Cabinet of rarities, & that of the best collection, especialy Medails, books, Plants, natural things, did exceedingly refresh me'.[22]

Samuel Hartlib not only provided Evelyn with information about matters associated with husbandry, but also put him in touch with others in his circle. One such was John Beale, a native of Herefordshire who, after studying at Cambridge and travelling in France, became rector of Sock Dennis in Somerset. Beale was particularly concerned about the cultivation of apple trees and the encouragement of the cider industry. In 1657 he published *Herefordshire orchards, a pattern for all England*, a slim volume made up of two letters he had written to Hartlib the previous year. Although the book contained practical advice on looking after fruit trees, Beale introduced spiritual thoughts, and in another letter to Hartlib he talked of all kinds of spirits 'whether they may all at all times bee properly called Angels or not that run parallel & have their offices in & over every part of the creation ... Some to Mineralls, some to Vegetables, some to Animalls, To several Elements, & to several Orbes, or Planets'.[23] This animist theology was highly unorthodox and certainly not to Evelyn's taste, yet the two men conducted a long and thoughtful correspondence.

Evelyn also had many discussions both by letter and personally with professional gardeners, such as John Rose. In the preface to *Sylva* he described how one day, 'refreshing my self in the garden at Essex-house', he had a discussion with Rose about the cultivation of vines. Essex House on the Strand was the London home of the Capels, a great gardening family. When Lord Essex committed suicide after being implicated in the 'Protestant Plot' (p. 51), the garden passed to his sister, Mary, who was to become Duchess of Beaufort. John Rose was then her head gardener, and Evelyn clearly had a high opinion of him, for he went on to describe how 'he reason'd so pertinently upon that subject [viticulture] (as indeed he does upon all things, which concern his hortulan profession) that ... I was easily perswaded to gratify his modest and charitable inclinations, to have them communicated to the world'. The result was a book, *The English Vineyard Vindicated*, published in 1666, with John Rose credited on the title page as the author and as the royal gardener, for he had been put in charge of the gardens of St James's Palace. In fact, while Rose provided the material, Evelyn wrote the text under the pseudonym of Philocepos. This interchange between Evelyn and professional gardeners, where he provided help with publishing material while they gave him practical information and supplied him with seeds, plants and trees, was to continue over the years, in particular with George London, who was trained by Rose, and his colleagues Henry Wise and Moses Cook, who in 1681 together founded the famous nursery of Brompton Park.

Evelyn was a prolific writer on every aspect of gardens and gardening. Apart from his great interest in the subject, he felt that there were all kinds of gaps to be filled and ideas to be developed. His library catalogue shows that he owned a comprehensive collection of works on horticulture, including herbals, practical manuals and books on garden design. In a letter written late in life, he advised that aspects of husbandry had been well covered by English authors, especially by Samuel Hartlib and his circle.[24] But returning from Europe in the early 1650s and beginning on his Sayes Court garden made him appreciate how far English gardening had fallen behind its Continental counterparts – something that comes through in his remark about the painted and formal projections of cockney gardens quoted earlier, for instance. This situation was hardly surprising given the years of political tumult, but, being Evelyn, he resolved to rectify it. In December 1658 he recorded in his diary: 'Now was published my French gardiner the first and best of that kind that introduced the olitorie [kitchen garden]'.[25] The treatise had been published in Paris in 1651 as *Le Jardinier François*, and although no name appeared on the title page, it was generally known to be the work of Nicolas de Bonnefons, valet de chambre du Roi. Bonnefons had dedicated his book to women, and particularly the managers of households, but Evelyn decided to make his version more masculine and practical. While Bonnefons chose the format 'so that you could carry it without inconvenience, to compare the work of your gardeners with this small book, and judge their capacity or negligence', Evelyn may have felt that English gardeners would not appreciate such interference.[26]

In his intriguing little book, *Fumifugium*, published in 1661, Evelyn described the threats posed by the polluted atmosphere of towns and cities from sea coal, so called because it was brought down to London by ship from Newcastle upon Tyne and other ports on the north-east coast of England. Speaking from bitter experience, he talked of the dire effect of the 'Hellish and dismall Cloud of SEA-COALE', which was

Avernus [infernal] to Fowl, and kills our Bees and Flowers abroad, suffering nothing in our Gardens to bud, display themselves, or ripen; so as our Anemonies and many other choycest Flowers, will by no Industry be made to blow [blossom] in London, or the Precincts of it, unlesse they be raised on a Hot-bed, and govern'd with extraordinary Artifice to accellerate their springing imparting a bitter and ungrateful Tast to those few wretched Fruits, which never arriving to their desired maturity, seem, like the Apples of Sodome, to fall even to dust, when they are but touched.

To counter this, he proposed that plantations should be set around London 'supplied with such Shrubs as yield the most fragrant and odoriferous Flowers, and are aptest to tinge the Aer upon every gentle emission at a great distance'.[27] When much of the City was destroyed in the Great Fire in 1666, there was a moment when such a radical approach might have been considered, but in vain. The problem would only get worse with the onset of the Industrial Revolution.

Evelyn, meanwhile, had embarked on a much more ambitious project, his *Elysium Britannicum*. The first mention of this comes in a letter written in 1659 to Jacques le Franc, a Protestant divine in Norwich, in which Evelyn enclosed a note about the project to be passed to Thomas Browne, whom he described as 'a magazine of erudition'. Evelyn explained that he was familiar with Browne's books, or as he put it in his inimitable way, 'better knowne to me by his incomparable elucubrations'.[28] He also had a broadside prospectus printed for private circulation, garnering ideas from Hartlib and his circle, experts in Oxford such as Jacob Bobart, the superintendent of the University's Botanical Garden, and the gardening writer Robert Sharrock.

Elysium Britannicum represents nothing less than an attempt to compile a comprehensive encyclopaedia of gardening. Although its title made reference to the Elysian Fields, the abode of the blessed in Greek mythology, the book was profoundly Christian in theme, with first principles about Paradise and the Fall of Man (as quoted on p. 160). Evelyn sought to bring together the spiritual and aesthetic. In one remarkable section, he offered a description of the perfect English garden. The concept emanated from John Beale, who had told Hartlib how he had spent a night on Backbury Hill near Ledbury in Herefordshire, and there dreamt of a garden. In edited form, Evelyn included this in *Elysium Britannicum*, evoking a lofty hill associated with ancient British tribes, with paths in trenches winding their way to the summit. Here an area, roughly square, had been cleared, looking down on precipices and desolate countryside, the Vale of Misery. This was 'a Place so blessed by Naturall Situation . . . it were capable of being made one of the most august and magnificent Gardens in the World, as far exceeding those of Italy & France, so prodi-gall of Arte and full of Ornament'.[29] Not only is this a striking image, a garden superimposed upon an ancient hill fort, it also suggests that in this garden, nature should take precedence over art, and its design should complement the natural features of the place, thus anticipating one of the important ideas of eighteenth-century landscape gardening.[30]

In other sections, *Elysium Britannicum* is practical, including draw-ings of seventy essential garden tools, from forks and spades to a knife grinder and a book in which to write the names of plants. The most extraordinary object in this group is a bedstead 'furnished with a tester and Curtaines of Green' to protect tender flowers from 'the parching beames of the Sunn' (Plate 44). Ways of protecting tender plants from the more likely aspects of English weather are provided by descriptions of conservatories and orangeries. Evelyn's fascination with special effects is covered by accounts of waterworks, cascades, fountains and pools with water-traps for aquatic practical jokes, 'artificial Echo's, Musick, & Hydraulick motions'. His notes on the best times for planting include reflections on 'the Celestial influences, particularly the Sun and the Moon', pointing out that 'the moone as being most neere to Earth has greate operation on Vegetables'.[31] Evelyn had no time, however, for what he describes as 'Astrological niceties', warning readers against the ideas of the radical apothecary, Nicholas Culpeper, whose famous and very popular herbal is conspicuous by its absence from his library cata-logue. Culpeper is described as a 'Figure-flinger', a term Evelyn applied to Sir Kenelm Digby, who also held astrological beliefs.

When they met in November 1665, Evelyn not only showed Pepys his *hortus hyemalis* but also 'read to me . . . of his discourse he hath been many years and is now about, about Guardenage; which will be a most noble and pleasant piece'.[32] But so huge was the undertaking, with constant additions, that *Elysium Britannicum* never made it to the printing presses. In a letter to John Beale in 1679, Evelyn revealed how he felt overwhelmed by the task:

> When againe I consider into what an Ocean I am plung'd, how much I have written, and collected, for above these 20 yeares, upon this fruitfull and inexhaustible Subject (I meane of Horticulture) not fully yet digested in my mind, and what insuperable paines it will require to insert the (dayly increasing) particulars into what I have already in some measure prepar'd, and which must of necessitie be don by my owne hand; I am almost out of hope, that I shall ever have strength and Leasure to bring it to Maturity, having for the last ten-yeares of my life ben in perpetual motion.[33]

Instead, Evelyn explained that he intended to extract the information about salads from the manuscript, and publish it as a separate treatise: in fact, it was to take him a further two decades to do this. He had already separated out *Kalendarium Hortense*, a gardener's almanac providing a thorough grounding in the horticultural year. This he inserted into his book of forest trees, *Sylva*, alongside *Pomona*, a treatise on the growing of fruit trees to make cider provided to him by Beale. As noted in Chapter 5, the idea for *Sylva* arose from concerns about the viability of naval timber supplies, but it developed into a wide-ranging account of the cultivation of trees, including aesthetic considerations, practical advice on planting and maintenance, and even the social use of different woods. Divided into thirty-five chapters, it described eighty species, some of which the reader would not expect to find in a discourse on forest trees, such as mulberry, arbutus and the tulip tree. Evelyn not only extolled the sweet chestnut for lining the 'Avenues to our Countrey-houses' where 'they are a magnificent, and royal Ornament', but also recommended that the nuts be eaten with salt and wine, 'being first roasted on the Chapplet'; being cheap and long-lasting, they could provide sustenance for 'our common people'. In a later edition, Evelyn suggested that the leaves be used as mattress-stuffing, though he warned that they crackled when the sleeper turned – which was why the French called them 'Licts de Parliament'.[34]

Although Sir Francis Bacon had laid out tree-lined walks in the gardens of Gray's Inn in London back in the 1590s, and there were similar walks in the colleges at Oxford and Cambridge, the fashion for avenues of trees really took off during the Restoration, after Charles II and his circle of courtiers returned from exile in Europe. Edmund Waller, who established a woodland garden with walks and groves at Hall Barn in Buckinghamshire, wrote a panegyric to the King for his layout of a formal landscape in St James's Park:

> For future shade young trees upon the banks
> Of the new stream appear in even ranks ...
> Near this, my Muse, what more delights her, sees
> A living gallery of aged trees;
> In such green palaces the first kings reigned,
> Slept in their shades, and angels entertained;
> With such old counsellors they did advise
> And by frequenting sacred groves grew wise.
> Free from the impediment of Light and Noise,
> Man thus retired his nobler thoughts employs.[35]

Sylva, first published in 1664, proved a great success. When a second edition was issued in 1670, John Evelyn proudly informed the King in the dedication that 'more than a thousand copies had been bought up ... of the first impression, in much lesse time than two years', which, according to booksellers, was 'a very extraordinary thing in volumes of this bulk'. Evelyn had become famous, as had Sayes Court. Even before the publication, the King came to visit, honouring 'my poore Villa with his presence, viewing the Gardens & even every roome of the house'.[36] But royal attention had its drawbacks, for Evelyn complained in a letter to Sir Richard Browne how the King's gardeners from Greenwich helped themselves to his elm trees, 'at least 40 of my best'.[37] Ironically, the gardeners may well have learnt how elms could easily be transplanted, even when quite well established, from Evelyn's own words in *Sylva*.

Avenues of trees, along with groves, were introduced into estates all over the country in the decades that followed. In his book *Man and the Natural World*, Keith Thomas ascribes this national planting to a mixture of social assertiveness, aesthetic sense, patriotism and long-term profit, comparing it to the English aristocrat's obsession with dogs and horses.[38] *Sylva* was to influence the fashionable gardens of the nation, but with its folio format and elaborate language, it was a book for the elite. John Pell, who had been part of the circle of Samuel Hartlib, commented in a letter, 'I wish that some body, without any Embellishments & Flourishes, would give us the *plaine precepts* for planting & ordering of woods, hedge-rowes, Orchards & Gardens: and the *Examples* of as many true Dendrophils as he can heare of in any county of England.'[39]

Evelyn did provide a glossary of difficult words in the third edition of 1679. This edition was the subject of what was probably the first book review in England to appear in a public newspaper rather than a learned journal. *The True Domestick Intelligence* contained a notice on 31 October 1679, declaring how

> *Sylva* and *Pomona* is come forth in a 3rd Edition, very much improved, and with considerable Additions. Tis esteemed by the Judicious, the most accomplished Volume that ever was published in any Language (and fittest for the Learndst of our Nobility and Gentry). To increase and to encourage the Planting of Grove Woods and Forrests for Fuel and Timber, to adorne the stateliest Pallaces and fairest Mansions, and withal to reclaime Wast Lands to bear a perpetual and permanent profit.

With brave optimism the review also noted that Evelyn was at work on his *Elysium Britannicum*, which when published, 'the three kingdoms ... will on a suddain become as the Garden of Eden, the most Flowery and flourishing Kingdomes of the Known World'.[40]

At Sayes Court, Evelyn had a gardener or gardeners to help him, but we know almost nothing about them, not even their names, until

Jonathan Mosse was brought in as an apprentice in 1686. Evelyn compiled a manuscript for him giving 'Directions for the Gardiner at Says-Court'; the title goes on to say, 'But which may be of Use for other Gardens', which suggests that he also intended it for publication. The manuscript covers all aspects of running a self-sufficient garden, beginning with the 'Termes of Art used by Learned Gardeners', defining techniques and the seasons, and the times attached to fruit and flowers, such as 'præcoce' (early blossoming and ripening), 'median' (middle-term, applied particularly to tulips) and 'serotine' (late flowering and ripening). Following these are long lists of different fruit trees, and notes for the kitchen garden. Mosse is advised to set the plants for the physic garden in alphabetical order, 'for the better retaining them in memorie'. He was given a full weekly regime, starting with a walk 'aboute the whole Gardens every Monday-morning duely, not omitting the least corner, and so [to] observe what Flowers or Trees & plants want staking, binding and redressing, watering, or are in danger; especialy after greate stormes, & high winds and then immediately to reforme, establish, shade, water &c what he finds amisse, before he go about any other work'.[41]

We can only guess at how Jonathan Mosse, probably from a humble background, received this mountain of information from a man who combined scholarship with skill at gardening. However, it does clearly demonstrate, as do parts of *Elysium Britannicum* and the *Kalendarium Hortense*, that Evelyn had a profound knowledge of the practical aspects of gardening. Such was the usefulness of *Kalendarium Hortense* that it was also published separately from *Sylva*. In 1690, when Flower Hyde, the Countess of Clarendon, wanted to obtain the eighth edition, Evelyn explained how it was almost forty years since 'first I writ it, when Horticulture was not in that Ascendent in our Country'.[42]

With his wide-ranging knowledge, Evelyn advised others on their gardens. For example, among his papers are letters from Elizabeth Murray, who married Henry Newton from Charlton House in Kent some time in the early 1640s. Evelyn made their acquaintance through friends in Greenwich in 1653, and in their subsequent correspondence Elizabeth and Evelyn refer to each other as 'best neighbours', for Charlton was not far from Sayes Court. In a letter dated 30 October

1654, Elizabeth described how she was enriching Charlton with 'tres of hard names wich possibly you may find for their rarity to deserve a place in your garden'. Two years later, Henry, having inherited his uncle's estate, changed their name to Puckering and the couple moved up to Warwick. Elizabeth missed Evelyn's company, writing to him that she could think only of Deptford and what she had lost by being at so great a distance. Her Warwick garden did not prosper, so Evelyn sent her a design for it which he hoped might 'contribute to your wonted passion for the Horticultural entertainments'.[43]

Evelyn had hoped in 1652 to purchase Albury in Surrey, but Henry Howard changed his mind about selling (p. 164). Instead, he was asked to help with the design and layout of the estate, which had been acquired by Howard's grandfather, Lord Arundel, in 1638, and terraced into vineyards with grottoes set into the terraces. Evelyn and Howard were both familiar with the great hillside gardens around Rome, and from 1662 created at Albury a highly Italianate garden, with echoes of the antique. In September 1667, Evelyn recorded in his diary that 'I accompanied Mr Howard to his Villa at Alburie, where I designed for him the plat for his Canale and Garden, with a Crypta thro the Hill &c'. In a later entry he mentioned 'such a Pausilippe is no where in England besides'.[44] This is a reference to a grotto in the form of a tunnel cut into the rock next to Virgil's tomb, which he had seen on a visit to Naples in February 1645. A pausillipo had been created at the Villa Aldobrandini in Frascati, leading out of a niched exedra with a pool, and Evelyn modelled his scheme on this with a bath house, rather than a grotto, set into the terrace below. Another tribute to a Roman garden came with two long terraces based on the Temple of Fortune at Palestrina.

Henry Howard became 6th Duke of Norfolk in 1677, but had inherited the title de facto at the Restoration because his elder brother Thomas was adjudged insane. Part of his inheritance was the ducal palace in Norwich, and he decided that he wanted to have a pleasure garden, connected to the palace by river. Howard may have been inspired by the London garden laid out by his grandfather, Lord Arundel, on both sides of the Thames, so that he could look out from Arundel House across the water to a piece of land in Lambeth where he had installed some of his fine collection of antique statuary. In the autumn of 1663, Mary Evelyn's cousin, Samuel Tuke, reported that Howard had paid £700 'for a plot of ground to make a spring garden at Norwich'. Shortly afterwards, Howard sent a plan of the plot to Tuke, asking him to pass it on to Evelyn as he

> desires your advice how we shall dispose it for a Garden to entertaine the good company in the Towne. He intends to have in it a Bowling ground & the rest to be cast into walks with fruit trees against the walls, with such pert words as you shall judge proper, the figures is irregular but that is not to be helped. Therefore I pray combine it the best you can.[45]

'Pert' in this context mean 'pertinent', and the 'words' would seem to be classical mottoes on doorways and gates, like 'Purgatorium' on Evelyn's gateway into the great garden at Sayes Court.[46]

When creating the garden, Evelyn may have thought back to the similarly 'public' garden of the Luxembourg Palace which he had admired on his visit to Paris in 1644. The one surviving description of the Norwich garden comes from Edward Browne, a physician like his father Thomas. He noted during the winter of 1663–4 the work progressing on 'a place for walking and recreations, having made already walkes round and crosse it, forty foot in breadth. If the quadrangle left bee spatious enough hee intends the first of them for a fishpond, the second for a bowling green, the third for a wildernesse, and the forth for a Garden.'[47] 'My Lord's Garden' in Norwich was redeveloped in the eighteenth century, but the garden at Albury has fared better. Although the canal and vineyard are gone, the grass terraces, yew walk and Evelyn's 'Pausilippe' tunnelled through the hill all remain, the one surviving example of his garden design.

In his own garden in Deptford, Evelyn not only encountered problems with the site, he had also to contend with the fact that he was gardening in what is now known as the Little Ice Age, the cooler temperatures during which meant that there was a much greater variability of climate. The hot summers of 1665 and 1666, when London saw the great epidemic of the plague, occurred in the midst of the coldest century of the last millennium. The summer of 1676, the hottest on record, was followed by a very cold December, when the Thames froze over. However, the most extreme weather came during the winter of 1683–4. In December, Samuel Pepys took time off from his duties in Tangier to spend three weeks in Spain with William Hewer. Throughout their stay they experienced torrential rain and flooding, ruining their cherished chance to visit cities and look at some of the famous picture collections. In London, meanwhile, the icebound Thames was frozen to such a depth that a frost fair was held. Evelyn described in his diary how booths were set up on the ice, and activities such as 'Bull-baiting, Horse & Coach races, Pupet-plays & interludes, Cookes & Tipling, & lewder places; so as it seem'd to be a bacchanalia, Triumph or Carnoval on the Water, whilst it was a severe Judgement upon the Land'. He travelled down to Deptford to see how the garden was coping and found 'many of the Greenes & rare plants utterly destroyed'.[48]

The fellows of the Royal Society, ever curious, asked Evelyn to present a paper on the state of the garden. He observed that 'the past winter has played the French King in my territories', a remark that was to have ironical overtones a decade later when the Russian Czar wreaked havoc on Sayes Court (p. 67). The report gives a good picture of the variety of trees, shrubs and flowers that Evelyn was cultivating, as well as the devastating effect of the frost and 'rigorous weather':

I fear my cork trees will hardly recover . . . my cedars I think are lost; the ibex and scarlet oak not so, the arbutus doubtful, and so are the bays . . . Among our shrubs, rosemary is entirely lost, and to my great sorrow; because I had not only beautiful hedges of it, but sufficient to afford me flowers for making a considerable quantity to hungary water; . . . Attriplex or sea purslane of which I had a hedge, has also perished, and so another of French furzes; the cypresses are most of them destroyed, especially such as were kept shorn in pyramids . . . The arborescent and other sedums, aloes &c, though housed, perished with me; but the yucca and opuntia escaped; tulips many are lost, and so the Constantinople narcissus, and such turberosae as were not kept in the chimney corner, where was a continual fire; some anemonies appear but I believe many are rotted.

The final, poignant loss was his tortoise, 'found quite dead after having for many years escaped the severest winter'.[49]

This was not the only horticultural calamity that Evelyn had experienced. Shortly after planting up his Morin oval parterre in 1652, he reported to Sir Richard Browne that he had lost half of his young plants, and throughout his diary he recorded bad weather, which he ascribed to judgment from on high. He had tried to predict the weather with a form of hygroscope and a thermoscope or weather glass, making drawings of them in *Elysium Britannicum* (Plate 43).[50] Sayes Court was not in a good position, with the smoke and noxious smells from the City, so graphically described in *Fumifugium*, trapped by the hills rising above the Thames valley as they moved towards the sea. When Evelyn set about replanting his garden after the devastation described above, he drew a plan, dating it 3 February 1685.[51] This time he recognised that the ideas that he had brought back from his European tours would have to be modified to take into account the climate and the site. He constructed a grand yet simple axial layout of lawn, hedgework and fruit trees, using the hardy holly for new hedging and eliminating topiary, broderie and tender exotics. Fruit trees were an important element, with cherries around the half circle, dwarf pears in the east triangle, existing trees from the former orchard in the west triangle, golden pippin and damsons along the wall facing north, and vines along that facing south.

One way of finding out about both the horticultural and the design details of gardens was to visit them, which Evelyn did – but so, with his insatiable curiosity, did Pepys. The fashion for 'garden tourism' had developed in Elizabethan times, with the Queen during her progresses appreciating the magnificent gardens created by her leading courtiers, men such as William Cecil, Lord Burghley, Robert Dudley, Earl of Leicester, and Sir Christopher Hatton. And Cecil, Dudley and Hatton visited each other's gardens in turn, picking up ideas and often exchanging plants. It was in this spirit that Evelyn went in 1662 to Hampton Court Palace to meet Charles II's new queen, Catherine of Braganza, and also took the opportunity to look at the gardens and grounds. With his particular interest in trees, he observed the rows of limes that the King had planted in the park, and a cradle walk of intertwining hornbeams in the gardens. In general, however, he did not think much of the formal parterres, one of which he called Paradise, feeling that they were too narrow.[52]

As a garden visitor, Evelyn was often critical of what he saw, and brief in his comments. Pepys, on the other hand, went with an open mind and thus gives a more vivid picture. Both men visited the gardens of Brooke House in Hackney. Evelyn went there in May 1654, noting merely that they were 'one of the neatest, & most celebrated in England', and on a second visit two years later, 'well furnished & kept'.[53] Pepys, who had spent some of his childhood in Hackney, took a trip by coach in June 1666 and declared the gardens 'excellent'. Having already seen orange trees in St James's Park, he was particularly interested at Brooke House in the way that they grew:

> some green, some half, some a quarter, and some full ripe on the same tree, and one fruit of the same tree doth come a year or two after the other. I pulled off a little one by stealth (the man being mighty curious [painstaking] of them) and eat it; and it was just as other little green small oranges are; as big as half the end of my little finger.

He also noted 'a great variety of other exoticque plants, and several Labarinths and a pretty Aviary'.[54]

Gardening burgeoned following the Restoration and the return of relatively peaceful and prosperous times. A 'good gardens guide' compiled at the end of the seventeenth century reflects this development, providing information about, and criticism of, gardens to visit in and around London. Sayes Court is described as

> a fine garden for walks and hedges (especially his holly one, which he writes of in his 'Sylva'), and a pretty little greenhouse, with an indifferent stock in it. In his garden he has four large, round philareas, smooth clipped, raised on a single stalk from the ground, a fashion

now much used. Part of his garden is very woody, and shady for walking; but his garden, not being walled, has little of the best fruits.[55]

This was written two years before Evelyn left for Wotton, so it is possible that he was finding the garden exhausting both physically and mentally.

The guide is comprehensive, covering commercial nurseries close to the City in Hackney and the extensive establishment of Brompton Park, where George London and Henry Wise were providing the plants and trees for many of Britain's most prestigious estates. There is one strange omission, the garden of Henry Compton, Bishop of London, at Fulham Palace. Compton, who had played a key role in the future of England by ensuring that Princesses Mary and Anne remained within the Church of England, was suspended from his episcopal duties by their father James when he became King. Retiring to Fulham Palace and with the help of his former head gardener, George London, Compton developed one of the capital's most important gardens. This development continued after the succession of Mary and William in 1688, for Compton did not get the hoped-for promotion to the archbishopric of Canterbury. As his biographer recorded: 'The Bishop had a great Genius for Botanism, and having . . . more leisure than usual, he apply'd himself to the Improvement of his Garden at Fulham, with new varieties of Domestick and Exotick Plants.'[56]

Compton's particular interest was in trees, and as Bishop of London and thus Head of the Church in the American Colonies, known as the Plantations, he was able to commission some of his curates to obtain exotic trees for Fulham. One curate in particular acted as a very effective plant hunter: this was John Banister, who had studied with Robert Morison at Oxford. Arriving in Virginia in 1679 to become rector of the parish of Charles City, he wrote to Morison enumerating the wealth of American oaks that might supplement Britain's impoverished stock, including white, red, black and dwarf. When Evelyn revised his book, now titled *Silva*, for the fourth edition in 1706, his addition of details of trees from Virginia and New England had probably been provided by John Banister.[57]

Evelyn was constantly asking his contacts in all parts of the world for information about their local flora and gardens, and Pepys was able to help, using his naval connections. In 1686, for example, he acted as the go-between for Evelyn with Captain Francis Nicholson. As Evelyn explained to Pepys: 'When I had last the honor to see & dine with you, there was a Captaine … who going to command some forces in New-England, was so generous as to offer me his assistance, in procuring for me, anything which I thought curious, & rare among the plants of those Countries'.[58] Within the letter, he enclosed a note to Nicholson with a list of twenty-five trees, half from New England, half from Virginia, asking him to gather seeds, plants, nuts and stones. His detailed instructions on how to ensure their safe journey back across the Atlantic shows the care and ingenuity employed by plant hunters:

> The seedes are best preserv'd in papers: their names written on them and put in a box. The Nutts in Barills of dry sand; each kind wrap'd in papers written on.
> The trees in Barills their rootes wraped about mosse: The smaller the plants are, the better; or they will do well packed up in matts; but the Barill is best, & a small vessel will containe enough of all kinds labels of paper tyed to every sort with yr name[.][59]

Evelyn had visited Compton at Fulham in 1682, recording in his diary how he was shown the natural history collection of Alexander Marshall, the first skilled botanical artist that we know of in Britain, although it may be significant that he had been brought up in France. Marshall never seems to have had a home of his own, but at one stage lived in South Lambeth with John Tradescant the Younger. He is recorded as preparing a book of flowers for Tradescant, which is now lost, and he began to compile his own florilegium, which is in the Royal Library. He spent the last part of his life with Compton at Fulham, and some of the exquisite illustrations in the florilegium depict the Bishop's dogs, his greyhound alongside a sunflower, and a beagle with 'Tradescant's Turkie Purple Primrose' and an iris. Evelyn was particularly taken by Marshall's insect collection, comparing it with that of Pierre Morin which he had seen in Paris in 1644 (p. 162).[60]

In 1692, George Evelyn's last surviving son died, and the Wotton estate passed by entail to John Evelyn. Mary and John did not move to Wotton for another two years, but were thinking of what could be done about the estate, which had declined from woodland into a series of coppices for local industry; in John's words, it was 'naked and ashamed almost to own its name'.[61] John wrote to his brother assuring him that he had no ambitions beyond 'the care & supervisal of your Gardens, and the Culture & Adornment of the place of our worthy forefathers'. Recognising that at his advanced age he could not contemplate a major overhaul of the gardens, he sent George a sketch 'representing my thoughts in order to a Grove of Evergreens', and suggested that they should build a conservatory, 'a temporary shead of boards and thatch', for his orange and myrtle trees.[62]

This last idea may have occurred to him as a result of his latest foray into garden publishing, a translation of Jean-Baptiste de la Quintinie's *Compleat Gard'ner* that appeared in 1693. De la Quintinie had been in charge of the gardens of the Prince de Condé at Chantilly, and Louis XIV's magnificent *potager* at Versailles. Although he corresponded with members of the Royal Society and came to England, visiting Sayes Court in 1673, de la Quintinie turned down the King's invitation to become one of his royal gardeners. Evelyn recommended that George's gardener, Abraham, should be given sight of his translation of what he considered the best publication on fruit-growing in existence. The book included words of praise for George London and Henry Wise and their nursery at Brompton Park. In a letter to 'Honest Abraham', Evelyn promised that he would bring with him to Wotton the best plants that London and Wise could provide. He explained that they

> think themselves obliged to furnish me with whatever they have of choice, for some kindness I have don them; and would have come with me to Wotton to direct me for the setting up of a Greenehouse, which with very little expense of Loame, boards & thatch and other warme Clothing, would have served the Orange Lemon Myrtil & other pretious shrubs which I also thought to send.

Just as he had sought to reassure his brother George, he told Abraham that he would be no more than 'an under Gardner with you', though given Evelyn's long horticultural experience, this would seem an unlikely role in practice.[63]

Evelyn's final gardening publication, in 1699, was *Acetaria*, his book on salads about which he had talked to Beale some twenty years earlier. It has been suggested that Evelyn's advocacy of a 'herby-diet' meant that he embraced vegetarianism. His contemporary, Thomas Tryon, who wrote *The Way to Health*, did indeed give up meat and fish, but it is clear from his diary that Evelyn enjoyed eating both. He did, however, dislike cruelty to animals, referring to cock- and dog-fighting, and bear- and bull-baiting, as 'butcherly Sports, or rather barbarous cruelties', and avoiding participation in stag hunts.[64] In this, he was at one with Pepys, who described animal sports as 'a very rude and nasty pleasure' and expressed boredom at the 'silly stories' that huntsmen were wont to tell.[65] Evelyn also found the vivisection of animals in experiments conducted by the Royal Society deeply upsetting, noting of one such experiment on a dog: 'This was an experiment of more cruelty than pleased me'.[66] Nonetheless, as Mark Laird has pointed out, he was implacable in his determination to stop birds, 'winged choristers', eating his fruit and vegetables.[67]

Evelyn's message in *Acetaria* was that vegetables were a healthy addition to the diet, and he gave clear instructions on how to cultivate a wide range, native and exotic, along with herbs and fruit. He also discussed what made for good food. This was particularly important for 'those who dwell in the Middle and Skirts of vast and crowded Cities, inviron'd with rotten Dung, loathsome and common Lay Stalls'. On the other hand, good practice brought with it improved taste, 'most powerfully in Fowl, from such as are nourish'd with Corn, sweet and dry Food'. Citing the camel and the elephant, he argued that ruminants had longer lives than carnivorous animals.[68] The book ends with a series of recipes for salads and dressings 'from an Experience'd Housewife', who undoubtedly was Mary Evelyn.

Right at the end of his life, Pepys did acquire a garden, when he moved to rural Clapham and the home of William Hewer. Henry Hyde, Lord Clarendon, wrote to him in 1700: 'I hope your being thus long at Clapham (for I thinke you were never soe long in the countrey before since you knew the world) will make you relish the pleasure of a garden'.[69]

That September, Evelyn described taking his family to visit Pepys in his new surroundings, a 'very noble, and wonderfully well furnished house with Offices and Gardens exceedingly well accommodated for pleasure and retirement'.[70] William Nicolson described the gardens in his own diary when he visited Clapham in the summer of 1702: 'Walks and Bowling-Green, Ponds, & unanswerable to the House. Hedges of different heights and woods, bay, yew, holly and hornbeam'. Nicolson probably explored the gardens with John Evelyn, for he noted that he 'own'd himself the causer of a deal of Luxury in these matters'.[71]

Given this remark and the components listed – all favourites of Evelyn – it is possible that he advised Hewer and Pepys on their purchase of plants, and may have also designed the garden for them. However, Pepys had become friendly with another distinguished botanist and gardener, Charles Hatton, to whom he always referred in his correspondence as Captain Hatton. The Captain came from a great gardening dynasty: an ancestor was Sir Christopher Hatton, Lord Chancellor to Elizabeth I, who created magnificent gardens at Holdenby and Kirby Hall in Northamptonshire, and at Hatton Garden in London. During the 1650s, Charles Hatton worked in the famous gardens of the Duc d'Orléans in Blois under the guidance of Robert Morison, Charles II's future Professor of Botany at Oxford. Even after the Restoration Hatton remained in France, buying plants for his brother to restock the family's gardens.[72] No correspondence has survived between Hatton and Evelyn, but in a letter in Latin written by Jack Evelyn from Oxford in 1699 to Pepys, he refers to both men:

> Hatton naturas herbarum callet et usus
> Et quantas vires parvula planta tenet.
> Hortum Evelyn tradit rectè praecepta colendi,
> Et scitè condit, quas habet ille, dapes.

> [Hatton takes care of the production and use of herbs
> And carefully tends [each] little plant.
> Evelyn directs the care of his garden
> using his knowledge for the food for his table.][73]

Hatton's connection with the Clapham garden comes in a letter from Pepys to his nephew John Jackson, who was in Cadiz as part of his Grand Tour in October 1700. Hatton, 'observing your having taken care for some Lazarolls [medlar trees] for me, wishes that you would this winter-season procure to be sent hither by shiping from Naples some young trees of the several kinds there, where, he says, they are almost as common as haw-trees here, producing a pleasant fruit, and such as would thrive very well at Clapham'. As an untried horticulturalist, Pepys goes on to say, 'This I tell you from him, and leave you to take what notice you see fit of as being myself wholly a stranger to the matter.'[74] A stranger to the matter he may have been, but Pepys had access to the best of gardening advice from both Hatton and Evelyn.

As he approached his eighties, Evelyn's energy as far as gardening was concerned proved phenomenal. In the few years that he looked after Wotton, he began to repair the damage to the estate, although his efforts were knocked back yet again by calamitous weather. In late November 1703, a hurricane struck. Evelyn recorded in his diary:

> The dismall Effects of the Hurecan & Tempest of Wind, raine & lightning thro all the nation, especial[ly] London, many houses demolished, many people killed: & as to my owne losse, the subversion of Woods & Timber both left for Ornament, and Valuable material thro my whole Estate, & about my house, the Woods crowning the Garden Mount, & growing along the Park meadow; the damage to my owne dwelling, & Tennants farmes & Outhouses, is most tragicall.

As earlier in his diary, he attributed the disaster to the wrath of God, 'with acknowledgement of his Justice for our National sins, & my owne, who yet have not suffered as I deserved to: Every moment like Jobs Messengers, bring(s) the sad Tidings of this universal Judgement'.[75]

Despite this note of despair, Evelyn looked to the future. In his new edition of *Silva* he not only included details of the Great Storm of 1703, but also ended the manuscript: '[I] shall, if God protract my Years, and continue Health be continually planting 'till it shall please him to transplant me into those glorious Regions above, the Celestial

Paradise, planted with Perennial Groves and Trees, bearing Immortal Fruit.'[76]

He also, perhaps more importantly, inspired his grandson Jack to preserve the gardens. In a little practical manual written just before he died, he exhorted Jack to plant trees 'which in a few years will prove of incredible Emolument & restore the Name of Wotton, otherwise in danger to be lost and forgotten, planting of Timber-trees being in truth the onely best and proper Husbandry the Estate is capable of'.[77]

Just nine years after Evelyn's death in 1706, Stephen Switzer wrote a tribute to him that sums up well the breadth of his 'hortulan affairs', and also the legacy that he bestowed upon the gardeners of the new century:

> One of the greatest writers we have had in gard'ning, as well as in several other matters ... This ingenious and learned person ... was appointed for the retrieving the calamities of England, and re-animating the spirit of planting and sowing of woods in his coun-trymen ... Howe he has acquitted himself is very well known at present, his books being almost in all hands; and 'tis to be hop'd will be continued down to the farthest posterity amongst the most ingenious and useful writings of that age.
>
> Neither was his labour less in matters nearer relating to gard'ning, in his translations, and in his *Kalendarium Hortense* ... He translated Quintinye's *Compleat gardener*, with another smaller tract, from French; was in his time the best linguist, and to him it is owing that gardening can speak proper English. His *Philosophical discourse of earth* is accounted amongst the best writings of the Royal Society.
>
> As he began, so he continued till his death, a great lover and observer of gard'ning; and tho' not at his own expense, yet in his readiness to give advice, he merited general thanks. In short, if he was not the greatest master in practice [this, Switzer thought, was John Rose] 'tis to him is due the theoretical part of gard'ning.
>
> But I need say no more, his own works, which are publick, are a clearer demonstration of the greatness of his genius, than any monument I can raise to his memory.[78]

8

EXOTIC EXTRAVAGANCES

I N NOVEMBER 1690, Samuel Pepys wrote in some excitement to John Evelyn, telling him of a grand dinner that the latter had missed at the house of the merchant, James Houblon: 'Hee and I dranke your health and earnestly wish'd you there as believeing the Meale would have pleas'd you noe lesse then it did mee, as hardly consisting of one dish or glasse (besides bread and beere) of nearer growth than China, Persia and the Cape of Good Hope.'[1]

This was an era of expanding horizons. Both Pepys and Evelyn were fascinated by the new worlds that were opening up, and the goods that were available as a result. Raising a glass suggests alcoholic drinks were being dispensed at the dinner in the Houblon mansion, but it was three non-alcoholic beverages that were taking seventeenth-century Britain by storm. The three, moreover, came from very different parts of the world: coffee from the Middle East, tea from China and chocolate from Central America.

The first European to describe the preparation and drinking of coffee was the Augsburg physician Leonard Rauwolf, who made an expedition in the Levant to look for medicinal plants in the 1570s. He noted:

A very good drink by them called Chaube that is almost as black as Ink, and very good in illness, chiefly that of the Stomach; of this they drink in the Morning early in the open places before everybody, without any fear or regard, out of China cups, as hot as they can, they put it often to their Lips but drink little at a time.[2]

Coffee arrived in England via Holland, with the first recorded coffee-house opening in Oxford in 1650, in a back room at the Angel Inn on the High Street under the proprietorship of Jacob, a Jewish entrepreneur from Lebanon. Evelyn, however, suggests in his diary that the beverage reached the city thirteen years earlier. While he was a student at Balliol, a Greek named Nathaniel Conopios joined the college, and Evelyn said he was 'the first that I ever saw drink Caffè, not heard of then in England, nor til many yeares after made a common entertainment all over the nation'.[3] Evelyn was not a fan of coffee-consumption, referring in his *Character of England* to the 'deplorable' habit of gentlemen spending 'much of their time; drinking of a muddy kind of Beverage', and his diary makes no reference to visits to coffee-houses.[4] But he would seem to have been rather a lofty exception. At Oxford in 1655 a gathering of students and fellows persuaded an apothecary, Arthur Tillyard, to prepare and sell coffee for their consumption. His coffee-house next to All Souls became a meeting point for the Oxford Coffee Club, which included leading scientists such as Robert Boyle: this informal confraternity was thus one of the groups that evolved into the Royal Society.

In London, the first coffee-house was opened in 1652 by Pasqua Rosee, an Armenian servant whose duties had included making a cup of coffee each morning for his master Daniel Edwards, a Levant merchant. Rosee's coffee-house was located in St Michael's Alley, just off Cornhill in the heart of the City. A second house was opened soon after, the Rainbow in Fleet Street, and similar establishments began to pop up like mushrooms all over the capital. Pepys's 'local' when he lived in Westminster was the Turk's Head in New Palace Yard, and here he attended meetings of the Rota Club (p. 21). The Rota, unsurprisingly, failed to survive the Restoration, but its political character set the pattern for London coffee-houses of the future, where newsbooks and newspapers could be read and topics of the day discussed (Plate 61).

Coffee-houses were open to anybody who could pay for a dish of coffee, usually set at a penny: in this context 'anybody' means any man, for women were not welcome. A poem written in 1674 by Paul Greenwood as part of a broadsheet advertising his establishment selling coffee in Smithfield gives some idea of the social mores. It mimics the 'Rules and Orders' issued for keeping the peace:

First, Gentry, Tradesmen, all are welcome hither,
And may without Affront sit down Together:
Pre-eminence of Place, none here should Mind,
But take the next fit Seat that he can find:
Nor need any, if Finer Persons come,
Rise up for to assigne to them his Room;
To limit Mens Expence, we think not fair,
But let him forfeit Twelve-pence that shall Swear:
He that shall any Quarrel here begin,
Shall give each Man a Dish t'Atone the Sin[.]

The idea of a 'common table' where members take the next seat available is maintained in some London gentlemen's clubs to this day. Coffee-houses became known as 'penny universities' because of the access to pamphlets and newspapers, with 'runners' or 'mercuries' announcing the latest news (Plate 63). The progress of William of Orange along the Channel in 1688 is an example of how quickly news could reach the capital (p. 61). The relaxed attitude to status, along with the acquisition of political information, was inimical to Charles II, who in 1675 issued a proclamation ordering the closure of coffee-houses, claiming that they wasted men's time. With 3,000 establishments in England, 250 of which were in London, this was an impossible task, and besides, they were providing the Crown with valuable revenue through the duties payable on the import of the coffee: in 1660 this had been set at fourpence per gallon.

Coffee-houses were also developing as centres for the transaction of business, acting as postes restantes, which even Evelyn was obliged to use at times. As England's colonies developed along the eastern seaboard of North America, for instance, merchants met at houses called the

Carolina, Virginia, Pennsylvania and New York, clustered around the Royal Exchange. Lloyd's became the office for shippers and investors, and thus for marine insurance. The Grecian coffee-house in Threadneedle Street, conveniently placed for the Royal Society at Gresham College, was a meeting place for scientists and the craftsmen, such as instrument makers, who helped them. The Temple in Fleet Street was the location of the Botany Club, where the horticultural enthusiasts of the Royal Society, such as Nehemiah Grew and Hans Sloane, met and debated with amateur botanists and practising nurserymen, and head gardeners such as George London brought their apprentices to observe and to build up networks. To find out the latest literary gossip, Pepys went to a coffee-house in Covent Garden where the dramatist John Dryden held court. In all, there are about eighty references in his diary, often with a note of the conversation that he had there, for example with Sir William Petty (p. 111). Robert Hooke's diary contains hundreds of references because coffee-houses served as his office base. His favourite establishments in the 1670s were Garraway's and Jonathan's, and in these he held many meetings with Christopher Wren and the craftsmen responsible for the rebuilding of London after the Great Fire.

When coffee first arrived in Oxford, its purveyors extolled its virtues for keeping students awake, while later broadsheets highlighted its benefits for health. One such described it as a sober and wholesome drink, with 'Incomparable Effects in Preventing or Curing Most Diseases incident to Humane Bodies'. Similar benefits were claimed for another new beverage, tea. This had been discovered in the mid-sixteenth century by Spanish and Portuguese priests in China, arriving in Europe in the early seventeenth century on the ships of the Dutch East India Company. The first reference to tea in London comes in September 1658 when an advertisement appeared in *Mercurius Politicus* for a 'China drink, called by the Chineans Teha, by other nations Tay alias Tee'. This new commodity was available for sale at the Sultaness Head coffee-house by the Royal Exchange.

Pepys mentions in his diary for September 1660 how in the middle of the working day he 'did send for a Cupp of Tee (a China drink) of which I never had drank before'. This would appear to have been only a moderate success, for his next reference comes seven years later, when he returns home to 'find my wife making of Tea, a drink which Mr. Pelling the pothecary tells her is good for her cold and defluxions'.[5] Sir Kenelm Digby, on the other hand, seems to have been more favourably disposed. Among his papers, which were published as a cookery book after his death in 1665, is a recipe for a tea caudle:

> Take two yolks of new-laid eggs, and beat them very well with as much fine sugar as is sufficient for this quantity of liquor; when they are very well incorporated, pour your Tea upon the Eggs and Sugar, and stir them well together. So drink it hot. This is when you come home from attending business abroad, and are very hungry; and yet have not conveniency to eat presently a competent meal.

His source for this was a Jesuit priest returned from China, who warned him against letting the hot water 'remain too long soaking upon the Tea, which makes it extract into itself the earthy parts of the herb. The water is to remain upon it no longer than whilst you can say the *Miserere* psalm very leisurely'.[6]

Women did not accept their exclusion from coffee-houses without a protest. A quarrel in broadsheet form arose when in 1674 an anonymous writer published *The Women's Petition Against Coffee Representing to Publick Consideration the Grand Inconveniencies Accruing to their Sex from the Excessive Use of that Drying, Enfeebling Liquor*. This writer is believed to be the playwright Aphra Behn, and the claim was that coffee was emasculating men. Within weeks there was a male riposte from, it has been suggested, the philosopher John Locke. His counter-argument was that the coffee-house provided a refuge for henpecked men who could not get a word in edgeways at home.

This war of words did not result in the doors of coffee-houses being flung open to women. Instead, tea became the fashionable drink to be consumed at home, following the example of Charles II's Queen, the Portuguese Catherine of Braganza. Apothecaries, such as Elizabeth Pepys's Mr Pelling, and grocers stocked tea for their female customers. Coffee-house proprietors also dealt in tea, serving it in their establishments and selling the leaves for husbands to take home to their wives. Thomas Garraway, whose coffee-house was in Exchange Alley, sold his teas for prices between 16s and 60s per pound. Robert Hooke, a prodigious tea-drinker who started each day with a dish, bought it in fifteen-pound boxes at the bargain price of 5s.6d per pound. Obsessed with his health, Hooke defined twenty qualities of tea, from purifying the blood and vanquishing heavy dreams to sharpening the wit and strengthening the 'use of due benevolence'.[7]

Brought to England by the East India Company from Bantam on Java, tea was a luxury item, only to be enjoyed by the wealthy, but chocolate was even more expensive because of the growing conditions of the beans and the high risk of damage as it travelled over the seas to Europe. After 'the food of the gods' was offered to the conquistador Hernán Cortés by Moctezuma, the Aztec emperor, the Spanish tried to keep secret the source of the cacao tree, processing in secluded monasteries the beans shipped back from New Spain, until the monopoly was broken in the early seventeenth century by an Italian traveller. Chocolate arrived in London in the 1650s, with an advertisement appearing in the *Publick Advertiser* in 1657 announcing that in 'a Frenchman's house' in Queen's Alley off Bishopsgate customers could enjoy 'an excellent West India drink'.

From the outset, chocolate represented the height of the exotic, and sometimes a frisson of danger, particularly given the *cause célèbre* of the 1660s after the death of Lady Denham, one of the mistresses of the Duke of York; Pepys and others speculated whether Duchess Anne, out of jealousy, had administered poison to Margaret Denham's chocolate. But it could also cure, with Pepys detailing in a 1661 diary entry how he 'Waked in the morning with my head in a sad taking through the last night's drink, which I am very sorry for. So rose and went out with Mr. Creed to drink our morning draught, which he did give me in chocolate to settle my stomach.'[8] The morning draught was consumed with wine in a tavern. A more enjoyable experience came in 1664, when he recorded going to a coffee-house 'to drink Jocolatte, very good'.[9]

Aphrodisiac powers were attributed to chocolate. One of the frankest letters penned by Evelyn was to John Beale complaining about the physician and scholar Henry Stubbes, who regularly attacked the Royal Society over a range of issues. One of Evelyn's complaints was that Stubbes, 'so foule-mouthed a Whifler', had written a book, *The Indian Nectar, or a Discourse concerning Chocolate*, in which he had recommended consumption to encourage 'venery', advising that it was much better than other aids offered by apothecaries, such as anchovies or 'Bononia [Bolognese] sausages'.[10] The Aztecs served chocolate cold, without sugar, although they sometimes added honey and spices such as chilli and vanilla. To produce a froth, they poured the liquid from one vessel held aloft into another. The Spanish found this time-consuming and awkward, so invented the *molinillo*, a small wooden swizzle stick. One seventeenth-century English recipe recommended adding milk and then, using the *molinillo*, adding sugar and eggs. Henry Stubbes advised dipping in a 'wig', a bread with spices such as nutmeg, cloves or caraway seeds.

These three exotic beverages were originally brought to Europe by the Spanish and Portuguese, the Venetians and more recently the Dutch. In the early seventeenth century the bulk of English commerce was with the Continent, although some London merchants had abandoned the traditional cloth trade with Germany and the Low Countries in favour of importing luxury goods from the Mediterranean and the Far East. John Evelyn's grandfather, John Stansfield, was an example of such a trader; so too was the Houblon family. In terms of trade, as well as colonisation, the English had been slow to get into the act, but as the century developed they were catching up with increasing rapidity.

England's first overseas colony, if Ireland is discounted, was in Virginia. Despite his desire to encourage England's trade, James I was not particularly interested in this swampy outpost, even though the main town was named in his honour. James held a particular aversion to tobacco, the principal cash crop of Virginia, and was also keen to appease the Spanish; thus, when English settlers arrived in Guiana and Surinam around the mouth of the Amazon in South America, he decreed that attempts to colonise lands claimed by Philip III should be 'left unto the peril which they should incur thereby'.[11] James's lack of enthusiasm for Virginia was shared by the merchant grandees of London. Some did invest in the Virginia Company, but once they realised that they would not find precious metals there, nor the holy grail of the passage to the East Indies, they lost interest. Instead it was merchant outsiders who developed the Virginian tobacco trade which became so lucrative that the King was obliged to suppress this particular prejudice. His pro-Spanish stance had meanwhile alarmed the Puritans among his subjects, so that a group that was to be known as the Pilgrim Fathers left England to settle in Holland. In 1620, when war broke out between the Spanish and the Dutch, they decided to sail to the 'howling wilderness' of what was to become New England, well away from any territorial ambitions of the Spanish King.

While the Spanish were preoccupied with fighting the Dutch, England began to gain its first island colonies in the Americas: Bermuda, Nevis, Montserrat, Antigua, Barbados, half of St Kitts (shared with France) and St Croix (shared with the Dutch). Daniel Defoe was later to describe these West Indies islands as 'the Dregs of the Spaniards first Extraction, the Refuse Part of their Conquests, their meer leavings'.[12] These were, however, secure locations because they were protected from the Spanish colonies to the west by the clockwise patterns of the winds. Although tobacco was their first successful export, in the early 1640s it was discovered that Barbados in particular was well suited to the cultivation of sugar cane. Brazil had been the prime source of sugar, but it was now the scene of a bitter war between Portuguese settlers and their Dutch conquerors. The Dutch, moreover, recognised that they could return a healthy profit by providing the English settlers in Barbados with both the technology to refine raw cane and the requisite labour by selling them slaves, and then shipping the sugar to Europe. Recipe books from Stuart England, such as that of Sir Kenelm Digby, attest to the nation's sweet tooth, and by the 1650s exports from Barbados alone were worth more than £3 million per annum, making it the wealthiest place in the English-speaking world. The acquisition of Jamaica in 1655 just added to the potential for the sugar trade.

Dutch commercial dominance had to be challenged, and this was accomplished through protectionist legislation in the form of the Navigation Acts. The first was passed in 1651, stipulating that all imports from outside Europe coming to England or its colonies were to be carried exclusively in English ships (not Scottish or Irish). This was not only aimed at hurting the Dutch, it also enabled resources to be built up to maritime strength and, by nurturing overseas commerce, strengthened state power. It was not surprising, therefore, that at his restoration Charles II augmented the legislation with two further acts, making it illegal for colonies to export products like tobacco and sugar anywhere except to England and other English colonies, or for foreign goods to go to English colonies except via England. This brought about a huge rise in commerce and wealth to a widening community of English merchants.

One of the 'new merchants' from outside London's mercantile elite was Martin Noell. It is thought that Noell was originally apprenticed to a London scrivener, an unlikely start for a shipowner and merchant, but he was clearly a man of steely determination who was able to take advantage of the English Civil War to play a prominent role in the finances of the Interregnum and become adviser and moneylender to Oliver Cromwell. Not only did Noell own sugar plantations in Barbados and Jamaica with many African slaves, he also was able to gain a foothold in the East India trade and in the setting up of colonies around the Indian Ocean. In 1659, during the parliament of Richard Cromwell, Noell's career looked to be jeopardy when he was accused of making an illicit profit out of transporting captured Royalist soldiers and convicted criminals to Barbados. This, however, turned out to be a lucky break, for he returned to favour with the restoration of Charles II the following year, able to resume his role as a West India lobbyist and creditor to the government. When Noell received a knighthood in 1662, Pepys expressed surprise, given his closeness to the Lord Protector: 'I this day heard that Mr. Martin Noell is knighted by the King, which I much wonder at; but yet he is certainly a very useful man.'[13]

But Sir Martin's luck did not last: in September 1665 he fell victim to the Great Plague. Such was the complexity of his sources of wealth that his executors and beneficiaries were stymied. As Pepys noted, 'It seems nobody can make anything of his estate, whether he be dead worth anything or no, he having dealt in so many things, public and private, as nobody can understand whereabouts his estate is, which is the fate of these great dealers at everything.'[14] However, the inventory of the contents of Noell's mansion in the parish of St Botolph's Bishopsgate does record the luxuriousness of the furnishings and Noell's taste for exotic objects. In the 'New Dining Room', for instance, there were Spanish tables, and Turkish and Persian carpets, while the 'Green Chamber' contained two cabinets, one of ebony, the second an Indian cabinet set on a frame. Many of the most exotic objects were to be found in 'Yr Lady's Chamber or Closet'. These included Spanish tables, 'Jappan trunks', '5 Jappan figures of wood', '2 China Jarrs and a snakes skinn', East India flower pots, furniture decorated with 'East Indiabeasts and birds', '2 pieces of Currall' and '1 Estridge (Ostrich) Egg'.[15]

Many of the objects and furniture were clearly acquired by Noell through his connections with the East India trade. This had been dominated in the sixteenth century by the Spanish and the Portuguese, who through improved naval technology had taken over the existing routes of Arab merchants and established trading relationships with Indonesia, China and Japan. These countries demanded silver in return for their spices, silks and porcelain, which Spain could satisfy through its mines in Mexico and Peru. The English lacked maritime expertise and government support, trading instead in the Levant for goods brought overland from the Far East on the Silk Road. By the end of the century the Dutch had come on the scene, bringing goods at lower prices round the Cape of Good Hope to Europe. Concerned about this threat, in 1600 Elizabeth I was prevailed upon to issue a royal charter establishing 'The Governor and Company of Merchants of London, trading into the East-Indies'; in short, the East India Company (EIC), with the monopoly of English trade between the Cape of Good Hope and Cape Horn. Two years later, the Dutch founded the Vereenigde Oost-Indische Compagnie (VOC), with ten times the capital of its English counterpart.

Following the lead of the Portuguese and the Dutch, the EIC obtained permission to establish 'factories' or permanent trading stations combined with warehouses at strategic points around the Indian Ocean. For the first twenty years a good trade was maintained, with factories at Muscat on the Red Sea, Masulipatam on the east coast of India, Bantam on Java in the Indonesian archipelago, and even at Hirado in Japan. But the Dutch instituted an aggressive policy, causing the English to abandon many of their trading stations and concentrate instead on India, opening factories at Madras on the Coramandel coast and Hugli in Bengal. Bombay, part of the dowry of Catherine of Braganza, was added in 1662. From these the EIC not only supplied the home market with textiles, especially calicoes and chintzes, but also used these goods to trade with the Far East, bringing back to London tea and porcelain from China and lacquerwork from Japan (Plate 51). In the long run, the VOC's seizure of the spice trade actually played into English hands, for while the demand for pepper and spices remained static, that for oriental textiles increased hugely in the second half of the seventeenth century, with a market not only in Britain but in North America too.

In 1664, when he was in Paris, John Evelyn had spotted a market on one of the quays of the Seine, by the Pont Neuf: 'and here is a shop cal'd Noahs-Arke, where are to be had for mony all the Curiosities naturall or artificial imaginable, Indian or Europan, for luxury or Use, as Cabinets, Shells, Ivorys, Purselan [porcelain], Dried fishes, rare Insects, Birds, Pictures & a thousand exotic extravagances'.[16] He acquired a taste for these 'exotic extravagances', and proved a keen shopper during his travels in Europe. This taste was to continue on his return to England. In 1651, for instance, he wrote to Samuel Tuke in Paris, acknowledging receipt of a Chinese garment.[17] When the East India Company regained its charter as a joint-stock enterprise in 1657, Evelyn became an investor, paying his first contribution at its headquarters in Leadenhall Street and offering a prayer that his investment might return safely and profitably. The Company was about to embark upon a phase of prosperity that answered his prayer, and also gave him access to the exotic goods brought to London; Evelyn noted in his diary how he took his wife Mary and Margaret Godolphin to inspect Indian curiosities in the Company's warehouse at Blackwall, on the Thames.[18]

Pepys, too, was a keen shopper, recording in his diary his purchases of both exotic clothes and furnishings for his new home in Seething Lane. On the morning of 7 January 1661, for instance, 'I went up and down into the City to buy several things (as I have lately done for my house) among other things, a fair chest of drawers for my own chamber and an Indian gown for myself. The first cost me 33s, the other 34s.'[19]

Pepys's 'Indian gown' and Evelyn's 'Chinese garment' were in fact based on the Japanese kimono. After the Dutch established exclusive trading rights with Japan early in the seventeenth century, each year the shogun presented a single kimono, beautifully folded and borne on a lacquered tray, to the representative of the VOC. The cachet of this robe, of patterned silk, spread to Europe, and as the demand grew, new sources were found in India in a variety of fabrics, including painted and printed cotton. When Pepys had his portrait painted by John Hayls in 1666, he hired an 'Indian gown' of golden brown silk in the kimono style, with no collar or shoulder seams (Plate 14). Such exotic garments were referred to by a range of names, including 'banyan', the term employed for merchants of West India, 'Cambay' from the Indian port, and nightgown, not for wearing in bed, but informal dress for the sophisticated cosmopolitan man to wear at home. Thus Pepys describes going to visit Sir Philip Howard, 'whom I find dressing himself in his night-gown and Turban like a Turke'.[20] Etiquette stipulated that only someone of superior rank could receive a person of lower rank in a state of undress, while that person of lower rank had to be formally dressed for the occasion.

Pepys makes a couple of references in his diary to oriental gowns for Elizabeth. In November 1663 he mentions how John Creed, Lord Sandwich's servant, had sent him a 'token, *viz.* a very noble parti-coloured Indian gowne for my wife'. Three weeks later, 'one Abrahall, who strikes in for the serving of the King with ship=chandlery ware, hath sent my wife a Japan gowne, which pleases her very well'.[21] These references, made rather nonchalantly, suggest that they were sweeteners, for Pepys had patronage within his power as Clerk of the Navy Board.

It is difficult to know what these gowns were like, for it is the men's seventeenth-century banyans that have survived and can be seen in museums, such as the fine silk gown belonging to William III that is in the Rijksmuseum. East India merchants were not only bringing ready-made banyans to Europe, but also the fabrics that could be made up for clients. In his shop in the parish of St Clement Dane's, Edward Gunn specialised in men's Indian gowns. The inventory taken at his death in

1672 lists a range of styles in 'coloured Indian sattin', and 'flowered' gowns for men. There is no reference to Indian gowns among these for women.[22] In the Victoria and Albert Museum, however, are two late seventeenth-century dolls, Lord and Lady Clapham, with a variety of costumes. One of Lady Clapham's is a loose gown of silk in oriental patterns (although the fabric was woven in Europe) worn over stays and a matching petticoat (Plate 53). Elizabeth Pepys's Indian and Japanese gowns may have looked like this, and would have been appropriate for her to wear on informal occasions at home. For instance, Pepys describes how 'this day [Elizabeth] put on her Indian blue gown, which is very pretty', when she played cards with some of his friends after an informal dinner party at Seething Lane.[23]

The early 1660s saw an interesting development in the style of men's dress, apparently influenced by the taste for the exotic. After a brief sartorial rush to the head, when some adopted the French fashion of petticoat breeches so voluminous that, as Pepys reported, one man 'put both his legs through one of his Knees of his breeches, and went so all day', a more sober and elegant fashion was introduced, indeed commanded, by Charles II.[24] 'The King hath yesterday in council declared his resolution of setting a fashion for clothes, which he will never alter', Pepys reported in October 1666. 'It will be a vest. I know not well how. But it is to teach the nobility thrift, and will do good.'[25] Evelyn certainly knew well how, for he had written in 1661 a pamphlet entitled *Tyrannus or the Mode* that he presented to the King. In this he had praised 'the usefulness of Persian clothing' in contrast to the French fashion. In his diary in October 1666 he noted: 'To Court, it being the first time of his Majesties putting himselfe solemnly into the Eastern fashion of Vest, changing doublet, stiff Collar, [bands] & Cloake &c: into a comely Vest, after the Persian mode, with girdle or shash, & Shoe strings & Garters, into bouckles'.[26] Having observed the new style when he visited Westminster, Pepys described the vest as being like a cassock, and decided that he would have one made by his tailor. This took place just after the Great Fire had destroyed much of the City, and England was at war, so the King was moved to undertake the revolution in dress as a gesture of anti-French economy. It was an unusual stance for him, but one that proved long-lasting, for the style became the prototype of the later coat and waistcoat, in place of the jerkin and doublet.

In the autumn of 1663 Pepys was organising the decoration of Elizabeth's study in Seething Lane, recording how he had gone 'to Cornhill and after many tryals bought my wife a Chinke: that is a paynted Indian calico'.[27] 'Chinke' may well have been a mistake on Pepys's part in writing his shorthand, and more properly should be 'Chint'. This was later to become 'chintz', derived from the Sanskrit for sprinkled or sprayed, the pattern being applied on the calico with a bamboo 'pen' and dyed with mordant and resists. Pepys describes the calico as very pretty, suggesting that it might have been a floral print based on a tree pattern for the repeat. A more unusual design, anticipating the fabrics and wallpapers of the eighteenth century, was admired by John Evelyn in 1665 when he visited Lady Mordaunt: 'here was a roome hung with Pintado full of figures great and small, prettily representing sundry Trades and occupations of the Indians with their habits &c; very extraordinarie'.[28] Pintado was a Portuguese term meaning 'spotted'.

Pepys does not make clear whether he bought his Indian calico from an individual shop or from a 'boutique' in the Royal Exchange in Cornhill, the shopping hub for luxury goods in the City. It had been the brainchild of the Elizabethan financier, Sir Thomas Gresham, who had been impressed with the Bourse in Antwerp and felt that there should be a similar trading centre in London. Opened in 1570, the Exchange consisted of covered walks with shops or boutiques surrounding a courtyard. A similar establishment was created forty years later by Robert Cecil, Earl of Salisbury. Situated on the Strand, the New Exchange offered luxury shopping for those who were moving out of the City and into the West End. To celebrate its opening in 1609, attended by the royal family, Ben Jonson wrote *The Entertainment at Britain's Burse*. The exotic contents of the shops were spelt out by a shop boy with his patter:

What do you lack? What is't you buy? Very fine China stuffs of all kinds and qualities? China chains, China bracelets, China scarves, China fans, China girdles, China knives, China boxes, China cabinets . . . crystal globes, waxen pictures, ostrich eggs, birds of paradise,

musk-cats, Indian mice, Indian rats, China dogs and China cats?
Flower of silk, mosaic fishes? Waxen fruit and porcelain dishes?

Jonson was suggesting that the world was the shopper's oyster, with a
series of fantasies:

[porcelain] tralucent as amber and subtler than crystal ... carpets
wrought of *paraquitos'* feathers; umbrellas made of the wing of the Indian
butterfly; ventolas of flying fishes' fins; hangings of the island of Cochin,
which, being but a natural cobweb of that country, last longer than your
gilded leather; paper made of the barks of trees and inks to carry dry in
your pocket; and thousand such subtleties which you will think to have
cheap now at the next return of the Hollanders' fleet from the Indies.[29]

Moreover this retail paradise was available to women as well as men,
and it is clear from contemporary accounts that they took full advantage
of being able to visit both Exchanges with their friends without being
accompanied by their husbands. Although the Royal Exchange was
destroyed in the Great Fire, the shopping had to go on, so Gresham
College was commandeered as temporary retail premises while a new
building arose from the designs of the architect Edward Jarman.

When Jonson wrote his entertainment in 1609 the trio of exotic
beverages – tea, coffee and chocolate – had not yet reached England, but
with their arrival in the middle of the century, a whole new tranche of
luxury goods was required for their consumption in the home, and in
particular in the closet or private apartment of fashionable ladies. In
Mundus Muliebris, or the Ladies Dressing-Room unlock'd, we get a picture
of the furnishings of such an apartment. This little satire on contemporary manners was described as anonymous, but is attributed to Evelyn's
clever eldest daughter, Mary, and was published in 1690, five years after
her death. A series of verses entitled 'A Voyage to Marryland' advises a
potential husband what was required for his bride:

You furnish her Appartment,
With *Moreclack* [Mortlake] Tapestry, Damask Bed,

Of Velvet richly embroidered:
Branches [hanging candlesticks], *Brasero*, [a moveable hearth of
silver for coals, from Spain], *Cassolets* [perfuming pots or censors],
A *Cofre fort*, and Cabinets,
Vasas of Silver, *Porcelain*, store
To set, and range about the Floor:
The Chimney Furniture of Plate,
(For Iron's now quite out of date)
Tea-Table, *Skreens*, Trunks, and Stand,
Large Looking-Glass richly *Japan'd*.

The list of contents closely resembles a 1683 diary entry by Evelyn in which he describes the dressing room of the Duchess of Portsmouth, the King's mistress, in Whitehall: 'Then for Japon cabinets, Skreenes, Pendule Clocks, huge Vasas of wrought plate, Tables, Stands, Chimny Furniture, Sconces, branches, Braseras &c they were all of massive silver, & without number'.[30]

The table in Mary's verse was part of a set of tea furniture consisting also of a kettle, teapot, canister, a basin for slops, a bowl for sugar, spoons, and cups of Chinese or Japanese porcelain. The tea was usually green, although a small amount of black, known as bohea, was being imported. It was customarily taken with sugar, and right at the end of the seventeenth century references begin to appear to 'milk bottles'. The Duchess of Lauderdale lived in great state at Ham House, near Petersham on the Thames. She received general visitors in her White Closet. According to an inventory in the National Trust's archives, in 1679 the closet contained 'one scriptoire of princew[o]od garnish'd wt silver, one little cedar table, six armechayres Japannd, with black cane bottomes, one Indian furnace [kettle] for tee garnished with silver'. She would serve tea to her most intimate friends in her private closet, and an inventory records 'six Japann'd backstools with cane bottomes', a 'Japan box for sweetmeats and tea' and a tea table 'carv'd and guilt' that had been imported from Java. Backstools meant that the chairs were not set against the wall, but around the table, and the National Trust has recreated this arrangement with the furniture that, remarkably, has survived from the late seventeenth century (Plate 54).

47. Hendrick Danckerts's view of Greenwich from the south-east. The Queen's House, designed by Inigo Jones for Anne of Denmark, can be seen on the left, and the King's Pavilion, commissioned by Charles II from Jones's nephew, John Webb, in the centre. Pepys recorded in his diary on 16 March 1669 how he visited Greenwich 'to see the prospect [from] the hill to judge of Dancre's picture which he hath made thereof for me; and I do like it very well – and is a very pretty place'. Pepys had ordered from the artist paintings of the four royal residences, Whitehall, Hampton Court, Windsor and Greenwich.

48. A map of the world from Willem Blaeu's *Theatre du Monde*, published in Amsterdam in 1638–40. Evelyn recorded in his diary how he called in at Blaeu's shop during his visit to

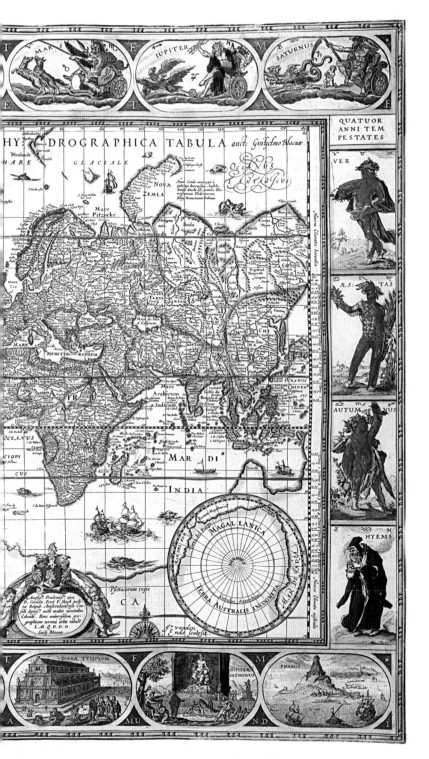

Holland in 1641, and a copy of the atlas was in his library. The borders are decorated with the four elements and seasons, the planets and landscapes from various parts of the world.

49. An illustration from Robert Knox's *Historical Relation of the Island of Ceylon*, published in 1681, showing a man and his son eating and drinking with a talipat tree in the background. Knox explains: 'Their common drink is only water … When they drink they touch not the Pot with their mouths. [Wives] wait and serve their Husbands while they eat … During their eating they neither use nor delight to talk to one another.'

50. 'Nieu Amsterdam', from a series of prints of Dutch colonies published in about 1680 by the printer Johannes de Ram. In this scene are two settlers, the woman holding a box of tulips, the man next to a barrel of tobacco leaves, indicating the trade between Europe and North America carried in ships of the Dutch West India Company. By the time this print was published, the settlement on Manhattan had passed from the Dutch to the English, renamed New York after the King's brother, James.

51. The interior of a merchant's shop dealing in luxury goods from Asia, such as ceramics, furniture and lacquerwork. Originally intended as a fan leaf, this image was painted in around 1700, probably in the Dutch Republic.

52. A bedcover or wall hanging of cotton embroidered with silk, made in Gujarat for the export market to Europe in about 1700.

53. Pepys refers in a November 1663 diary entry to his wife Elizabeth being given a 'Japan gowne', but such a garment for women has not survived from the 1660s. However, a doll dating from the 1690s, known as Lady Clapham, has survived. She is wearing a loose gown of oriental style (albeit of silk woven in Europe) over stays and a petticoat – appropriate dress for entertaining at home.

54. The Duchess of Lauderdale's private closet at Ham House. The room, hung with 'Dark Mohayre bordered with flowered Silke with purple & gold fringe', was where the Duchess entertained her intimate friends to tea. The japanned chairs are probably the 'backstools with cane bottomes' listed in the inventory of 1683. The tea table is a composite piece: the upper section is Javanese, made to take tea cross-legged; the lower section is Anglo-Dutch, added to bring the table up to a height more convenient and conventional for Europeans. The teapot is Dehua, from China, but with mounts of European silver gilt.

55. Designs printed at the back of Stalker and Parker's *Treatise of Japaning and Varnishing*, published in 1688. These designs were particularly aimed at ladies of leisure who could make themselves items for their closet such as combs, clothes brushes and 'a Pincushing Trunke for Pendents Necklace Rings & Jewells'.

56. Tuberoses (nos. 1 and 2) from John Parkinson's *Paradisi in Sole*, published in 1629. Parkinson has identified them as hyacinths, *Hyacinthus Indicus maoir* and *minor*, taking his cue from the Flemish botanist Clusius. He noted that they were not bulbous, but rather had a tuberous root. He also noted that they came from the West Indies, and did not flower in England until the middle of August – if the gardener was lucky. Their scent, he wrote, was 'very sweet … or rather strong and headie'.

57. A painting traditionally described as John Rose, the royal gardener, presenting a pineapple to Charles II – though the only elements that we can be sure of are the King and the fruit. It is thought that the gardener George London commissioned a series of versions, probably from Hendrick Danckerts, as a tribute to the skills of Rose, who was his mentor. Pineapples were first imported from Barbados in the 1650s, and Charles II certainly tasted them, but gardeners were not able to raise them in England until the early eighteenth century. The pineapple was a horticultural holy grail, as well as the symbol of hospitality.

58. An eighteenth-century engraving of Westminster Hall by Hubert-François Gravelot, showing the walls lined with bookstalls. When Pepys was living in Westminster in the late 1650s, Ann and Miles Mitchell were his local booksellers, from whom he bought newsbooks and political pamphlets, and at whose stall he ate bread to keep himself going during the coronation of Charles II in 1661.

59. An engraving by Abraham Bosse of the Gallery of the Palais de Justice in Paris, about 1638, showing some of the 'boutiques', with a bookshop next to sellers of fans and lace. The two London Exchanges, the Royal in the City and the New Exchange in the Strand, were similarly laid out, with a variety of retailers side by side. As in this Parisian scene, women could shop without their husbands as escorts. Pepys took advantage of this by suggesting that Deb Willet might leave messages for him at Henry Herringman's bookshop in the New Exchange, thus escaping the scrutiny of his wife.

60. 'Come who buys
my New Merry Books',
a woodcut showing a
chapman selling his wares.
This illustration is from
one of Pepys's 'Penny
Merriments', published in
about 1680 and entitled
Make Room for Christmas.

61. A London coffee-
house, from an
advertisement for 'Will's
Best Coffee Powder',
about 1700. The customers
are enjoying not only the
coffee but also newspapers
such as the *London Gazette*
and the *Post Boy*.

Will's Best Coffee Powder at
Manwarings Coffee House in
Falcon Court over against St
Dunstans Church in Fleet Street

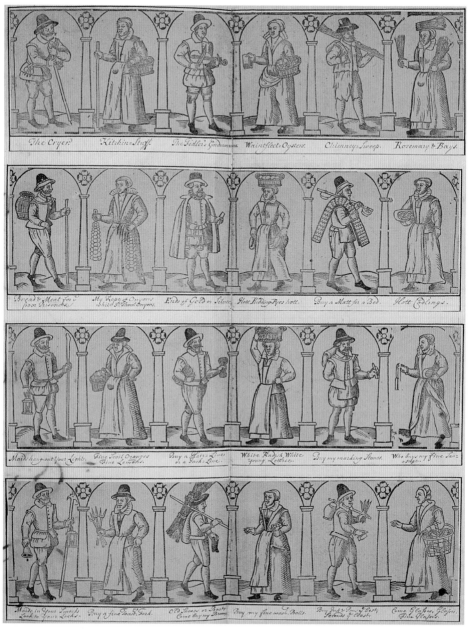

The Cryer?   Kitchin=Stuff.   The Fidler: Goodmorrow.   Wraintfleet=Oysters.   Chimney=Sweep.   Rosemary & Bays.

Bread & Meat for ye poor Prisoners.   My Lope of Onyons White St Thoms Onyons.   Ends of Gold or Silver.   Hott Pudding Pyes hott.   Buy a Matt for a Bed.   Hott Codlings.

Maide hang out your Lights.   Fine Sevil Oranges Fine Lemons.   Buy a Haire=Line or a Jack=Line.   White Radish White young Lettice.   Buy my marking Stones.   Who buys my fine Sau=sedges.

Maide in Your Smocks Look to Your Locks.   Buy a fine Toast. Fork.   Old Shoes or Boots Come buy my Broom.   Buy my fine wash Balls.   Buy Inke & Pens ye best Secondes ye Clast.   Come Glasses, Glases Fine Glasses.

62. Pepys described this series of street vendors and officers as 'A very antient Sett thereof, in Wood, with the Words then used by Cryers', which he pasted into albums for his library. The series, dating from the early seventeenth century, shows twenty-four male and female figures, suggesting a procession through time from the town-crier at daybreak to a woman selling glassware in the early evening.

Cryes.

Delicate Cowcumbers to pickle
Cencombres a confire
Cocomeri q mettere in composta

Hott Bak'd Wardens Hott
Pommes cuites Poires cuites
Mele Pera cotte

4 Paire for a Shilling Holland Socks
Achetez des Chaussons
Chi vuol Scapini d'Holanda

Londons Gazette here
Nouvelle Gazette
Chi Gabro d'venir de Londra

63. A page from Marcellus Laroon's *Cryes of the City of London Drawne after the Life* published in 1687, showing four female vendors. Above left: cucumbers for pickling; above right: baked wardens, hard pears that were only edible when cooked; below left: shilling Holland socks; below right: the *London Gazette* – the women selling such newspapers were known as 'mercuries'.

64. The first page of Pepys's diary, with his characteristic mixture of shorthand and longhand for names (such as 'Axe Yard' and his maidservant, Jane). It is headed 1659/60 because the new year did not start until Lady Day, 25 March.

65. The opening page of Evelyn's diary, or 'Kalendarium', dated 1620, the year of his birth, and giving details of his family, especially of his father, Richard.

Pepys lost the chintz and other furnishings when his home in Seething Lane was destroyed by fire in 1673, but he did not lose his taste for the exotic. As he gained influence as the Secretary of the Admiralty, so the presents given to him became more extravagant. In his diary for January 1661 he mentions quite by chance that he had a pet monkey. Coming home late one night, he found that she had got loose and beat her into submission, which he later regretted. His predilection for exotic animals may have been generally known, for a week later a naval officer, Captain Rooth, gave him two cages of canaries.[31] Perhaps the zoological acme was reached in 1674 when Samuel Martin, the Consul in Algiers, sent to accompany some naval intelligence a tame lion 'which is the Onely rarety that offers from this place'. Somehow Pepys kept him in his lodgings in Derby House in Westminster, reporting to Martin that he was 'as tame as you sent him, and as good company'.[32]

Sir John Wyborne, the Deputy Governor of the East India Company, and his wife Katherine sent a range of gifts from Bombay in 1687. One mysterious item was 'a jaspar Antonia stone of eight ounces' that Wyborne had acquired from a Goan Jesuit; this is thought to have been a precious medicine. Other gifts included 'a very Grave [plain] Walkeing Cane' and 'fifteene fine Little Birdes in a small Cagge'. A year later 'a very pritte velvet Carpett' arrived from Katherine, who jokingly noted that Bombay lacked the shopping facilities of the London Exchanges. She also sent Pepys 'a piece of Atlass' and 'a China lackered desck'.[33]

Hard lacquer from the Far East was much prized and, although sometimes referred to as 'Japan', more often came from China. Imitations were also produced by European craftsmen, based on Chinese models, and there was a vogue for decorating furniture, toilet sets, boxes and shelves with lacquer. The reference to Robert Hooke supplying 'white varnish' for 'Mrs Pepys' was probably for this purpose rather than for Mary Skinner's paintings (p. 96). Lacquering became such a fashionable recreation, especially for ladies, that a book was produced on the subject in 1688, *A Treatise of Japaning and Varnishing*. It was written by a craftsman, John Stalker, who had his workshop at the sign of the Golden Ball in St James's Market in London, with George Parker, who lived near the Sheldonian Theatre in Oxford. As the book was printed in

Oxford, Parker may have acted as a ghostwriter, as the style is very high-flown. Despite the loftiness of the prose, it was a practical book, giving rules for counterfeiting tortoiseshell and marble, as well as staining and dyeing wood, ivory and horn, and outlining required equipment (Plate 55). In a letter to his uncle from Paris late in 1699, John Jackson referred to Mary Skinner and 'her book of Japanning', and a copy of Stalker and Parker's work is still in Pepys's Library in Magdalene College.[34]

When William Nicolson visited the home that Pepys, Mary Skinner and Will Hewer shared in Clapham in the summer of 1702, he noted how it was filled with Indian and Chinese ornaments. This brief reference does not give us much detail, but Mary Skinner's will of 1714 provides a glimpse of what the house contained. Among the goods she left was 'the great Skreen of Six-leaves Indian' given to her by Pepys, 'two Indian Silver Guilt perfuming Bottles, and an Indian cabinet'.[35] The cabinet was probably one that John Evelyn talked about to his wife in a letter written in 1695. He told her that 'Mrs Skinner (Mr Pepp's Inclination)' had bought a cabinet for the substantial sum of £50. She had been 'all over the Towne & could no where find any like it, & would have given 60*l* if it had been asked, for she payd the 50*l* immediately without any chafering for abatement'.[36]

Among Evelyn's own collection of cabinets was one that he described as a 'Japan Indian', which, given his position as an investor in the East India Company, suggests that it did indeed come from the Far East. He mentions it in a letter to his son John in 1696, when he was telling him to help himself to items from Sayes Court for his London house in Dover Street. While his son could take 'the inlaid Cabinet of curiosities, ... the other Japan Indian I rather keepe in the Country ... because of the Carving, which the aer of London would prejudice'.[37] The first cabinet could have been either the piece decorated with *pietra dura* that Evelyn had commissioned from Florentine craftsmen during his stay in Italy in 1644 (p. 15) or the ebony cabinet commissioned by his young bride in Paris in 1652 (p. 18). All three cabinets, along with one made in Antwerp, appear in the inventory made by Evelyn of the contents of Wotton in 1702.[38] The term 'cabinet of curiosities' refers not only to a piece of furniture, but also to the room in which it might appear. Evelyn had just such a room at Wotton, and among the contents he lists a range of objects placed within one of his cabinets. These include pieces of porcelain from China, bowls of marble and crystal, 'flagons of Jasper', all displayed on loops or circles of small shells. Other pieces are arranged on black japanned shelves, and it may be that these were made for Evelyn by his artistic daughter Susanna.

Evelyn's cabinets of curiosities could be said to extend beyond the house to the garden. Indeed, he referred to parts of the garden at Sayes Court as cabinets; similarly, Henry Compton considered the trees in his garden at Fulham Palace as a collection of curiosities from North America, as described in Chapter 7. Two garden-owners in particular – William III and Mary, Duchess of Beaufort – collected and cultivated tender exotics on a grand scale. William's interest in gardening had been propagated in Holland, having been richly supplied by the servants of the two great Dutch trading companies, the VOC in the East Indies and the WIC in the Caribbean. Merchants, ship's captains and physicians working in the factories were encouraged to send exotic plants back to Amsterdam, with a garden in the settlement at the Cape of Good Hope acting as a stopover to allow for acclimatisation. In 1675, William, as Stadtholder, put out a request for 'all sorts of animals, birds, herbaria, cabinets and other curiosities'.[39] The resulting treasures were installed in the garden and menagerie at Honselaarsdijk, one of several gardens belonging to the House of Orange. When he arrived in England, William made Hampton Court Palace his favourite residence and garden. Mary Evelyn visited the palace in the summer of 1691, and reported rather breathlessly to her husband how the greenhouses were

> filled with the most rare plants of the Indies things wonderfull in the kind some with leaves ¾ of a yard long and a quarter broad others of different forms not to be described easily the name I know not . . . I wish you there a day with all my heart and hope you will go the gardners are holanders.[40]

The Duchess of Beaufort was born Mary Capel, from a distinguished horticultural dynasty. A group portrait painted in about 1639 by Cornelius Johnson shows the family posed in front of the Italianate garden created by Sir Arthur Capel at Much Hadham in Hertfordshire.[41] Three of his children were to become enthusiastic gardeners: Arthur, Earl of Essex, at Cassiobury Park; Henry at Kew; and Mary at the gardens of her husband at Beaufort House in Chelsea and Badminton in Gloucestershire. Their sister Elizabeth became a skilled flower painter. Despite her status and possessions, the Duchess suffered from melancholia, or 'mopishness' as one of her friends put it. She took comfort in horticulture, and Mark Laird draws an interesting parallel with John Evelyn, who threw himself into gardening activities while mourning the death of his children.[42] When her husband inherited Badminton in 1662, Mary's interest was focused on medicinal plants, but she became fascinated by florists' flowers, especially the carnation, the auricula and the polyanthus, growing them at Beaufort House. Her greatest period of gardening came in the 1690s, when she began to collect tender exotics, many of them arriving via Leiden and Amsterdam, with the expert help of two botanical enthusiasts from the Royal Society, the apothecary James Petiver and the physician Hans Sloane. Like Pepys, she retained Sloane as her doctor. A third botanist, William Sherard, became tutor to her grandson for two years from 1700 to 1702. Both Sloane and Sherard had studied with the distinguished French botanist Joseph Pitton de Tournefort at the Jardin du Roi in Paris, so the Duchess had access to the very best of horticultural advice.

Two tender exotics stand out for their extravagance in the latter part of the seventeenth century: the tuberose and the pineapple. The tuberose (*Polianthes tuberosa*) is not a rose, but related to the narcissus and the jonquil, and native to Central America (Plate 56). The Aztecs called it 'omixochitl' or bone flower in tribute to its waxy blossoms of radiant white. It was described by Francisco Hernandez, physician to Philip II of Spain, who was sent in 1577 on a mission to New Spain (Mexico) to gather information on the natural history and population for the Council of the Indies in Seville. Hernandez got Indian artists to draw the omixochitl along with other exotic flowers that included what we now call the dahlia, but he died before his writings could be published, and an edited version was produced in Mexico City in 1628 that left

Europe largely in ignorance. The great Flemish botanist Carolus Clusius, meanwhile, included the plant in his history of rare flora in 1601, describing it as a kind of Indian hyacinth with a tuberous root, hence its modern name.

Hernandez had noted how, with its strong scent, it was used by the Aztecs for their garlanded wreaths, and it was this scent that entranced gardeners when the first plants arrived in Europe in the early seventeenth century. Louis XIV was one such enthusiast, ordering his gardener, Jean Baptiste de la Quintinie, to grow 10,000 for his garden at the Trianon at Versailles. Evelyn's first reference to the flower comes in a letter written in 1664 to Walter Pope, tutor and travelling companion to his nephew George on his European tour, asking him for 'rare tuberoses' along with jonquils and anemones that could easily be sent to him as roots and bulbs.[43] When giving instructions to his apprentice Jonathan Mosse, Evelyn advised him that alongside melons and gourds, he should grow in his hotbed amaranths, marvel of Peru, nasturtium indicum and tuberoses. 'The Hot-Bed should be in the warmest corner of the Nurserie, well secured from the weather by wall, pale, or reedepannells of five-foote high or more. Herein you raise all your choicer seedes, both for fruite flower, and many exotiq plants & Trees, under covers of Glasse frames, or Bels, Matresses &c.'[44] The heat would have been generated by dung, sometimes topped up with tan bark. When translating de la Quintinie's book in 1693, Evelyn suggested that the tuberose be used in June for decorating the house, with the flowers arranged in bough pots and placed in empty fireplaces, where their scent could fill the room.

As for the pineapple, Evelyn recorded in his diary for 9 August 1661 how 'I first saw the famous Queen-pine brought from Barbados presented to his Majestie, but the first that were even seene here in England, were those sent to Cromwell, four-yeares since'. It comes as a nice irony that the Puritan Oliver Cromwell should be the first to enjoy such an extravagance. Charles II acquired a taste for the fruit, and in 1668 Evelyn recorded how 'His Majestie having cut it up, was pleasd to give me a piece off his own plate to tast of'. Evelyn, however, expressed modified rapture saying that it 'falls short of those ravishing varieties of deliciousness' recorded by writers, hardly surprising considering it had endured the long journey from the West Indies.[45] Fruiting pineapples, however, were not successfully raised in Europe until the wealthy owner of a Dutch garden, Agneta Block, did so on her estate at Vijverhof near Amsterdam in 1687. The clue to her success was the invention during the 1680s of the first true hothouses. While tuberoses could be grown using the cross between a hotbed and a glass frame, the pineapple, like other very tender exotics, had to be raised in glasshouses equipped to generate sufficient heat for the plants to survive northern winters.

The Dutch were pioneers in this field, first developing iron stoves at floor level within orangeries and greenhouses, but then turning to the idea of supplying the heat underground. Following a visit to Leiden, John Watts installed a system in the garden of the Society of Apothecaries at Chelsea, where he was the Keeper. On 11 November 1684 Hans Sloane wrote to John Ray describing how Watts

> has a new contrivance, at least in this country: viz. he makes under the floor of his greenhouse a great fire plate with grate, ash-hole, &c., and conveys the warmth through the whole house, by tunnels: so that he hopes, by the help of weather-glasses within, to bring or keep the air at what degree of warmth he pleases, letting in upon occasion the outward air by the windows. He thinks to make, by this means, an artificial spring, summer and winter.[46]

The following year Evelyn went to see the system, admiring the ingenuity of the 'subterranean heate, conveyed by a stove under the Conservatory, which was all Vaulted with brick; so as he [Watts] leaves the doores & windowes open in the hard(e)st frosts, secluding onely the snow &c.'[47] Even so, when he included a greenhouse in his 1691 edition of *Kalendarium Hortense*, Evelyn warned that with the hypocaust system 'Plants . . . rarely pass'd their Confinements, without Sickness, a certain Langour or Taint discoverable by their Complexions', and suggested instead having the stove outside the greenhouse.[48]

Another drawback of the hothouses was that they were very expensive. The Duchess of Beaufort, who converted her greenhouse into a hothouse in 1698, was able to afford the running costs, as was the King, but Henry Compton on his episcopal salary was obliged partly to abandon his stoves. Moreover, despite every effort, William III's gardeners at Hampton Court were unable to replicate Agneta Block's success in raising pineapples, and it was to be another twenty years before they could be cultivated to grace the dinner tables of the wealthy in England. When Agneta had her portrait painted with her second husband, children and pet dogs in the garden at Vijverhof, a pineapple is shown in the foreground.[49] The English parallel, an image of the royal gardener John Rose presenting a pineapple to Charles II, is not so straightforward (Plate 57). As both Rose and the King were dead before the first pineapple was grown in Holland, it is thought that the painting, which is known in several versions, represents instead George London's tribute to the horticultural skills of Rose, who was his mentor.

Just as Dutch enthusiasts of horticultural exotics got their plants, roots and seeds from merchants and others working for the great trading companies, so too did the English. In 1671, John Evelyn was appointed a member of the Council for Foreign Plantations, which added 'Trade' to its title the following year. The idea of such an executive council had been suggested to the King a decade earlier by the merchant Martin Noell, urging that it was 'of the highest Consequence' that a body should be established 'solely dedicated to the Inspection, Care, and Regulation of all forreigne Plantations belonging to the Crowne of England . . . to which Government they ought to bee accountable'.[50] The terms of reference for the Council were broad, with members required to inform themselves on the state of trade overseas and the means by which to encourage it. Evelyn served on the Council until 1674, participating in discussions of commodities that included slaves traded by the Africa Company, and receiving reports from the Caribbean and North America, and from the East India Company. In this way, he was able to garner information about plants from very different areas, and to contribute his expertise on the acclimatisation of exotics.

The Church also played its part, through Henry Compton as the Bishop responsible for the American plantations. As noted in Chapter 7, he was able to use botanically minded curates to hunt for plants and to send them back to him. One of his best contacts was John Banister, who went first to Barbados and then in April 1679 to Virginia, where he served as rector of the parish of Charles City. He had learnt his botany while at Oxford, studying with Robert Morison, and put it to good use when searching out plants for both Compton and Jacob Bobart the Younger, Superintendent of the Oxford Botanic Garden. Contemplating the compilation of a natural history of Virginia, Banister sent drawings to James Petiver and papers to the Royal Society. Unfortunately, all this enterprise was abruptly ended when he was accidentally shot while exploring the lower Roanoke River in 1692. Compton immediately wrote to Bobart in Oxford asking him to recommend another naturalist as Banister's successor.

At this time Bobart was compiling lists of seeds and plants, and offering them to the owners of famous gardens for exchange or sale. Thus, when plants were brought back from Jamaica by James Harlow in 1692, Compton received a share to increase the probability of survival. When *Pelargonium inquinans* was introduced from South Africa, the Bishop received some of the plants, which were to become one parent of our bedding geranium, while the other, *Pelargonium zonale*, was grown by the Duchess of Beaufort. Bobart also operated a network of plant collectors scattered around the world. One such collector was a Scottish surgeon, Samuel Browne, working for the East India Company based in Fort St George at Madras. Browne travelled to Zhou Shan in China and sent back large specimens of *Rhus chinensis*, the China Sumac tree. James Petiver recorded how it arrived in England still bearing its ripe berries, and was given to Compton, who raised several small trees from those berries at Fulham Palace. Like Banister in Virginia, Browne sent back dried plants from India along with information that Petiver was able to incorporate into *Philosophical Transactions* for the Royal Society.

Hans Sloane, following his botanical studies in France, sailed for Jamaica in September 1687 as physician to the Duke of Albemarle. While in Jamaica he carefully recorded every plant he found, employing a local clergyman to draw the specimens that he was unable to dry, in preparation for a planned publication of the natural history of the island. When Albemarle died two years later, Sloane returned to England with around 800 plants, some of which were given to Compton, others to the Duchess. Sloane was later able to purchase Petiver's collection of preserved plants for the substantial sum of £4,000, and to incorporate it with his own, creating the basis for the British Museum of Natural History. The other great herbarium of this period was compiled by the Duke of Beaufort's erstwhile tutor, William Sherard, and left to the University of Oxford along with his library.

Sloane and Petiver were just two of several botanical enthusiasts who were members of the Royal Society. But, thanks to Robert Hooke, the institution itself also played an important role in the acquisition of knowledge of exotic plants and the countries from which they came. Although Hooke spent his entire working life in London, he was fascinated by distant lands, taking an increasing interest in travel narratives, cartography and exotica which he collected for the Repository of the Royal Society, mostly housed in his rooms at Gresham College. In 1681 he became friendly with Captain Robert Knox, recently returned to England having escaped from nineteen years' captivity by Rajasinha II, the ruler of Ceylon. On his voyage home, Knox began to compose *An Historical Relation of the Island of Ceylon, in the East Indies*, which came to the attention of the directors of the EIC who recommended publication. Hooke helped him to shape the text, which included descriptions of the plants, animals and minerals to be found on the island, as well as the customs of the inhabitants (Plate 50). The book proved very popular, and was translated into French, German and Dutch.

Hooke recognised how useful Knox's eye for detail could prove for the Royal Society as part of ongoing investigations into peoples, cultures and trades. When the Governor of the EIC, Sir Josiah Child, commissioned Knox to undertake an expedition to Vietnam and Java to collect a cargo of pepper, Hooke took the opportunity to request that he gather interesting specimens for the Society. Knox more than fulfilled his brief, returning in 1683 with a substantial collection of exotic curiosities. Among the botanical items was the root of a tea tree that he had planted in a pot of earth aboard his ship, and a wide variety of seeds and cuttings: 'the seed of the Tunquin oranges, the best in the world', 'of a certain bean or pease that grows in Java' and 'of water-melons, which grow in the island of St Jago'.[51] Knox became a celebrity, being presented to Charles II at Whitehall and having 'an hours discourse' with him.

Hooke and Knox developed a close friendship, spending many hours talking of the latter's adventures over cups of chocolate in Hooke's favourite coffee-houses. Hooke tried one particular exotic extravagance: 'bangue', or cannabis, which Knox had acquired in Mauritius, recording in his diary for 26 October 1689: 'at Jon. [Jonathan's] Cap. Knox choc. ganges strange intoxicating herb like hemp, takes away understanding and memory for a time frequently used in India with benefit: rice not injurious to the Sight nor harmful to the teeth'.[52] Two months later, at a Cutlerian lecture at the Royal Society, attended by Evelyn and Pepys, Hooke talked about 'bangue':

It is a certain Plant which grows very common in India, and the Vertues, or Quality thereof, are there very well known; and the Use thereof (tho' the Effects are very strange, and at first hearing, frightful enough) is very general and frequent; and the Person, from whom I received it, hath made very many Trials of it, on himself, with very good Effect.[53]

A Preface was provided by Christopher Wren for Robert Knox's description of Ceylon, in which he wrote, 'I conceive it may give great Satisfaction to the Curious, and may be well worth your Publishing'. The book was just one part of a voyage of discovery in words, pictures and maps being made available to men like Pepys and Evelyn. The latter had begun his voyage in 1641 when he visited Hendrik Hondius's shop In den Atlas in Amsterdam, pronouncing in his diary that he was 'greately pleasd with the designes of that indefatigable Person'. He added that 'Mr. Bleaw, the setter-forth of the Atlas's & other Workes of that kind is worthy seeing'.[54] This was Johannes Blaeu, who with his father Willem had bought up the copperplates of many maps from the Hondius family and had begun to produce atlases that were to prove a landmark in publishing. Evelyn bought the French edition, *Theatre du Monde, ou Nouvel Atlas*, containing 208 maps in two volumes. This atlas gives not only detailed maps in colour of the known world, but also engravings of the various indigenous peoples (Plate 48).

During his years in Europe, Evelyn began to build up his collection of books on travel, such as *Le Voyage de Levant fait par le Commandement du Roy en l'année 1621*, by Louis des Hayes, published in Paris in 1645, and he continued to add to it when he returned to England. Following the Restoration, the number of travel accounts published in English increased markedly, aimed at a market concerned with the expansion of the nation's overseas interests and the development of empire. The popularity of travel literature is shown by the output of John Ogilby, who described himself on the title pages as 'His Majesty's Cosmographer, Geographick Printer, and Master of Revels in the Kingdom of Ireland'. Ogilby gathered various sources about a particular area of the world and published them in lavishly illustrated folios, often sold by subscription lottery (p. 239). Evelyn acquired from him *Africa* (1670), *America* (1671) and *Asia* (1673), as well as an atlas of Japan.

Pepys likewise built up an impressive collection of books on travel and, with his interest in naval matters, he acquired more than 1,000 maps and charts. In 1695 he began meticulously to organise them in a catalogue with three main categories – land, sea, and miscellaneous – and grids drawn out in manuscript on each map, alphabetically indexed to facilitate finding places. One 'travel' book in his library is *The Isle of Pines* by Henry Neville, a fictional tale published in 1668, but with the plot set a hundred years earlier, as narrated by a Dutchman writing to a friend in London. It tells of George Pine and four females who are wrecked on a desert island, and how their descendants are discovered by Dutch explorers. This, along with the non-fictional account of Ceylon by Robert Knox, which Pepys also acquired, is thought to have been inspiration for Daniel Defoe's *Robinson Crusoe*. The subtitle of *The Isle of Pines* runs 'A late Discovery of a 4th Island near Terra Australis Incognita'.

Terra Australis Incognita was a source of much speculation in the late seventeenth century. In August 1698, Evelyn recorded dining with Pepys at York Buildings along with William Dampier, 'a famous Buccaneere' who had 'brought hither the painted Prince Jolo'. Jolo, or Jeoly from Mindanao, one of the islands of the Philippines, had been the source of much interest when he was exhibited in England, before his death from smallpox in 1692. Dampier subsequently published an account of his adventures, *A new voyage around the world*, in the year before his dinner with the two diarists, and was preparing to set out again on his travels 'by the Kings Incouragement'. Evelyn unexpectedly found him a more modest man 'than one would imagine, by the relation of the Crue he had sorted with. He brought a map, of his observations of the Course of the winds in the South-Sea, & assured us that the Maps hitherto extant were all false as to the Pacific-sea.'[55] Dampier's book was a great success, not only because it was a tale of buccaneering adventure but also because it gave clear details of the flora, fauna and people that he had encountered, together with navigational information.

In addition to Pepys and Evelyn, Dampier also impressed Hans Sloane and other members of the Royal Society. With his new journey he aimed to circumnavigate Terra Australis, which he judged distinct from New Holland, and to investigate its commercial potential. In the event, hindered by a difficult crew, he was only able to explore the barren north-west coast of Australia before sailing towards New Guinea. Although his ship, the *Roebuck*, foundered at Ascension Island in February 1701, Dampier was able to return to London on an East Indiaman, bringing back with him material for a new book, *A Voyage to New Holland*, and specimens of some forty Australian plants that are now in the Sherardian Herbarium in Oxford. The book, which Dampier described as being for those 'who are curious to know the Nature of the Inhabitants, Animals, Plants, Soil, etc in those distant Countries, which have either seldom or not at all been visited by any Europeans', was published in 1703, by which time Pepys was either gravely ill or dead. Nevertheless, the volume is in his library, which suggests that he felt it imperative that John Jackson should purchase and bind it up to complete his collection.[56]

Pepys's book collection reflected an interest in both naval matters and descriptions of distant lands, their peoples and cultures. These interests are in fact complementary, for the aim was to both protect Charles II's kingdoms and develop their trading power. In 1672, the Duke of Buckingham wrote, 'The undoubted interest of England is Trade, since it is that only which can make us either Rich or Safe; for without a powerful Navy, we shall be Prey to our Neighbours, and without Trade, we could neither have Sea-Men nor Ships.'[57] In the mid-seventeenth century the Dutch enjoyed naval supremacy, but also depended for their enduring prosperity on being at peace with their European neighbours. With the reforms of the English navy undertaken by Pepys and his colleagues, this Dutch supremacy was threatened not only in Europe but also along trade routes around the world, making possible the development of a British Empire.

Perhaps the final tribute to Pepys for his work in building up the navy was to have his own island. This was discovered by the English buccaneer, William Ambrose Cowley, on a voyage to the South Atlantic in 1683. In a manuscript atlas originally owned by Hans Sloane, the island is shown in glowing greens with the Stuarts commemorated by Mount Charles and Mount James, Prince George, Princess Ann (*sic*) and Catherine Points, but to Pepys goes the honour of Mr Secretary's Point, and the name of the island itself.[58] No one since 1683 has been able to find it, and it is now officially classed as a phantom island, possibly one of the Falkland Islands. It is rather like the dramatic imaginings of Ben Jonson, and there is no doubt that it is the most exotic extravagance associated with Samuel Pepys.

9

THE AFFECTION WHICH WE
HAVE TO BOOKS

A T THE VERY outset of their personal acquaintance, John Evelyn gave Samuel Pepys a book that he had translated, inscribing it, 'Be pleased to accept this trifle'. The book, Gabriel Naudé's *Instructions concerning Erecting of a Library*, first published in France in 1627, had been aimed at wealthy collectors, so that at the time that he received the book, Pepys felt it to be 'above my reach'.[1] However, Evelyn had noted Pepys's interest and wanted him to join the network of book lovers. Evelyn translated Naudé's advice that such a person should publish and make known to everybody

> the affection which we have to Books, and the extraordinary desire which we have to erect a Library; for this being once divulged and communicated, it is certain, that if he who designed it to be in sufficient credit and authority to do his friends pleasure; there will not be a man of them but will take it for an honour to present him with the most curious Books that come into his hands; and that will not [vo]luntarily admit him into his Study, or in those of his friends.[2]

The friendship that was to develop between Evelyn and Pepys was to be strongly enhanced by their shared love of books.

Neither inherited a library, and both men began to collect books early in their lives. Evelyn became a serious book-buyer during his travels in Europe in the 1640s, making note of the date and place of purchase; the flyleaves of his early acquisitions show that he acquired works in Paris in 1643, Rome in 1644 and Venice in 1645, all centres of bibliographical excellence. He also added his motto taken from 1 Thessalonians 5:21, *Omnia Explorate, Meliora Retenite* ('Prove all things: hold fast that which is good'). Pepys began in a modest way while at Magdalene, purchasing his books from the Cambridge bookseller William Morden. In one book he wrote the inscription 'musaeo Samuelis Pepys'. This is unusual for two reasons: first, because Pepys rarely marked his books, and second, because he was indicating that the volume was part of a collection of interesting objects, a cabinet of curiosities.[3] In the early years of his collecting, Pepys referred in his diary to 'my books', but in 1668, when the number had reached 500, he talked of his 'library'. By the end of their lives, Pepys had amassed a library of 3,000 titles whilst Evelyn's stood at over 4,000 plus 800 pamphlets; not prodigious numbers, but substantial, on a par with those of Robert Hooke, Robert Boyle and John Locke. This was a period when most gentlemen numbered their books in hundreds, whilst tradesmen would be lucky to own enough titles to fill a shelf.

In 1689, alarmed at the number of notable book collections that had been sold up, Evelyn wrote a long letter to Pepys in which he praised him for his intention to 'secure what (with [so much] Cost and Industrie) you have Collected, from the sad dispersions, many noble Libraries [and Cabinets] have [suffered] in these late times: One Auction [I may call it diminution] of a day or two, having scatter'd what has ben gathering many [years]'.[4] It is ironical, therefore, that Evelyn's own library suffered just such a fate. The process had in fact begun in his own lifetime, but gathered speed in the nineteenth century, ending in a dramatic climax with the sale at Christie's in 1977 and 1978. However, we have a good record of what was in his library with the manuscript catalogue that he compiled in about 1687, and in the twentieth century the bibliographical scholar Geoffrey Keynes was given access to the collection and wrote a detailed account.[5] As a result of the twentieth-century auction, Evelyn's books are to be found in libraries across the world, but nearly 300 volumes, including many of his horticultural books, were bought by the British Library.

Evelyn's collection of books, as shown in the catalogue to his library, reflected his personality and his particular interests. He considered his library to be for edification, instruction and devotion; thus, more than a quarter of the books recorded were theological titles, while a fifth were histories. Sections were devoted to poetry and drama, philology, law, grammar, rhetoric and logic, mathematics and music, medicine, philosophy and politics. These were conventional areas for gentlemen's libraries of the time, but Evelyn also had a special subject category, 'Historiae Materiarum & Oeconom: Rei Rustici Mechanologici, &', consisting of 127 books and 36 pamphlets. These were works on horticulture, botany, husbandry and forestry, including books published in Europe, which not only showed Evelyn's particular interest in 'hortulan affairs' but also served as important reference for his own writings.

Although Evelyn's library was largely conventional, it was also modern. He did not collect antiquarian books and manuscripts, preferring to concentrate on his own times and the works of his contemporaries. When the first part of Edward Hyde, Lord Clarendon's *History of the Rebellion* was published in 1702, Evelyn and Pepys were fascinated to read his take on the era that they had both lived through. In a letter to Pepys, Evelyn applauded Clarendon's elegant style and his lack of desire for revenge for the shabby treatment meted out to him in 1667 when he had been forced into exile (p. 43). Evelyn went on to declare:

> I acknowledge myself so transported with all the parts of this excellent History; That knowing (as I did) most of the person[s] then Acting the Tragedy, and thos against it; that I have no more to say, but much, very-much to Admire . . . and that by the time he has don, there will need no other History or Account of what past during the Reigne of that suffering and unfortunate Prince [Charles I], to give the World a piece equal to anything Extant, not onely in our owne poorely furnish'd Historys of this, but of any Nation about us.[6]

This is the last surviving letter from Evelyn to Pepys, as the latter died four months later. But we do know that Pepys was equally enthusiastic about the book, writing to Clarendon's son, Laurence Hyde, expressing his pleasure in a less convoluted manner.

Some of the same titles appear in the library of Samuel Pepys, but his collection is based on a very different remit. The proportion of religious books, for instance, is smaller than in Evelyn's library. Whilst Evelyn remained a staunch Anglican throughout his life, Pepys pursued a much more complex path as far as his religious views were concerned. He grew up in London during the Civil War and Oliver Cromwell's Protectorate, attending the most Puritan-minded of all the city's schools, St Paul's, and describing himself as a 'great roundhead'. His diary shows that with the Restoration he regularly attended Anglican services, but did not take communion, was easily distracted from boring or poor sermons by the sight of pretty women, and recorded critical remarks concerning members of the clergy. It was music rather than words that transported him to another plane.

Kate Loveman, in her recent study of Pepys and his books, shows how he moved from anti-clerical views towards a thorough scepticism of scriptural authority and the ability of individuals or institutions to interpret it.[7] Both Evelyn and Pepys had in their libraries the great Polyglot Bible compiled by Brian Walton, Bishop of Chester, and involving the most learned scholars at Oxford. This immense work, funded by subscription, with texts in nine languages and six volumes of folio, kept the printing presses in London busy from 1654 to 1657. Despite, or perhaps because of, its immense size, Evelyn eventually donated his Polyglot Bible to the Cranston Library (pp. 233–4). But it was a work that was central to Pepys's theological study, for it enabled him to look at the priority and correctness of the different versions of the scriptures. In the end he was not persuaded that Walton had proved his case, and continued to regard the scriptures as unstable, and to doubt the authority of the Church, Protestant or Catholic, to adjudicate. These were, however, difficult times. In the 1670s he had been obliged to refute in Parliament the accusation of closet Catholicism, and had lied about having 'papist' books in his library. When in the 1680s he came to catalogue his library, Pepys divided his religious books into five categories: liturgies, 'Liturgick Controversies', scripture, sermons and preachers, and 'for private devotion'. By separating those of his books concerning inner conviction from those to be observed by visitors, he was avoiding the perilous waters in which he had earlier swum.

Pepys's books reflect his interests in the theatre, music and science. Writing to his Oxford friend Arthur Charlett in 1694, he described himself as

being (God knows) not only noe prætender to, much lesse Professor of, any of the learned Facultys, but on the Contrary, a Person knowne to have pass'd the greater and more docible part of my Life, in one unintermitted Cours, or rather Tumult of Businesse, I have had very little Selfe-Leasure to read, and as few Temptations therefore, as Opportunitys of lookeing-out for Curiositys on any other Head, then that whereto I have thus singly beene given-up. I mean the Sea.[8]

Indeed, his collection of maritime works was large and comprehensive, reflecting his long career in naval administration and his research for his book, *Memoires*. The collection included manuscript descriptions of great voyages, such as Edward Fenton's account of his travels with Martin Frobisher, given to Pepys by John Evelyn. One of his great treasures was part of the Anthony Roll, a gift from Charles II, recording in 1546 the forty-six ships of Henry VIII's navy, including the only representation that we have of the ill-fated *Mary Rose*. Pepys also managed to take home with him on his retirement no fewer than seventeen volumes of Admiralty letterbooks, despite appeals from his successor for their return.

But Pepys was being unduly modest when he claimed he was not well read. Nor was he accurate in saying that he did not look for curiosities beyond those connected with the sea, for his collection includes many examples of incunabula. The term comes from the Latin for swaddling clothes and refers to the infancy of printing, reckoned to be before 1501. He defined his criteria in a table, 'Of the Origine & Growth of Printing in England', that he bound into his copy of Joseph Moxon's

Mechanick Exercises. This was based on his own observations, along with advice from Moxon himself, who kept a shop selling maps, globes and scientific instruments, and from John Bagford. Bagford was born in Fetter Lane in London around the year 1650, and worked as a shoe-maker. Despite his lack of academic education, by 1686 he was engaged in the book trade around Holborn, collecting early printed editions for a history that he planned to write. At the same time, he was looking out for incunabula for some of the leading collectors of the day, including Pepys's physician, Hans Sloane, and for Pepys himself. Pepys's collection contains six books by William Caxton, and seventeen examples of the work of Caxton's assistant and successor to his business, Wynkyn de Worde. In the letter quoted above, Pepys was probably being evasive because Charlett was asking for details of what he owned to include in a planned catalogue of medieval manuscripts currently in private hands. Pepys was concerned that he would be subject to constant demands for access to his library, so prevaricated: 'How farr a Masse of Papers, for the most part unconnected, and those out of any of the trodden Roads of common Reading, can bee thought convertible to publick use, I must acknowledge I cannot see'. Nevertheless, he agreed to try to help once he had sorted out his papers. In a letter to Evelyn, he quoted Charlett: 'We must not forget Mr Evelyn's MSS; and what became of Sir Richard Browne's?' Evelyn's response was: 'As for Manuscripts, my stock is so trifling.'[9]

Other collections in Pepys's library are very unusual. By the time of his death, he had built up a collection of over 1,700 ballads, constituting the largest single collection of its kind. Ballads were single sheets, printed with the words of songs, usually accompanied by a picture, sold for a penny or two in the streets. Pepys sometimes mentions in his diary that he bought sheets to perform the songs, but then probably threw away the paper or copied the words into a commonplace book. However, he started to make his collection quite late in his life, at a period when he could see that black-letter printing (Gothic) with pictures was fast giving way to white letter (Roman) and no pictures. It was a prescient thing to do, because the ephemeral and fragile form of the ballads means that they have often perished; after all, paper was at a premium, being used to wrap cheese, light pipes, and to line the pie dishes of pastry cooks. Over half the items in Pepys's collection are the only known copies in existence.

Alongside the ballads, Pepys built up a collection of 215 chapbooks, which are also unusual. A chapbook was a book of between four and twenty-four pages, roughly printed on cheap paper and sold at under sixpence. Pepys owned some in quarto format, but the majority were smaller, in octavo and duodecimo, and with his customary orderliness he divided them into 'Vulgaria', 'Penny Merriments' and 'Penny Godlinesses'. His collection includes almanacs, 'penny dreadfuls', histories and practical books, among which are some cookery titles, and a few pious booklets.

Quite different in style is his collection of calligraphy. In the 1690s Pepys met Humphry Wanley, a haberdasher's apprentice from Coventry, who shared his passion for codes, handwriting and ancient texts. Pepys not only introduced Wanley to his friends in Oxford and London with library connections, but also sent him samples of calligraphy from medieval manuscripts for comment. Wanley's replies, with notes on dates and contents, were transcribed into albums along with the samples. These seem to have been acquired by Pepys as he trawled through the capital's bookshops and wrote to libraries asking them to supply the gaps in his collection, with remarkably successful results. Wanley was to become a leading curator, expert on Anglo-Saxon manuscripts and a founder, with John Bagford, of the Society of Antiquaries.

These various genres seem an odd miscellany, but there is method behind their collection. The clue appears to lie in the inscription that Pepys put in one of his earliest books bought in Cambridge, 'musaeo Samuelis Pepys'. Gradually, through his acquisition of books, manuscripts and ephemera, he was building up a museum of his own life and times, seizing chances offered to preserve technologies that were rapidly changing. The record of his own life is also to be seen in his collection of prints. He was introduced to this genre by Evelyn, one of the first British collectors.[10] Evelyn's enthusiasm for prints began when he went on his European travels: the earliest reference to an acquisition in his 1687 catalogue is a set of cartouches which he bought in Paris in 1643, and he bought avidly during his visit to Italy. Some idea of the subjects he chose to acquire is given in a letter that he wrote many years later: 'Nor was I onely curious of antiquities, but of all modern edifices, gardens, fountains, prospects of cities, countries, sieges, battels, triumphs, publique and famous solemnities, sports, executions, cavalcades; the effigies and portraits of greate persons; habits, machines, inventions, emblems, devises, animals, pictures, chart and maps innumerable.'[11] Evelyn's collection of 'effigies and portraits of greate persons' also included engraved images of himself, his wife and her parents, commissioned in 1650 after drawings 'ad vivum' from the Parisian artist, Robert Nanteuil (Plates 22 and 23).

From an early age, Evelyn loved drawing and would have liked to have studied art formally, but met opposition from his father, with his tutor at Oxford, George Bradshaw, reporting: 'As for his drawing and painting I shall be care[ful] to see him use it as his recreation, not as his businesse'.[12] He was, however, able to fulfil at least part of his ambition by learning the art of etching when he returned to London in the late 1640s. Louis XIV and Prince Rupert were both amateur etchers, and a knowledge of the principles was regarded as part of noble education. Evelyn produced etchings not only to give as gifts to his friends and family but also, albeit briefly, in 1649 to be published and sold on the open market in London. The publisher of Evelyn's first prints, a set of imaginary landscapes, was Thomas Rowlett, one of a group of printmakers who had struggled to make a living as the Civil War drew to a close – a period hardly conducive to the success of their enterprise, especially as some of the artists had Royalist connections.[13] It is not known who taught Evelyn to etch, but it was probably one of the group, and Evelyn may have helped to finance Rowlett.

Evelyn's career as an engraver was a brief one, and his serious print collecting came to an end in 1655. In the letter quoted above he explained: 'as it took up a great deale of time and no little mony; and that the thirst of still augmenting grew upon me, I at last gave it over, contenting my selfe with a competent number, and very seldome since enquiring after more of any sort'.[14] Instead, he began to write a monograph on the subject, entitled *Sculptura*, which was published in London in 1657. In this Evelyn attempted to write a history of a subject that had been previously ignored, beginning with technical terms, taking the reader from antiquity through to the invention of printmaking, with what Antony Griffiths terms 'a breathless list of its greatest masters'.[15] Then followed a chapter on drawing and another on the newly invented art of the mezzotint, although this was radically truncated as Prince Rupert would not give permission to publish any useful information. Evelyn intended to accompany this text with a translation of a practical treatise written in 1645 by his friend, the French engraver Abraham Bosse, but he was pipped to the post by a translation made by the English printmaker William Faithorne.

Visiting Evelyn at Sayes Court in November 1665, Pepys described in his diary how his host showed him some engravings, and also 'the whole secret of Mezzo Tinto and the manner of it'.[16] This was early in their friendship, but Evelyn recognised Pepys's interest in prints. Four years later, when Pepys was planning to take Elizabeth on holiday to France, Evelyn supplied him with letters of introduction to Abraham Bosse and Robert Nanteuil in Paris. He assured him that they 'will abundantly satisfy your Curiosity; and you will do well to purchase of them what they have of most rare of their own Works, as well Books as Tailles-Douces'.[17]

Pepys built up a collection that included the subjects quoted by Evelyn in his letter, concentrating particularly on the topography of Rome, Paris and London. But he extended the range beyond what Evelyn might have thought of acquiring, especially in his London section. In his catalogue, Pepys listed for London 'maps, buildings & monuments, churches, Thames and its views, magistracy & justice, solemnitys, habits, crys'. The last category was three series of the Cries of London, which he had pasted on successive pages in a large album. The earliest set, dating from the beginning of the seventeenth century, has woodcut illustrations of male and female criers set in arcaded niches. Their order suggests a procession through time, beginning with the town-crier at daybreak, with interruptions by the bellman and watchman (Plate 62). A second set, also of wood engravings, probably dates from 1640. The third is made up of individual prints in metal, created by Marcellus Laroon and published in 1687 (Plate 63). Although Pepys described the first two sets as 'antient', Laroon's prints were so 'moderne' that he was able to caption some of them with the names of criers known to him. Laroon, a Frenchman born in The Hague, came to London as a costume painter in the studio of Sir Godfrey Kneller. Not only is it highly likely that he painted the drapery in Kneller's 1689 portrait of Pepys, he may also have painted an earlier portrait of the diarist with Harwich in the background.[18]

If the London cries are equivalent to the ballads and chapbooks in Pepys's library, another genre echoes his grander books: engraved portraits of distinguished people. During the 1690s, Pepys and Evelyn conducted a detailed correspondence on this subject. In his *Numismata*, published in 1697, Evelyn provided a survey of the people whose portrait the reader would like to know, and most of the groups he mentioned can be found in Pepys's print collection. One of the most poignant pages in Pepys's album entitled 'Gentlemen, Virtuosi, Men of Letters & Merchants' is made up of a group of five men arranged in a circle around Pepys himself. He had always had the capacity for conviviality, but these were what he felt to be his closest lifetime friends (p. 98 and Plate 26).[19]

The diary of Samuel Pepys, kept for so tantalisingly short a period of time, nevertheless gives us a great deal of information about his books, as well as rare details about attitudes to books and to reading within his household.

As with his playing of music, Pepys would read at all hours of the day. In October 1660, he recorded how he began to read an English version of a novella by the French writer, Paul Scarron, *The Fruitless Precaution*, 'which I read in bed till I had made an end of it and do find it the best-writ tale that ever I read in my life'.[20] Reading in bed cannot have been easy, even with the best-quality wax candles that provided a steady white light and little smoke, unlike their tallow alternative. Just nine days later, Pepys found a solution when he met up in an alehouse with the instrument maker Ralph Greatorex, who showed him 'the manner of the Lamp glasses, which carry the light a great way'. This was possibly a concave glass set behind a lamp or candle, but whatever its arrangement, Pepys realised that it was 'Good to read in bed by and

I intend to have one of them'.[21] More usually, he read in his closet or chamber where he housed his books, sometimes reading aloud with friends. In June 1663, for example, he noted how with Lord Sandwich's servant John Creed he 'spent the most of the afternoon reading in Cicero and other books' and discussing the texts.[22]

Again, as with his music-making, Pepys had no hesitation in reading on the move. Returning from Woolwich by public coach in October 1664, 'an ordinary woman prayed me to give her room to London, which I did, but spoke not to her all the way, but read as long as I could see my book again'.[23] This rather unchivalrous behaviour contrasts with another coach journey out to Epping Forest in Essex in May 1668, when one of his travelling companions was a lone lady, 'whom I took great pleasure in talking to, and did get her to read aloud in a book she was reading in the coach, being the King's Meditations [the prayers of Charles I printed at the end of his *Eikon Basilike*]'. It no doubt helped that the said lady was 'tolerable handsome, but mighty well spoken', whilst the shunned woman on the Woolwich coach was dismissed as 'ordinary'.[24] Pepys read on horseback and while being rowed up and down the Thames. He also read while walking, ensuring in the summer of 1663, as he prepared to set out for Walthamstow, that he had with him a 'book of Latin plays which I took in my pocket, thinking to have walked it'.[25] Perhaps his most perilous walk while reading was over fields on an icy December night 'by light of link, one of my watermen carrying it and I reading by the light of it, being a fine, clear dry night'.[26] He also read books in taverns and shops. Barbers offered not only musical instruments but also books for their waiting customers. In December 1664, Pepys recorded going to have his hair cut and finding 'a copy of verses, mightily commended by some gentleman there'.[27]

Elizabeth Pepys shared Samuel's love of books, in particular enjoying French novels. Pepys described how she sat up after he had gone to bed because she could not tear herself away from *Polexandre* by Marin Le Roy de Gomberville in no fewer than five volumes. Elizabeth was clearly made of stern stuff, because Pepys also records buying for her *Ibrahim, ou l'illustre Bassa*, a fashionable romance by Madeleine de Scudéry, in four volumes, and in the same year, 1668, *Cassandra* by Gaultier Coste

De La Calprenède, this time in ten volumes. On one occasion Elizabeth used her reading to point out the error of her husband's ways. On 19 December 1664, the couple came to blows over Elizabeth's management of the servants, and Samuel gave her a black eye. Elizabeth retreated to await the healing of her bruises and consider her position, coming to the conclusion that much of her trouble arose from her husband's bouts of jealousy. She turned to Philip Sidney's *Arcadia*, a text that was regarded as relevant in matters between the sexes and men's respect, or lack thereof, for women. Pepys returned home on 2 January,

> thinking to be merry [but] was vexed with my wife's having looked out a letter in Sir Ph. Sidny about jealousy for me to read, which she industriously and maliciously caused me to do; and the truth is, my conscience told me it was most proper for me, and therefore was touched at it; but took no notice of it, but read it out most frankly. But it stuck in my stomach.[28]

In happier times Samuel and Elizabeth enjoyed reading together. On one winter evening in 1666, after supper, Pepys read 'something in Chaucer with great pleasure' to his wife and his brother.[29] Husband and wife shared a love of the theatre, and together read plays. One of their favourites was Sir William Davenant's musical drama, *The Siege of Rhodes* (p. 144). One summer they took two of their servants on a trip upstream on the Thames, bringing with them a copy of the play. Pepys's verdict was that it had been 'a fine day – reading over the second part of *The Siege of Rhodes* with great delight'.[30]

Pepys was an inveterate buyer of plays, which were produced in quarto format for around a shilling, and he liked to read up in preparation for his visits to the theatre. In his diary he makes a clear distinction between the effectiveness of scripts read and plays seen. He read with pleasure a translation of Corneille's *Le Cid*, but when he saw it performed as *The Valiant Cidd* at the Cockpit in Whitehall, he thought it 'a most dull thing acted', adding that the King and Queen felt the same, not smiling once, despite its billing as a tragi-comedy.[31] A similar response came when he went to see Ben Jonson's *Catiline*: he judged it 'a play of much good sense and words to read, but that doth appear the worse upon the stage'.[32] He once decided to try to read the text during the performance, as if following a score at a concert: 'in Paul's churchyard I bought the play of *Henery the fourth*. And so went to the new Theatre [the Theatre Royal in Vere Street] ... and there saw it acted; but my expectation being too great, it did not please me as otherwise I believe it would; and my having a book I believe did spoil it a little.'[33] This was probably one of the parts of Shakespeare's *Henry IV*. Pepys did not repeat the experiment.

The two servants who went on the reading expedition on the Thames in 1666 were Mary Mercer, Elizabeth's current gentlewoman, and Jane Birch, who had been with the Pepyses since their marriage. Pepys felt it was important that his servants should be able to read. This was made almost embarrassingly apparent one time when Pepys brought guests home to dine. His wife and the servants had been particularly busy as it was washing day, and so decided to send out for food from a cookshop nearby, but 'had so little wit to send in our meat from abroad in the cook's dishes, which were marked with the name of the Cooke upon them; by which, if [the guests] observed anything they might know it was not my own dinner'.[34] This was not merely a social gaffe, for Pepys recognised that for shopping, cooking and keeping of accounts, it was helpful for his household to be literate. When Jane Birch's eleven-year-old brother, Wayneman, arrived from the village of Dymock in the Forest of Dean to serve as a footboy, Pepys recorded that he 'had the boy up tonight for his sister to teach him to put me to bed, and I heard him read, which he doth pretty well'.[35] Wayneman's successor as footboy, Tom Edwards, read to Pepys to help him sleep after the upsetting experience of seeing London in flames in September 1666, while Pepys got Will Hewer to read passages from a Latin testament to improve his knowledge of the language.[36]

As Pepys's eyesight deteriorated, he required Tom Edwards to read texts out to him. In his diary for 27 May 1668 he noted that he

then made the boy to read to me out of Dr. Wilkins his *Real Character*, and particularly about Noah's arke, wherein he doth give a very good account thereof, showing how few the number of the several species of beasts and fowls were that were to be in the arke, and that there was room enough for them and their food and dung.

On Christmas Day that year, Pepys made him read a life of Julius Caesar, and 'Des Cartes book of music – the latter of which I understand not, nor think he [probably Lord Brouncker] that writ it'.[37] These sessions must have been meaty fare for the young boy. Elizabeth was also roped in to read complicated texts to her husband, and one reference in Samuel's diary talks of 'hiring' her, in other words, bribing her to spend two evenings on Robert Boyle's *Origine of Formes* that Pepys himself had admitted to finding hard going.[38]

Naudé proposed a form of etiquette among book lovers (as noted on p. 218), which Kate Loveman, in *Samuel Pepys and His Books*, calls 'book hospitality'. John Evelyn embraced the concept with enthusiasm. His correspondence shows that he was constantly presenting copies of his own writings to friends and to those whom he wished to impress. Carefully compiled lists of intended recipients for his works survive among his manuscripts, sometimes stipulating special bindings for the most eminent. He noted in his diary 'Being casualy in the Privy Gallery at White-hall, his Majestie [Charles II] gave me thanks (before divers Lords & noble men) for my Book of *Architecture* & *Sylva* againe: That they were the best designd & usefull for the matter & subject, best printed & designd ... that he had seene'.[39] In turn, Evelyn's library contained a remarkably high proportion of presentation copies from others, across a wide range of subjects. Samuel Hartlib, for instance, gave him the third edition of his *Legacy of Husbandry*, published in 1655. Jeremy Taylor, who wielded the greatest influence on Evelyn's spiritual life, presented him with a copy of his *Collection of Offices or Forms of Prayer* in 1658. Robert Boyle, whom he greatly admired, gave him no fewer than ten of his works, and Evelyn inscribed in each 'ex dono Authoris illustriss[imi]'. Giles Mandelbrote suggests that this assiduity was not just a result of Evelyn's sense of honour and obligation, but may also reveal 'a somewhat tiresome persistence in seeking out such opportunities'.[40]

In the 1660s, Pepys was still learning the etiquette of 'book hospitality', as illustrated in a sub-plot running through his diary concerning his dealings with Abigail Williams, the mistress of his superior on the Navy Board, Lord Brouncker. Pepys discovered in 1665 that Williams had got one of the navy clerks to transcribe a book on the rates of navy ships without permission, and was concerned that she was intending to make a gift of it to a 'gallant'. Pepys felt that 'The book was a very neat one and worth keeping as a rarity' and therefore should be destined for the Navy Office. When Brouncker and Pepys asked Abigail to deliver the book to them, she arrived in person and asked that the copy should be destroyed, 'which was a plaguy deal of spite'. Six months later, after a dinner at Brouncker's home, Williams showed Pepys her closet, where 'endeed a great many things there are – but the woman I hate'.[41] The lady does seem to have aroused strong feelings of antipathy (as shown on p. 123), but the appropriate response as laid down by Naudé on being shown somebody's closet and the collections therein should be to express admiration, and to offer a gift of a book. This Pepys refused to do, and was told by mutual friends how Williams spoke 'mighty hardly of me' in particular for 'not giving her something to her closet'.[42] Her interpretation of his behaviour was that he was treating her as a whore rather than as a learned and cultured lady, and Pepys certainly had 'form' in this area, as shown by his attitude towards the mistress of Lord Sandwich (p. 90). More efforts to show him her closet are noted in the diary, but Pepys continued to refuse to play the elaborate game. The final twist in this story came in 1673, when Abigail accidentally knocked over a candle in the naval residence at Seething Lane and Pepys lost his home. Luckily he was able to get his library and papers out of the building before the fire took total hold.

John Evelyn's diary does not give us the rich detail about reading that can be gleaned from that of Pepys. However, it does make clear his championship of the idea of the public library. When he submitted to the King his ideas about rebuilding the City of London after the Great Fire, Evelyn's suggestions for the re-creation of St Paul's Churchyard included a public library to sit alongside the houses for clergymen, shops for stationers and a grammar school. The concept of a public library was not envisaged as in modern times: when Sir Thomas Bodley founded his 'Publique Librarie in the Vniversitie of Oxford' in 1602, graduates and 'sonnes of Lordes' were permitted entry by right, and any 'gentleman stranger' might apply to study. This meant that it was generally accessible to the cultured and the well-born. Evelyn's desire for a library in St Paul's Churchyard was to satisfy the needs of young, unbeneficed clergy. His plan of 1666 never got off the ground, but he continued to seek opportunities for men (never women) of culture but modest means to have access to books. Nearly twenty years later, Evelyn recorded in his diary how his friend Thomas Tenison, vicar of St Martin's in the Fields, told him of 'his intention of Erecting a Library in St Martines parish for the publique use' and asked him to persuade Christopher Wren to design such a building:

> [Tenison] told me there were 30 or 40 Young Men in Orders in his Parish, either, Governors to young Gent: or Chaplains to Noble-men, who being reprov'd by him upon occasion, for frequenting Taverns or Coffe-houses, told him, they would study & employ their time better, if they had books: This put the pious Doctor upon this designe, which I could not but approve of, & indeede a greate reproach it is, that so great a Citty as Lond: should have never a publique Library becoming it: There ought to be one at S.Paules, the West end of that Church (if ever finish'd), would be a convenient place.[43]

Dr Tenison's library in Castle Street is regarded as the first of its kind in London, surviving until the nineteenth century.

Evelyn may have influenced the founding of two other early 'public' libraries. Andrew Cranston, the vicar of Reigate in Surrey, was determined to promote education within his community. He was the earliest local correspondent of the Society for Promoting Christian Knowledge, the headmaster of the local school and the founder of the library 'for the use & perusal of the freeholders, vicar and inhabitants' of Reigate. Cranston founded his library in March 1701, and began to solicit books and monetary contributions from the local community, and also from his contacts in London. Six months later, John Evelyn, then based at

Wotton, obliged with the monumental Polyglot Bible in six volumes. Edited by Brian Walton in the 1650s, the bible offered parallel texts of scripture in nine languages, including Syriac, Arabic and Persian. Other books in the library suggest that Cranston was particularly interested in translations of the scriptures, and he noted in this gift 'Ex dono Ingeniossimi John Evelyn, Armiger' and his fellowship of the Royal Society.

Meanwhile, Thomas Plume, vicar of St Alphege in Greenwich and Archdeacon of Rochester, had decided to create a similar establishment in his native town of Maldon in Essex. In about 1699 he built a room especially to house his library for the education of gentlemen and for the use of the local clergy. In September 1665, when the plague was raging in London, both Evelyn and Pepys went to hear sermons given by Dr Plume; Pepys commented that he was 'a very excellent scholler and preacher'.[44] No direct connection has been made between Evelyn and Plume, but given that the latter was the former's local clergyman, it would seem highly likely that they met and talked about libraries. Plume collected approximately 7,400 books and 1,500 pamphlets for the library in Maldon – a huge number, covering a wide range of subjects. Both Cranston's and Plume's libraries are still housed in their original buildings.

Whilst Evelyn rarely records in his diary how he acquired his books, Pepys provides a rich seam of information about the booksellers that he used. When he was living in Westminster, Miles and Ann Mitchell were his local booksellers, with a stall in the great hall of the Norman kings. A mid-eighteenth-century engraving shows the interior of Westminster Hall with part of the walls lined by stalls and counters, along with courts of law, such as Chancery and the King's Bench, in session (Plate 58). Customers in the 1660s were obliged to make their purchases in the presence of the exhumed bodies of Oliver Cromwell and his generals, Ireton and Bradshaw, hung in irons. Pepys was clearly made of strong stuff, for he does not refer to these when recording his visits to the Mitchells' stall to buy newsbooks and political pamphlets.

The heart of London's book trade was based in St Paul's Churchyard and the streets just to the north: Warwick Lane, Little Britain and Duck Lane. Here, books, prints and pamphlets were sold from premises that ranged from narrow-fronted shops with the household living above to booths furnished with shutters that could be folded down to create a counter, sometimes squeezed in the spaces between the buttresses of the medieval cathedral. Some booksellers were not only retailers but owned the rights to certain texts, organising their printing, binding and distribution, making them like publishers in the modern sense.

In the early 1660s, Pepys's main bookseller was Joshua Kirton, to be found at the sign of the King's Arms in the easternmost area of the Churchyard by Paul's Cross. The range of books sold by Kirton is well covered by Pepys's entry for 10 December 1663:

> I did here sit two or three hours, calling for twenty books to lay this money [£2 to £3] out upon; and found myself at a great loss where to choose, and do see how my nature would gladly returne to the laying out of money in this trade. I could not tell whether to lay out my money for books of pleasure, as plays, which my nature was most earnest in; but at last, seeing Chaucer – Dugdales *History of Pauls*, Stow's *London*, Gesner, *History of Trent*, besides Shakespeare, Johnson, and Beaumonts plays, I at last chose Dr. Fuller's *worthys*, *the Cabbala, or collections of Letters of State* – and a little book, *Delices de Hollande* with another little book or two, all of good use or serious pleasure; and *Hudibras*, both parts, the book now in greatest Fashion for drollery, though I cannot, I confess, see enough where the wit lies. My mind being thus settled, I went by link home.[45]

In the 1660s, when Pepys was making his way in the world, and careful about the laying out of his money, he regarded buying books as a perilous exercise in self-indulgence, on a par with his sexual liaisons and visiting the theatre. On this occasion, he resisted the temptation of buying for pleasure and instead chose the more serious works. This moral caution was not to last, especially when he became a wealthy man.

Some booksellers specialised in particular subject areas and, given the variety of Pepys's library, it is not surprising that he patronised a wide range of shops. For his music, he went to his friend, John Playford, who traded out of the west porch of the Temple Church. For scientific books, he visited Joseph Moxon's shop in Warwick Lane, which also furnished him with terrestrial globes for Elizabeth. John Brown sold him his own manual on the use of the slide rule from his mathematical instrument shop in the Minories. His stationer, John Cade in Cornhill, supplied him with his first prints. For his ballads and chapbooks, Pepys would travel to London Bridge, the base for a group of specialist sellers known as the Ballad Partners. London Bridge was a teeming thoroughfare, the only bridge across the Thames and thus the main exit southwards to Canterbury and the Channel ports. Land was at a premium, so the shops and houses rose cliff-like, several storeys high. Pepys bought his 'Merriments and Godlinesses' from Josiah Blare at the Looking Glass and John Back at the Black Boy. The books may have been low in price, but they were produced and sold in bulk. When Blare died in 1707, the inventory of his shop showed he had over 31,000 'great and small books' including the highly profitable line of almanacs. It has been estimated that in the 1660s over 300,000 almanacs were produced annually, the equivalent of one for every three families in the kingdom. In 1668, John Back included at the end of one of his books, *Danger of Despair*, a trade list of further available publications, along with an announcement that he 'Furnisheth any Countrey Chapmen with all sorts of Books, Ballads, and all other Stationary-Wares at reasonable Rates'. The Ballad Partners were ideally placed to supply chapmen, hawkers and pedlars with their wares, often pre-packed for their convenience, before they set off around the country (Plate 60).

The Great Fire, which broke out in Pudding Lane, did not destroy the southern part of London Bridge thanks to a break provided by an earlier fire. The Ballad Partners were thus able to protect their wares, but the booksellers of St Paul's Churchyard were not so lucky. As the flames approached, George Tokefield, Clerk of the Stationers' Company, bundled the important records of the registrations made by booksellers and printers before the publication of titles into a barrow and wheeled them to safety at his house in Clerkenwell. His prescience was not shared by the booksellers, who decided for safety to put their stock in Stationers' Hall, in Christchurch, Newgate Street, and in the chapel of St Faith in the crypt of the cathedral. This proved a disastrous decision, for all three buildings perished, along with the stock. Pepys, in his diary entry for 26 September, reckoned that £150,000-worth of booksellers' stock had gone up in flames, while Evelyn put the figure even higher, at £200,000. 'Kirton, my bookseller, poor man, is dead', Pepys wrote the following year, 'I believe, of grief for his losses by the fire.'[46]

Some booksellers returned to St Paul's Churchyard and rebuilt their shops and their businesses. One such was James Allestree, whose cousin Richard was Dean of Christ Church, Oxford. In 1658, during the Commonwealth, Richard Allestree's book *The Whole Duty of Man* had been published anonymously because of its staunch Church of England stance. Come the Restoration, his name appeared on the work, which became such an outstanding success, a *sine qua non* for any Anglican household that could afford books, that it went on being reprinted right through to the early nineteenth century.[47] James was not his cousin's publisher, but Richard's financial help may have enabled him to build a well-appointed bookshop in St Paul's Churchyard. An idea of the layout is provided by his inventory taken at his death in December 1670. The ground floor was dedicated to business, with living quarters above. A counting house was placed at the back and the shop in front, furnished with presses and shelves. A decorative partition, consisting of a double arch with two doors, provided an inner sanctum where Allestree could entertain prospective authors, prestigious customers and members of the Royal Society, for with John Martin he was the institution's official printer and the publisher of John Evelyn's *Sylva* and Robert Hooke's *Micrographia*. During the diary years, Pepys became just such a prestigious customer.

Allestree's business partner, John Martin, did not return to the Churchyard, instead opening a shop at the sign of the Bell just west of Temple Bar. With Kirton's death, Pepys made Martin 'his' bookseller. In August 1667 he recorded meeting up with John Evelyn at Martin's bookshop and commiserating about the dire state of the nation. Evelyn, Pepys noted, 'tells me that wise men do prepare to remove abroad what they have, for that we must be ruined – our case being past relief, the Kingdom so much in debt, and the King minding nothing but his lust, going two days a week to see my Lady Castlemaine'.[48]

The modern concept of browsing through shelves of books did not pertain in the seventeenth century; when Pepys visited Kirton's shop, he mentioned in his diary how the bookseller would bring out titles from his stock that might be of interest to the customer. The apprentices would be sent out to paste notices of books on walls and on the door-posts of the shop, which may have resulted in an embarrassing incident in John Martin's shop in January 1668. Pepys confided to his diary how he 'stopped at Martins my bookseller, where I saw the French book which I did think to have had for my wife to translate, called *L'escholle de Filles*; but when I came to look into it, it is the most bawdy, lewd book that ever I saw ... so that I was ashamd of reading in it'. The apparently innocuous title belied a book that took the form of a conversation between an experienced woman and a virgin. When the book was published in France in 1655, the author, Michel Millot, was condemned and the book burned. Pepys, being Pepys, returned three weeks later, and bought the book in a plain binding 'because I resolve, as soon as I have read it, to burn it, that it may not stand in the list of books, nor among them, to disgrace them if it should be found'.[49]

In the 1660s, the leading publisher and bookseller of poetry, drama, prose romances and classical translations was Henry Herringman, who established his shop at the Blue Anchor in the Lower Walk of the New Exchange. He was the publisher of the leading English playwrights, including John Dryden. In June 1668, Pepys recorded visiting Herringman's shop and being warned that the playwright himself regarded his latest play, *An Evening's Love*, as fifth rate. The New Exchange encouraged women as well as men to do their shopping. Pepys took advantage of this by suggesting to Deb Willet that there she might leave a message about a possible assignation, away from the prying eyes of his wife, Elizabeth.[50] Pepys was even bolder when visiting the shop of the distinguished bookseller William Shrewsbury in Duck Lane. His first foray, according to his diary, came on 10 April 1668 when he bought *The Golden Legend*, a collection of lives of medieval saints by the thirteenth-century Dominican, Jacques de Voragine, and kissed the attractive Mrs Shrewsbury. Two weeks later he examined some of the books that had belonged to the disgraced French finance minister, Nicolas Fouquet, buying a Spanish book, *Summa de varones illustres* by Juan Sedeno, published in Toledo in 1590. At the same time he described in the language that he used for sexual exploits how he 'did find [Mrs Shrewsbury] sola in the boutique, but had not la confidence para hablar a ella. So lost my pains – but will have another time'. This proved wishful thinking, for no doubt the lady kept away when she saw Pepys approaching. The last time he saw her, she was pregnant, and he ungallantly pointed out that 'ella is so big-bellied that ella is not worth seeing'.[51]

It has been estimated that the booksellers suffered the greatest losses among London's tradesmen as a result of the Great Fire, and to pick themselves up used a variety of marketing ploys. One such was to run a lottery. This was a speciality of John Ogilby, one of the most colourful figures of the seventeenth-century book trade. In his *Brief Lives*, John Aubrey wrote that Ogilby began his career by paying off his father's debts in a lottery managed by the Virginia Company in March 1612, though this could well be apocryphal as Ogilby would have been twelve at the time. Pepys attended Ogilby's book lottery in February 1666, acquiring two books, a translation of Aesop's *Fables* and Ogilby's account of the coronation of Charles II. As both were finely illustrated, the first by David Loggan and the second by Wenceslaus Hollar, the tickets cost £2 each, with only one blank. Pepys avoided the blanks and triumphantly brought the books home in their white vellum bindings.[52] He would have found out about the lottery through a newspaper, *The Gazette*. An advertisement in 1668 runs: 'Mr Ogilby's lottery of books opens on Monday, the 25th instant, at the Old Theatre between Lincoln's Inn Fields and Vere Street, where all persons concerned may repair on Monday, May 18, and see the volumes, and put in their money.'

The issuing of catalogues was another means employed by booksellers to stimulate demand. The first general catalogue had been produced in 1595 by Andrew Maunsell, whose shop was located in Lothbury. He collected titles both in English and foreign languages as a guide to his customers, grouping them in subject categories, noting the originating bookseller, publication history and format, but quoting no prices. Maunsell was well ahead of his time, for the next bookseller to undertake such a project was William London, in 1657, in Newcastle upon Tyne. He was reaching out to 'the Wise, Learned and Studious in the northern Counties of Northumberland, the bishopric of Durham, Westmorland and Cumberland' with 'the most vendible Books in England Orderly & Alphabetically Digested'. London's catalogue, which took the form of a substantial 124 pages in quarto format, was recommended by John Evelyn to Sir Kenelm Digby in a copy of the only letter that survives between them.[53]

In 1668, Robert Clavell, whose shop was to be found at the Stag's Head near St Gregory's Church in St Paul's Churchyard, began to issue term catalogues, so called because they were published at the end of the law terms. These were distributed to his customers in London, but he also set out to exploit the provincial book market. Clavell had been a clerk in the Post Office under the administration of Lord Arlington after the Great Fire. In this capacity he was able to collect from local postmasters all over the country the names and addresses of provincial booksellers, and to dispatch to them parcels of title pages of books that were about to be published, which he had acquired, together with a fee for the service, from London publishers. He justified sending these parcels free of charge on the grounds that the Post Office revenues would ultimately increase as a result. This practice was challenged by a rival, the Fleet Street bookseller John Starkey, 'since Country Booksellers usually write by their Carryers, and post-masters do not much concern themselves with Bookes'. Starkey brought out a newspaper, *Mercurius Librarius*, at Michaelmas 1668, at sixpence per copy, where he carried advertisements from publishers but did not charge them for the service. Clavell, rattled, appealed via Arlington to the licensor of the press, Sir Roger L'Estrange, to rule that he should have sole licence to print catalogues of new books. L'Estrange diplomatically proposed that the two men should run *Mercurius Librarius* as partners, and so both names appeared on the Easter edition for 1669. However, given the commercial potential of the market, the quarrel between Clavell and Starkey rumbled on for many years.[54]

Pepys preferred to find out about his books through word-of-mouth recommendations, in coffee-houses, at dinner parties and talking to friends like John Evelyn. He called this 'crying up', a method still used today with reviews and bestseller lists. He may well have used specialist catalogues which were being developed at the very time that he had the financial means to add to his library. One of his booksellers in the 1680s was Robert Scott in Little Britain who produced catalogues of his anti-quarian books. In a letter to Pepys in June 1688 he sent him details and prices of various books that he had acquired for him, ending 'butt without flattery I love to find a rare boo[k] for you'.[55] We also know that Pepys bought books and manuscripts at auction.

The first auction identified for books occurred in 1676 when the bookseller William Cooper produced a sale catalogue and auctioned the library of Dr Lazarus Seaman, the former Master of Peterhouse, Cambridge. Cooper declared afterwards that the sale had been 'to the great content and satisfaction to the Gentlemen who were buyers'.[56] This marked the beginning of a hectic period for auctions, often involving the libraries of university scholars who did not have families to whom they could bequeath their books, and whose colleges already had similar collections. These sales often took place in coffee-houses, and it is interesting to note that some establishments became known more for their auctions than for their coffee. For example, Nathaniel Rolls set out advertising his coffee-house in Petty Canons Lane by the north door of the unfinished St Paul's Cathedral, but by the mid-1690s he was describing it as an auction house.

In a letter to Evelyn in November 1690, Pepys wrote how he 'was gone but to Covent Garden by Chaire, to try whither I could have layd out a little Mony well at an Auction of prints . . . but fayled, there coming no Heads [engraved portraits] in Play, dureing my stay, which was not above ½ an houre'.[57] This disappointment was tempered by the exotic meal that Pepys enjoyed later that day at the Houblon household (p. 189). He was by this time in poor health and often housebound, so it is not surprising that he made use of agents to attend auctions on his behalf. One of these was John Bagford; a letter from 1697 survives from Pepys asking him to acquire one of the last edition of *Stobaei Sententiae* at an auction to be held by the bookseller Robert Littlebury: 'I commis-sion you to secure it for me upon the easiest terms you can: letting me know, in the meantime, by a line or two, as soon as you may, whether I may expect to be supplied herewith from thence or no, that I may be at liberty to look out for it elsewhere.'[58]

One avid attendee of auctions was Robert Hooke. A paper in his hand lists no fewer than fifty-seven auctions and catalogues between August 1686 and August 1689, but apparently he went to even more than this impressive tally. He attended not only the dispersals of 'gentlemen's libraries', where he paid substantial sums, but also auctions held informally at open-air bookstalls in Moorfields, where volumes might be had for a few pence. Failures to pick up bargains were marked in his diary as 'MF o', but in March 1693 he came upon nearly 100 of the Dutch chemistry books of his late friend, Robert Boyle, 'exposed in Moorefeilds on the railes'.[59] The bookstalls were set up there against the railings of Bedlam Hospital that Hooke had designed.

One of the great practitioners in the art of auctioneering was Edward Millington, and a parody of his patter by Ned Ward, the 'London Spy', enables us to hear his voice:

> Here's an Old Author for you, Gentlemen, you may Judge his Antiquity by the Fashion of his Leather-Jacket; herein is contain'd for the Benefit of you Scholars, the Knowledge of every thing Written by that Famous Author, who thro' his Profound Wisdom, very luckily discovr'd that he knew nothing. For your Encouragement, Gentlemen, I'll put him up at Two Shillings, advance three Pence; Two Shilling once: What, no Body Bid? . . . Knock, and now you've bought him, Sir, I must tell you, you'll find Learning enough within him to puzzle both Universities. And thus much, I promise you further Sir, when you have Read him Seven Year, if you don't like him, bring him to me again, in Little Brittain, and I'll help you to a Man shall give you a Shilling for him to cover Band-Boxes.[60]

Rather surprisingly, Evelyn's library contained three of Millington's catalogues, for he cannot have been a fan of auctions, preferring to buy new rather than second-hand and referring to 'auction men' in disparaging terms to Pepys.[61] Nor, unlike Pepys and Robert Hooke, did he use his diary to record his visits to his booksellers. His correspondence, however, does cast occasional light on his relationship with them as far as his own books were concerned. One of the reasons that he gave for not continuing with the further volumes of his translation of Lucretius' *De Rerum Natura* was his disgust with the slovenly proofreading of the text during his absence in France in 1656, and he noted in his diary in 1661 how disappointed he was by the quality of the printing of *Erecting a Library*.[62] Thirty years later, he was still at odds with his publishers. In a very blunt letter in May 1691 to Richard Chiswell about the reprint of his *Kalendarium Hortense*, Evelyn complained about Chiswell's tardiness in sending him some author's copies to circulate among friends, something that he felt was very important. The letter ends: 'This delay has quite Spoild the Grace of it ... I therefore shall henceforth fore-warne all Scriblers, and impertinent Authors of Books (be they Profitable or Un-profitable) of what the Poet [Virgil] has said of other Animals *Sic vos non vobis* – Gentlemen, you have your labour for your Paines'.[63]

By 1666, Pepys's book collection had grown to such an extent that he needed to think about where to keep it, as his diary entry on 23 July attests:

> Up, and to my chamber, doing several things there of moment. And then comes Simpson, the Joyner, and he and I with great pains contriving presses to put my books up in; they now growing numerous, and lying one upon another on my chairs, I lose the use, to avoid the trouble of removing them when I would open a book.[64]

Thomas Simpson was the Master Joiner at the dockyards of Deptford and Woolwich, and together he and Pepys worked out how to produce presses with adjustable shelves and glass-panelled doors. Based on the design for ships' furniture, the presses could come apart, essential in the confined passageways of ships, with the doors in the lower section sliding upwards rather than opening outwards, to avoid the hazard of tripping. Pepys was so delighted with his new piece of furniture that he quickly ordered a second. The ability of the bookcases to be taken apart probably saved his book collection when Abigail Williams had her mishap with the candle, setting his home in Seething Lane on fire in 1673.

Each bookcase held about 250 books, with folios on the lowest shelves and octavo and quarto volumes ingeniously stepped on some of the other shelves to maximise space. With his growing wealth in the 1670s and 1680s, and his increased leisure time in the 1690s, more bookcases were added, so that by the time drawings were made of the library in York Buildings in 1699, there were seven lined up against the walls (Plate 28). Once a new press was acquired, Pepys drew up an alphabet and, a few months later, a catalogue or shelf list. In 1692 he decided to review and reorganise his collection, withdrawing to Clapham to put his papers in order. The following year he was ready for his 'Adjustment' of the books. They were marshalled in strict order according to size. If one did not match, out it went, unless a favourite, in which case it was made up to size with a wooden plinth disguised in gilt leather. There were three catalogues: one by name, a second by alphabet, and a third by subject. The three together were called *Supellex Literaria* ('literary furniture').

Pepys was able to draw on a group of assistants to help him organise his library. His clerk Paul Lorrain became Ordinary (chaplain) of Newgate Gaol in 1698, where one of the more lucrative aspects was to take down the last speeches of those condemned to execution at Tyburn and to publish them in ballad form; thus he shared Pepys's interest in ballads. Although employed at the prison, Lorrain continued to act as Pepys's library assistant, and sometimes is described as his footman. By the turn of the century, another member of the household, Daniel Milo, was also enrolled into library service. Further, and despite her spelling being described as of the picturesque school, Mary Skinner helped with scribing, for, like Elizabeth Pepys, she enjoyed reading. Her will made in 1715 refers to her library of two bookcases, and three specific bequests to Pepys's nephew, John Jackson, of books to which she had added her own illustrations.[65] Jackson played an essential role in purchases for Pepys's library. Sent off on his Grand Tour of Europe in 1699, he purchased a whole range of material for his uncle: books and manuscripts, sonatas by Corelli, guidebooks and engravings of Rome and its monuments. Evelyn commended Pepys on the breadth of his print collection as a result: he could think of no omissions.[66]

Pepys was a great organiser, a role that had been vital in his years as a naval administrator. This was not one of Evelyn's strengths, as was all too obvious in his cataloguing of his library, where his fascination with different methods sometimes bordered on the obsessional. By 1687 Evelyn's system had become very elaborate, arranged according to 'Intellectual Powers', and divided into six heads: three of Memory, three of Judgement, and then into nearly 120 subheadings. For the naming of his shelves, he tried letters and numbers for different subjects, abandoning this when he reached 'O'. He turned instead to the names of the Greek gods, Mercury and Apollo, and then moved on to the Nine Muses. This did not satisfy, so he took the twelve Roman emperors from Julius Caesar to Domitian, adding seven sages from Greece, and assigning subjects: poetry, for example, was given to the Muses; theology to the three Graces; military matters to the Furies; history and geography to the emperors, seasons and continents; science to the elements and the winds, and so on. There are echoes here of the ambitious approach of *Elysium Britannicum*, which eventually overwhelmed him, and in time the catalogue system proved so cumbersome that he had to revert to a more straightforward scheme.

It was the auction of the library of Lord Lauderdale that prompted Evelyn to write his letter to Pepys in August 1689 expressing his concern about the future of 'noble libraries'.[67] The future of his own library looked straightforward – it would be handed down through his family. Events in the 1690s seemed to strengthen this natural succession: in 1691 the death of his nephew made him heir to Wotton and he moved there three years later; in 1698 his surviving son also died, so that his grandson, Jack, became his heir. Jack was very interested in books, even enjoying his own little library when he came to stay with his grandparents at Wotton. John Evelyn downsized his library from the high-water mark of the 1687 catalogue, recommending to Jack that 'most of the trifling Books ... should be weeded out to give place to better till it were thro'ly purged'.[68]

Pepys, on the other hand, had rather different plans. In 1695 he wrote a memorandum encapsulating the principles that had guided him in the construction of his collection, making clear that he wanted it to be quite different from the 'Extensive, Pompous and Stationary Libraries of Princes,

Universities, Colleges and other Publick Societies', instead aiming for the 'Self-Entertainment onely of a solitary unconfined Enquirer into Books'.[69] Despite this statement, he was considering leaving his collection to one of the universities, coming down in favour of two colleges at Cambridge: Trinity, where there were traditional family associations, and Magdalene, his own college. He had retained a particular fondness for Magdalene, acting as a generous donor when in the mid-1670s a new building was proposed to house the fellows and relieve congestion. Although Robert Hooke was asked to design it, the style of the completed building looks old-fashioned, suggesting that it followed a plan drawn up in the 1640s by a local builder, and that Hooke's conception was cosmetic tinkering. Pepys not only contributed towards the new building, but gave £10 towards repairing one of the old buildings, with Mary Skinner adding her own donation of five guineas, marked in the college records as from 'Madm Pepys'.

In fact, the concern about the threat of overcrowding at Magdalene proved unfounded, and the fellows were at a loss as to what to do with the space in the new building. This could have been when Pepys suggested his own library might be housed there. With this in view, he began to lay down stipulations, finalising them in two codicils to his will in 1703. His nephew John Jackson was to enjoy the collection during his lifetime and to 'complete' the library by adding missing volumes or sets. On Jackson's death the library would go to Magdalene College, to be kept in a separate room, the *Bibliotheca Pepysiana*, and remain unchanged in perpetuity, without addition or subtraction. Should this stipulation be broken, then the library would go to Trinity.

Over the years, Pepys had built up an important library, as was recognised by his contemporaries. In 1708, when his collection was still in Clapham, John Bagford included it in his account of some of the major libraries 'in and about London'. His account neatly provides a bibliographical 'obituary':

> it consists of various Subjects, relating to English History, Maritime Affairs, the Power and Constitution of the Admiralty and Sea Laws. In his Life time he made a great Collection from our Records in the Tower and elsewhere, also our English Historians Antient and Modern.

There are the finest Models of Ships of all sorts, Ships painted by the best Masters, a Drawing of the Royal Navy of Henry VIII. There are Bookes of Musick, Mathematics and other subjects, rare in their kind; he spared no cost for compiling matters relating to the City of London, as Books, of Prints, Ground-plots, Maps, Views, Palaces, Churches, Great Houses, Coronations, Funerals, Publick Shows, Habits and Heads of famous Men, and all that could be collected, relating to London; and besides those that have been graved, he hath been at the Charge of Drawing those that never were in Print to illustrate the City of London, of which he was a Native, there is nothing in that Nature to compleat. He hath Heads of all sorts both English and Foreign, a Collection of Copy Books of all European Master, Italian, French, German, High and Low Dutch, Spanish and English, put in order of times and several Countries, and pasted on large Paper bound up. He hath likewise a large Book of Title Pages and Frontispieces, not only of our English Gravers, but of those of Italy, France, Germany, Flanders, Holland, etc. These are much augmented by Mr Jackson, his Nephew, in his Travels. There are any other scarce and valuable Books, dispos'd in an excellent order in 12 cases.[70]

EPILOGUE
And So to Bed

O
N 14 MAY 1703 Evelyn made the journey to Clapham to visit his
friend, despite having broken his shin bone, recording in his diary
that he found Pepys 'languishing with small hope of recovery which
much affected me'.[1]

This was the last time they saw each other, but John Jackson provided
Evelyn with a detailed account of Pepys's last days. When he died on 26
May an autopsy was performed on his body by the physicians Hans
Sloane and John Shadwell (son of the dramatist Thomas and one of
Pepys's godsons) with the surgeon Charles Bernard. They were following
John Jackson's wishes, 'for our own satisfaction as well as public good',
as he explained to Evelyn. Pepys would undoubtedly have approved of
this in the true Baconian spirit of scientific research. The findings
forcibly bring home the suffering Pepys must have endured in his last
years. The left kidney contained several irregular stones joined in a mass
adhering to his back. The surrounding areas, including his gut, were
much inflamed and septic, the bladder gangrenous and the old wound
from his stone operation had again broken open. The lungs were full of
black spots and foam.[2]

As soon as news reached him of Pepys's death Evelyn wrote a tribute
in his diary:

a very worthy, Industrious, & curious person, none in England exceeding him in the Knowledge of the Navy, in which he had passed thro all the most Considerable Offices, Clerk of the Acts, & Secretary to the Admiralty, all which he performed with greate Integrity: when K: James the 2d went out of England he layed down his Office, & would serve no more: But withdrawing himselfe from all publique Affaires, lived at Clapham with his partner (formerly his Cleark) Mr. Hewer, in a very noble House & sweete place, where he injoyed the fruit of his labours in g(r)eate prosperity, was universaly beloved, Hospitable, Generous, Learned in many things, skill'd in Musick, a very greate Cherisher of Learned men, of whom he had the Conversation . . . Mr: Pepys had ben for neere 40 years, so my particular Friend, that he now sent me Compleat Mourning: desiring me to be one to hold up the Pall, at his magnificent Obsequies; but my present Indisposition, hindred me from doing him this last Office.[3]

Evelyn was to survive him for almost three years, signalling his own end in his marathon diary on 27 January 1706 with: 'The Raine and a Thaw upon a deepe Snow, hindred me from going to Church. My Infirmitys increasing, I was exceeding ill this whole weeke.' His final entry runs: 'Let every one that names the L. Jesus depart from Evill, & increase in love of that profession.'[4] Evelyn died at his London house in Dover Street on 27 February.

A moving tribute to Evelyn was written by his widow in a letter to a friend:

it is not possible to be insensible of so great a losse. 58 years experience of the goodnesse kindnesse worth and virtue of such a friend, is not easily effaced . . . all is his due, I only comfort myself that having lived so long together wee may not be long parted, I cannot wish a happier state then to be where he is . . . I have obligation to him from my first being put into his hands, his way was tender fatherly and friendly and the continuance of his kindnesse held to the last moment, his memory must be precious to me.[5]

Mary was granted her wish to join her husband in February 1709. Wotton was duly inherited by his beloved grandson, Jack, who became Sir John Evelyn Bt in 1713. In his memoir written for his grandson, John Evelyn exhorted him to plant trees, 'which in a few years will prove of incredible Emolument & restore the Name of Wotton, otherwise in danger to be lost and forgotten, planting of Timber-trees being in truth the onely best and proper Husbandry the Estate is capable of'.[6] Jack did as his grandfather requested, adopting the new fashion of landscaping. He also followed his virtuosic interests, becoming a fellow of the Royal Society and of the Society of Antiquaries, although he never travelled abroad.

John Jackson, too, proved a worthy heir to Samuel Pepys. During his uncle's last hours, Pepys had asked Jackson to promise to be friends with Mary Skinner and to forget their former quarrels. By a codicil made shortly before his death, Pepys left an annuity of £200 to Mary as 'the most full and lasting acknowledgement of my esteem respect and gratitude to the Excellent Lady Mrs Mary Skyner for the many important Effects of her Steddy friendship and Assistances during the whole course of my life, within the last thirty-three years'. This last-minute addition to a will that had earlier made no reference to Mary suggests that he had intended a private arrangement to be worked out with Will Hewer as his executor, but then realised that this was inadequate provision. Mary herself may have insisted on her right to be acknowledged. Given her strength of character, the latter would seem likely, and as Claire Tomalin points out, 'you can only admire her spirit in the face of Pepys's persistent tendency to exclude women from the masculine world of the written word'.[7] The promise of friendship that Mary and John Jackson made at Pepys's bedside appears to have been honoured by both of them, for when Mary died in 1715, Jackson was her executor and she bequeathed almost everything that Pepys had left her to him and his family.

Jackson was unmarried when Pepys died, but in 1705 he expressed the desire to marry John Evelyn's granddaughter, Elizabeth Draper. His suit, however, was rejected, with Evelyn giving his reason as his inability to make a large enough settlement on Elizabeth. The idea of a dynasty that could be traced back to the two great diarists is a 'what if' beloved of historians. It is not quite on the same level as Richard III gaining a horse on Bosworth Field, or the Archduke Franz Ferdinand's chauffeur taking the correct route through the streets of Sarajevo in June 1914, but it is intriguing nevertheless.

Instead, Jackson married Ann Edgely, a cousin of William Hewer, and she proved vital in the arrangements for the future of Pepys's library. His cherished wish had been that his library should go to his old college, and he had laid down firm stipulations (as set out on p. 246). In the event, Magdalene kept to the terms, and the year after Jackson's death in 1723, his widow Ann arranged for the book collection to be transferred to the college. Jackson in fact died intestate, which could have caused problems for the fate of the library, but Ann, perhaps because of her closeness to Pepys through her cousin, ensured that the original terms were adhered to. The book collection was duly delivered to Cambridge, along with the furniture of the library – the bookcases, of course, but also double-sided portraits for the walls, terrestrial globes and Pepys's model ships. Just as the bookcases were original in concept, so too was his 'partner' desk, a central space to accommodate the knees of two sitters, and cupboards to hold outsize volumes.

Among the books was Pepys's diary. It seems extraordinary that he should have allowed this, given the explicit nature of some of its contents and the many entries that did not redound to his credit. Evelyn had carefully doctored his diary, often adding amendments years later, intending it to be a record of himself for future generations, but Pepys made no such revision in hindsight. Moreover, he carried out regular 'ejections' from his book collection, including the novel that he had written while at Cambridge that he probably felt was embarrassingly juvenile, and some of his purges were politically motivated. But the whole enterprise of his library was to stand as a monument to himself. In a paper, 'The Conditions of a Private Library', he explained that a library's subject holdings should be in proportion 'to the particular Genius [character] of their Owner'.[8] Among the stipulations that Pepys laid down to Magdalene was that only the Master had the right to borrow from the collection, just ten volumes at a time, and that they were to go no further than his Lodge. So Pepys had ensured that any readers of the diary, should they be able to decipher the shorthand, would be male, scholarly and in surroundings imbued with his spirit.

It is in some ways remarkable that the college was prepared to take on something that was so frozen in time. A German traveller, Nathanael Jacob Gerlach, visited Magdalene in 1728, just four years after the arrival of the collection. In his memoir of his travels in England he observed: 'The library has no *supplementa* [additions] and may not be moved from the spot but remains preserved *in honorem familiæ*. I look upon it as a *monumenta vanitatis*. After some time the whole lumber may grow out of date, the little gold blackened, and the use of the library vanish.'[9]

However, the Master of Magdalene at the time, Daniel Waterland, was delighted by the quality of the collection, exercising his privilege to take out the books. According to the Master's Borrowing Book, he took out publications on a wide range of subjects, around forty to fifty volumes annually, and the effect was to inspire the fellows to improve their own library provision, which was in a poor state.

Eventually, however, Gerlach's prediction was to prove accurate, and by the end of the eighteenth century the *Bibliotheca Pepysiana* had become a sleeping beauty. John Evelyn's collection, meanwhile, was kept in the room specially built by Sir John Evelyn at Wotton, experiencing the usual losses and additions of a family library. But then, in 1814, William Upcott came calling at the Evelyn family home. In the unlikely role of a fairy-tale prince arriving to wake the sleeping beauty, he changed the fate not only of the diary of John Evelyn, but also of Samuel Pepys. As a result, the two friends have become *the* commentators of Restoration England.

APPENDIX
The True Domestick Intelligence, or
News both from City and Country, published
to prevent False Reports, Friday,
31 October 1679
'Domestic Improvements'

SYLVA AND POMONA is come forth in a 3rd Edition, very much improved, and with considerable Additions. Tis esteemed by the Judicious, the most accomplished Volume that ever was published in any Language (and fittest for the Learnedst of our Nobility and Gentry). To increase and to encourage the Planting of Grove Woods and Forrests for Fuel and Timber, to adorne the stateliest Pallaces and fairest Mansions, and withal to reclaime Wast Lands to bear a perpetual and permanent profit: And to enlarge their Orchards for the best Fruit, and for the Richest Cider. The first Edition appeared Anno 1663. And it was then but a Prodromes [precursor] to what it is now grown to. And then it undertook the most difficult and hopeless of our Rural improvements, for it requireth the multitudes of hands at the Work, and considerable Charges, and making the slowest return of Profit; yet it hath prevailed among the Wisest and greatest in all the chief parts of England and Wales, and in Ireland amongst the Protestants, and in some parts of

Scotland amongst the Nobility. And now it appeareth very much to the honour and advancement of these three Kingdomes in Strength, Wealth and Health, and for most Innocent Delights, and most agreeable to all that have concerned themselves in these kinds of Culture; His Majesty giving the most perfect example and all other the most August Ornaments of his Royal Pallaces, and for the Advancement of his Kingdoms. You may see a Breviat of the 2nd Edit. in Phil Trans N.53.

The same most obliging Author hath given us the French Gardiner, and Mr Roses's English Vineyard, and a most excellent Kalender for all Curious Gardens, and a most profound and no less useful Discourse of Earths and Composts for all kinds of Agriculture and Hortinculture [*sic*]. And after all his other Learned Volumes which he hath published for the General good of all mankind, which are here forborn to be enumerated: he is now, I hear, finishing a most elaborate work for Princely Gardens, such as before was never offered to the World. And now if the Product and Effect shall answer the Noble Authors present Designs (as it hath done in some measure hitherto in these three kingdoms) will on a suddain become as the Garden of Eden, the most Flowery and flourishing Kingdomes of the Known World.

Printed by Nathaniel Thompson next the Cross-Keys in Fetter Lane.

NOTES

Introduction

1. Upcott's account, originally written in an autograph book, is reproduced in the first volume of E.S. de Beer, *The Diary of John Evelyn*, 6 vols, Clarendon Press, 1955 (hereafter JE diary), pp. 53–4.
2. 1821 edition, ii, Chapter 1.
3. *Memoirs of Samuel Pepys, Esq, FRS*, Henry Colburn, 1825.
4. Virginia Woolf, *The Common Reader*, vol.1, p. 83 in the Vintage Classics edition of 2003. The original essay had been written for the *Times Literary Supplement*, 28 October 1920.
5. *The Diary of Samuel Pepys*, ed R.C. Latham and W. Matthews, 12 vols, Bell & Hyman, 1970–83 (hereafter SP diary), vi, pp. 289–90, 5 November 1665.
6. Geoffrey Keynes, *A Study in Bibliophily*, Clarendon Press, 1984 edition, p. 3; SP diary, vii, p. 112, 29 April 1666.
7. JE diary; John Evelyn, *London Revived: Considerations for its Rebuilding in 1661*, ed. E.S. de Beer, Clarendon Press, 1938 (hereafter *London Revived*).
8. The Samuel Pepys Club official website, http://www.pepys-club.org.uk
9. Arthur Bryant, *Samuel Pepys: The Years of Peril* (1935), *The Saviour of the Navy* (1938), *The Man in the Making* (1939), all Cambridge University Press.
10. SP diary.
11. Frances Harris, *Transformations of Love*, Oxford University Press, 2003; *The Letterbooks of John Evelyn*, ed. Douglas C. Chambers and David Galbraith, University of Toronto Press, 2014 (hereafter *Letterbooks*). The originals are British Library (BL) Add. Mss 78298 and 78299.
12. Guy de la Bédoyère, *Particular Friends: The Correspondence of Samuel Pepys and John Evelyn*, Boydell Press, 1997 (hereafter *Particular Friends*); JE diary, v, p. 538, 26 May 1703.
13. Claire Tomalin, *Samuel Pepys: The Unequalled Self*, Penguin Viking, 2002; Gillian Darley, *John Evelyn: Living for Ingenuity*, Yale University Press, 2006.

1 Two Worlds

1. *Particular Friends*, p. 271, 22 July 1700.
2. JE diary, i, pp. 1–2.

3. Letter to Mary Evelyn, 29 January 1666, quoted in Harris, *Transformations of Love*, p. 58.
4. *Particular Friends*, p. 271, 5, 22 July 1700.
5. BL Add. Ms 78386, ff. 60–1, *Oeconomics to a newly married friend* (Margaret Godolphin).
6. William Bray (ed.), *Memoirs of John Evelyn*, i, London, 1819, p. 4.
7. BL Add. Ms 78315, f. 2, 31 May 1637.
8. JE diary, ii, p. 20.
9. JE diary, ii, p. 18.
10. Bodleian Library, Rawlinson A.182, p. 311, in the hand of Samuel's brother, Thomas.
11. Having survived the excruciating operation, Pepys celebrated its anniversary every year with a feast.
12. SP diary, ix, p. 218, 30 May 1668.
13. Quoting Henry de Bracton's treatise on the laws and customs of England.
14. *The Holy Commonwealth*, 1659, quoted in Christopher Hill's *The Century of Revolution, 1603–1714*, Cardinal Books, 1974, p. 110.
15. JE diary, ii, p. 79, 12 November 1642; p. 80, 7 December 1642.
16. Tomalin, *Samuel Pepys*, p. 21.
17. SP diary, i, p. 265, 13 October 1660; p. 280, 1 November 1660.
18. JE diary, ii, p. 547, 30 January 1649.
19. BL Add. Ms 78303, f. 34, 30 January 1649.
20. BL Add. Ms 78302, f. 4, Richard to John Evelyn, 3 May 1636.
21. JE diary, i, pp. 34–5.
22. JE diary, i, pp. 34–5.
23. JE diary, i, p. 30.
24. BL Add. Ms 78298, f. 124v, to Walter Pope, 20 March 1664.
25. 'A Device for the Gray's Inn Revels', in *The Major Works of Francis Bacon*, ed. Brian Vickers, Oxford University Press, 2002, p. 55.
26. The cabinet was acquired by the museum in 1977 when Evelyn's collections were sold by the family.
27. JE diary, ii, p. 230, 8 November 1644.
28. JE diary, ii, p. 287, 29 November 1644.
29. JE diary, ii, p. 475, February 1646. Today the tables are to be seen in the Hunterian Museum at the Royal College of Surgeons in London. Another set, better preserved and consisting of six panels, was brought to England by a Cambridge student, John Finch, who travelled in Europe in the seventeenth century with his friend Thomas Baines, and can be seen in the Royal College of Physicians in London.
30. JE diary, iii, p. 77, 29 September 1652, on the occasion of Elizabeth Browne's funeral.
31. BL Add. Ms 78315, f. 98, 5 February 1647.
32. BL Add. Ms 78392, f. 36.
33. BL Add. Ms 78431, 27 June 1648.
34. BL Add. Ms 78300, f. 1, 1 March 1652.
35. The cabinet was acquired by the Geffrye Museum following the 1977 sale.
36. John Rea in *Flora, seu de Florum Cultura*, London, 1665, p. 2.
37. John Evelyn, *Character of England*, London, 1659, p. 27.
38. College registry, B/422 p. 3a.
39. SP diary, v, p. 31, 30 January 1664.
40. David Masson, *The Life of Milton*, Macmillan, 1859–94, iv, p. 602.
41. Published in 1659, Pepys Library (PL) 1397 (3).
42. JE diary, iii, p. 224, 22 November 1658.

2 The Decade of the Diaries

1. Joanna Moody (ed.), *The Private Life of an Elizabethan Lady: The Diary of Lady Margaret Hoby, 1599–1605*, Sutton Publishing, 1998.

2. Alan MacFarlane (ed.), *Diary of Ralph Josselin 1616–1683*, British Academy, 1976; 'A Darker Shade of Pepys', lecture by Mark Goldie, Dr Williams Library, 2009; Mark Goldie (ed.), *The Entring Book of Roger Morrice*, Boydell Press, 2007, 6 vols.
3. JE diary, ii, p. 10, 1631.
4. 'Of Travel' in *The Major Works of Francis Bacon*, ed. Brian Vickers, Oxford University Press, 2002, p. 374.
5. SP diary, ix, p. 170, 21 April 1668.
6. H.W. Robinson and W. Adams (eds), *The Diary of Robert Hooke (1672–80)*, Taylor and Francis, 1935 (hereafter *Diary of Robert Hooke*); Hooke's diaries (1688–93) in R.T. Gunther, *Early Science in Oxford*, x, part iv, Oxford University Press, 1935.
7. SP diary, i, p. 144, 17 May 1660.
8. SP diary, i, p. 158, 25 May 1660.
9. JE diary, iii, p. 246, 29 May 1660.
10. Anthony Hamilton, *Memoirs of the Count de Gramont*, trans. Peter Quennell, Routledge and Kegan Paul, 1930, p. 103.
11. SP diary, ix, p. 342, 30 October 1668.
12. Dorset's words in Samuel Johnson's *Works of the English Poets*, London, 1779, vol. xi, p. 209.
13. SP diary, v, p. 35, 2 February 1664. The observation was made by Captain Cocke, a hemp merchant.
14. Quoted in Peter Earle, *The Life and Times of James II*, Weidenfeld & Nicolson, 1972, p. 72.
15. Henry Brouncker was said to have performed this remarkable act at the request of the Duchess of York, who was concerned about her husband's safety. Henry Brouncker distinguished himself badly in other ways, see p. 150.
16. SP diary, vi, p. 220, 10 September 1665.
17. SP diary, viii, p. 345, 19 July 1667.
18. SP diary, vi, p. 253, 5 October 1665.
19. SP diary, vi, p. 120, 8 June 1665.
20. JE diary, iii, pp. 417–18, 7 September 1665.
21. R.G. Howarth (ed.), *Letters and the Second Diary of Samuel Pepys*, J.M. Dent and Sons, 1932 (hereafter *Letters and 2nd Diary*), p. 25, 4 September 1665.
22. SP diary, vi, pp. 206–7, 30 August 1665; note 4, p. 283.
23. *Letterbooks*, i, letter 268, p. 403, 14 December 1665.
24. SP diary, vi, pp. 338–9, 25 December 1665.
25. In *Butcher, Baker, Candlestick Maker*, Museum of London and I.B. Tauris & Co., 2016, Hazel Forsyth explains that Saturday was a regulation baking day, and Farriner claimed that his oven was extinguished at around 10 pm that night, inspected at midnight when the embers that were still glowing were raked out, and the doors and windows of the bakehouse closed to reduce draughts. The fire could have started from a guttering candle, or even a spontaneous combustion of the flour.
26. See footnote 4, SP diary, vii, p. 280.
27. SP diary, vii, p. 269, 2 September 1666.
28. JE diary, iii, p. 451, 2 September 1666.
29. JE diary, iii, pp. 451–8; SP diary, vii, pp. 272–9, 3–6 September 1666.
30. JE diary, iii, pp. 454–5, 4 September 1666.
31. JE diary, iii, p. 464, 10 October 1666.
32. SP diary, vii, p. 279, 7 September 1666.
33. JE diary, iii, p. 449, 27 August 1666.
34. JE diary, iii, p. 459, 7 September 1666.
35. *Letterbooks*, i, pp. 420–1, 27 September 1666.
36. John Evelyn, *Fumifugium*, London, 1661 (hereafter *Fumifugium*), pp. 3–4.
37. *London Revived*, pp. 50–1.
38. SP diary, viii, 1 August 1667.

39. *London Revived*, pp. 34, 48–9, 52, 34.
40. The schemes of Newcourt, and what is believed to be that of Hooke, are now in the London Metropolitan Archives.
41. BL Add. Ms 78333, f. 5. For reference, see note 3 on p. 427, i, *Letterbooks*.
42. BL Add. Ms 78539, f. 13, Mary Evelyn to Ralph Bohun, 14 April 1667; SP diary, ix, p. 314, 23 September 1668.
43. *Particular Friends*, pp. 30–67.
44. SP diary, ix, p. 564–5, 31 May 1669.
45. *Particular Friends*, 8, 21 August 1669, pp. 68–75.
46. *Particular Friends*, 9, 2 November 1669, p. 76.

3 Prodigious Revolutions

1. J.R. Tanner (ed.), *The Further Correspondence of Samuel Pepys, 1662–1679*, G. Bell & Sons, 1929, pp. 256–7, letter to Captain Elliot at Aldeburgh, 19 August 1669.
2. Peter Earle, *The Life and Times of James II*, Weidenfeld & Nicolson, 1972, p. 95.
3. JE diary, iii, pp. 589–90, 14 October 1671: one of the first uses of the term 'misse'.
4. *Particular Friends*, pp. 79–80, 27 August 1672.
5. JE diary, iv, p. 26, 5 November 1673.
6. Anchitell Grey, *Debates of the House of Commons, from the Year 1667 to the Year 1694*, 10 vols, London, 1763, ii, p. 411, 10 February 1674.
7. BL Add. Ms 78299, f. 2v, to John Beale, 11 July 1679.
8. *Letters and 2nd Diary*, pp. 127–8, to James Houblon, 14 March 1682.
9. The list of the MPs taken from the Shaftesbury Papers (PRO Via/348) is printed in J.R. Jones, *Bulletin of the Institute for Historical Research*, xxx (1957). Old members are indicated by *o*, new members are *H* for honest (or pro-Shaftesbury), *B* for bad or base, and *D* for doubtful. Pepys and his naval associate Anthony Deane are marked *ov*: old and vile.
10. Samuel Pepys to Sir Richard Beach at Chatham warning him against designs on the fleet, 16 November 1678, printed in Bryant, *Samuel Pepys*, p. 240.
11. JE diary, iv, p. 169, 4 June 1679.
12. JE diary, v, p. 111, 25 July 1692.
13. Dryden was making a biblical allusion to the King as David and Monmouth as Absalom.
14. *Particular Friends*, p. 141, 7 August 1683; *Letters and 2nd Diary*, p. 158, letter to James Houblon, 14 October 1683.
15. *Letters and 2nd Diary*, p. 440, February 1684.
16. *Particular Friends*, p. 141, 7 August 1683.
17. JE diary, iv, pp. 271–2, 7 February 1682.
18. The phrase was used at Fox's funeral in 1716. See C.G.T. Dean, *The Royal Chelsea Hospital*, Hutchinson, 1950, p. 28.
19. *De Vita Propria*, in JE diary, i, p. 32.
20. SP diary, vii, p. 29, 29 January 1666.
21. JE diary, iv, p. 270, 27 January 1682.
22. JE diary, iv, pp. 409–10, 6 February 1685.
23. Huddleston had helped Charles escape from the Battle of Worcester in 1651; JE diary, iv, p. 408, 6 February 1685.
24. JE diary, iv, pp. 476–9, 2 October 1685.
25. Quoted in Earle, *Life and Times of James II*, p. 140.
26. JE diary, iv, p. 456, 15 July 1685.
27. *Letters and 2nd Diary*, pp. 435–6.
28. JE diary, iv, p. 484, 31 October 1685.
29. JE diary, iv, pp. 594–5, 20 August 1688.
30. *Letters and 2nd Diary*, p. 177, 23 February 1687. Nearly a year later Pepys did try to help him by recommending him for a naval chaplaincy with Lord Dartmouth, Admiral of

the Fleet, but Peachall turned it down, explaining, 'I had a little itch to such a service 30 yeare agoe, but now am as old againe, and incumbred with businesse': p. 195, 27 September 1688. Peachall was restored to his positions the following month.

31. JE diary, iv, p. 586, 8 June 1688.
32. Anne's letter to Mary, 14 March 1688, *Letters of Queen Anne*, ed. Beatrice Curtis Brown, Cassell, 1935, p. 34.
33. JE diary, iv, p. 591, 17 July 1688.
34. *Memoirs of John, Duke of Marlborough,* Longman, Hurst, Rees, Orme, and Brown, 1818, i, p. 27.
35. JE diary, iv, p. 600, 6 October 1688.
36. *Letters and 2nd Diary*, p. 81, 6 May 1679.
37. *Particular Friends*, p. 186, 12 December 1688.
38. *Letters and 2nd Diary*, p. 189, 2 January 1689.
39. SP diary, i, p. 139, 14 May 1660.
40. Tony Claydon, *Oxford Dictionary of National Biography*, 2004.
41. BL Add. Ms 78301, ff. 31 and 35, John Evelyn junior to John Evelyn.
42. JE diary, iv, pp. 624–5, 22 February 1689.
43. Quoted in Gila Curtis, *The Life and Times of Queen Anne*, Weidenfeld & Nicolson, 1972, pp. 55–6.
44. *Letters and 2nd Diary*, to Dr Charlett, p. 244, 4 August 1694.
45. *Letters and 2nd Diary*, pp. 211–12, 29 October 1689; 23 November 1689.
46. *Particular Friends*, pp. 94–141.
47. *Particular Friends*, p. 216, 11 June 1690.
48. J.D. Davies, 'Pepys and the Admiralty Commission of 1679–84', *Bulletin of the Institute of Historical Research*, lxii, 1989, pp. 34–53.
49. *Particular Friends*, p. 281, 19 September 1700.
50. BL Add. Ms 78291, 22 February 1691.
51. BL Add. Ms 78300, pp. 36 and 38, 21 July and 3 August 1691.
52. Quoted in JE diary, v, p. 289, note 5.
53. BL Add. Ms 78359, 17, f. 40.
54. *Particular Friends*, p. 234, 29 August 1692.
55. James Boswell, *Life of Samuel Johnson*, London, 1827, p. 127.
56. *Letters and 2nd Diary*, p. 253, 7 November 1694.
57. JE diary, v, p. 249, 30 June 1696.
58. BL Add. Ms 78299, f. 105, 3 August 1696.
59. BL Add. Ms 78300, Mary Evelyn to John Evelyn, f. 61, 16 July 1696.
60. J.R. Tanner (ed.), *Private Correspondence and Miscellaneous Papers of Samuel Pepys, 1679–1703*, G. Bell & Sons, 2 vols, 1926 (hereafter *Private Correspondence of Pepys*), i, p. 176.
61. *Letters and 2nd Diary*, pp. 291–4, Christmas Day 1699. Innocent XII survived until the following November.
62. *Particular Friends*, p. 242, 22 May 1694.
63. *Particular Friends*, p. 281, 19 September 1700.
64. *Particular Friends*, p. 290, 24 December 1701.
65. William III died on 8 March 1702, six months after James II.
66. 'Bishop Nicolson's Diaries: Part II', ed. Henry Ware, *Transactions of the Cumberland and Westmorland Antiquarian and Archaeological Society*, 2 (1902), pp. 155–230, p. 164.
67. BL Add. Ms 78403; Geoffrey Keynes (ed.), *Memoires for my Grand-son by John Evelyn*, Nonesuch Press, 1926 (hereafter *Memoires for my Grand-son*), pp. 50ff.

4 Private Lives

1. There is a mystery about where Pepys's parents married. In his diary for 31 December 1664 (v, p. 360), he says that they were married at Newington in Surrey. It is thought likely, however, that the marriage took place north of London, in Newington Green,

where Margaret's sister was in service. The parish records for St Mary's Stoke Newington make no reference to such an event.

2. SP diary, ii, p. 64, 1 April 1661.
3. SP diary, ii, pp. 89–90, 28 April 1661.
4. Helen Truesdall Heath (ed.), *The Letters of Samuel Pepys and his Family Circle*, Oxford University Press, 1955 (hereafter *Letters of Samuel Pepys and his Family Circle*), pp. 1–3, 16 May 1663.
5. *Letters of Samuel Pepys and his Family Circle*, p. 27, in which Balty was trying to help Pepys clear his name on accusations of papism, 8 February 1674.
6. Richard Ollard, *Pepys: A Biography*, 2nd edn, Sinclair-Stevenson, 1991, p. 58.
7. *Letters of Samuel Pepys and his Family Circle*, p. 183, Ester St Michel to Samuel Pepys, 28 September 1681.
8. *Letters and 2nd Diary*, p. 172, 11 December 1686.
9. *Letters and 2nd Diary*, p. 373, to Sir Geo Rooke, April 1703.
10. BL Add. Ms 15857, f. 62, Browne to John Evelyn, 13 November 1647.
11. Darley, *John Evelyn*, p. 113.
12. Quoted in Darley, *John Evelyn*, p. 266.
13. SP diary, ix, p. 94, 27 February 1668.
14. Daniel Rogers, *Matrimoniall Honour: or, the mutuall crowne and comfort of godly, loyall, and chaste marriage*, London, 1642, p. 32.
15. *A True Relation of the birth, breeding and life of Margaret Cavendish, Duchess of Newcastle, written by herself*, Lee Priory, 1814, p. 12.
16. SP diary, v, p. 222, 26 July 1664.
17. For example, Ephesians 5:22; 1 Peter 3:1–7.
18. BL Add. Ms 78430, ff. 6, 21, 26.
19. BL Add. Ms 78296.
20. University of Sheffield Library, Hartlib Papers, 29/8/10B; BL Add. Ms 78434, William Glanville, 1 June 1664.
21. BL Add. Ms 78431, letter 10 May 1652.
22. BL Add. Ms 78219, 23 January 1654.
23. BL Add. Ms 78430, f. 20, *Instructions Oeconomique*, 1648.
24. BL Add. Ms 78221, f. 77, John Evelyn to Richard Browne, 15 February 1658; f. 79, 11 March 1658.
25. BL Add. Ms 78219, to Browne, 6 March 1657.
26. *Particular Friends*, p. 90, 1 March 1677.
27. JE diary, iv, pp. 427–8, 14 March 1685.
28. BL Add. Ms 78539, 20 May 1685.
29. *Particular Friends*, p. 93.
30. *Particular Friends*, pp. 149–54, 29 and 31 July, 3 August 1685.
31. JE diary, iv, p. 464, 29 August 1685.
32. John Evelyn, *Sculptura* (1662), *Parallel of Architecture* (1664) and *Idea of the Perfection of Painting* (1668).
33. *Letterbooks*, ii, p. 917, letter 620, 14 August 1689.
34. For details, see Carol Gibson-Wood, 'Susanna and her Elders: John Evelyn's Artistic Daughter', in Frances Harris and Michael Hunter (eds), *John Evelyn and his Milieu*, British Library, 2003, pp. 233–54.
35. SP diary, i, p. 291, 12 November 1660.
36. SP diary, ii, p. 204, 30 October 1661.
37. SP diary, v, p. 267, 10 September 1664.
38. SP diary, ix, p. 56, 7 February 1668.
39. SP diary, ix, pp. 337–8, 344, 367, 25 October, 1 and 19 November 1668.
40. *Letters and 2nd Diary*, pp. 201–2, 9 and 10 July 1689.
41. BL Add. Ms 78219, to Richard Browne, 30 June 1657.
42. SP diary, vi, p. 182, 4 August 1665; *Letterbooks*, i, p. 403, letter to Lady Carteret, 14 December 1665.

43. SP diary, iv, p. 303, 9 September 1663.
44. SP diary, v, p. 179, 14 June 1664.
45. His brother, John Houblon, became the first Governor of the Bank of England and James one of the directors when it was established in 1694.
46. SP diary, ix, p. 65, 12 February 1668.
47. *Letters and 2nd Diary*, p. 42, 4/14 April 1673: letters from the Continent were dated by the New Style, a difference in ten days.
48. *Letters and 2nd Diary*, p. 136, 13 May 1682.
49. *Letters and 2nd Diary*, p. 261, 20 August 1695.
50. JE diary, iii, p. 529, 28 July 1669.
51. Quoted in Antonia Fraser, *The Weaker Vessel: Woman's Lot in Seventeenth-Century England*, Weidenfeld & Nicolson, 1984, p. 454.
52. BL Add. Ms 78298, to James Hamilton, 27 April 1671.
53. Harris, *Transformations of Love*, p. 152.
54. W.G. Hiscock, *John Evelyn and Margaret Godolphin*, Macmillan, 1951, pp. 24, 38–9.
55. John Evelyn, *The Life of Mrs Godolphin*, ed. Harriet Sampson, Oxford University Press, 1939, p. 52.
56. JE diary, iv, pp. 138–9, 23 July 1678; Evelyn, *Life of Mrs Godolphin*, pp. 72–3.
57. The account of the trial, Old Bailey Sessions Papers, 6–9 December 1693, is printed in H.B. Wheatley, *Pepysiana*, George Bell, 1899, pp. 45–7.
58. *Letters of Samuel Pepys and his Family Circle*, pp. 123–4, 28 May 1689.
59. Bodleian Library, Rawlinson A.170, f. 42, 27 September 1689.
60. BL Add. Ms 78431, to Mary Evelyn, 11 November 1695.
61. *Particular Friends*, p. 264, 14 January 1699.
62. *Letters of Samuel Pepys and his Family Circle*, p. 74, letter to Balthasar St Michel, 14 July 1679.
63. *Memoires for my Grand-son*, p. 34.

5 Take Nobody's Word for It

1. BL Add. Ms 78335, f. 6.
2. Deborah Harkness, *The Jewel House: Elizabethan London and the Scientific Revolution*, Yale University Press, 2007, p. 2.
3. Harkness, *The Jewel House*, p. 7.
4. Montagu Burrows (ed.), 'The Register of the Visitors of the University of Oxford, from A.D. 1647 to A.D. 1658', Camden Society ns, xxxix (1881), p. xc.
5. Bodleian Library, Ms Ashmole, 1810.
6. *Aubrey's Brief Lives*, ed. Oliver Lawson Dick, Nonpareil Books, 1999, p. 165.
7. Robert J. Frank, *Harvey and the Oxford Physiologists*, University of California Press, 1980, p. 57.
8. Michael Hunter, Antonio Clericuzio and Lawrence M. Principe (eds), *The Correspondence of Robert Boyle*, 6 vols, Pickering and Chatto, 2001, i, pp. 190–1, letter to Samuel Hartlib, 14 September 1655.
9. JE diary, iii, pp. 110–11, 13 June 1654.
10. Christopher Wren, *Parentalia: or Memoirs of the Family of the Wrens*, London, 1750, p. 206.
11. JE diary, iii, pp. 163–4, 27 December 1655.
12. Mark Greengrass, Michael Leslie and Timothy Raylor (eds), *Samuel Hartlib and Universal Reformation*, Cambridge University Press, 1994, pp. 12–13.
13. BL Add. Mss 78346, 78333, 78335–8.
14. *Letterbooks*, i, pp. 254–5, 3 September 1659. The drawing is reproduced in Michael Hunter's essay, 'John Evelyn in the 1650s: A Virtuoso in Quest of a Role', in his *Science and the Shape of Orthodoxy: Intellectual Change in Late Seventeenth-Century Britain*, Boydell Press, 1995, pp. 85–6.
15. SP diary, ii, pp. 21–2, 21 January 1661.

16. *Letters and 2nd Diary*, p. 4, 11 December 1656; see Michael Hunter, *The Royal Society and its Fellows, 1660–1700: The Morphology of an Early Scientific Institution*, The British Society for the History of Science, 1982.
17. SP diary, v, p. 151, 16 May 1664.
18. SP diary, v, p. 27, 27 January 1664.
19. Samuel Sorbière, *A Voyage into England, containing many things relating to the state of Learning, Religion and other Curiosities of that Kingdom*, London, 1709, pp. 36–7.
20. SP diary, viii, p. 243, 30 May 1667.
21. BL Add. Ms 78539, to Ralph Bohun, 29 March 1668.
22. SP diary, v, p. 27, 27 January 1664.
23. Thomas Birch, *The History of the Royal Society of London*, A. Millar, 1756, ii, pp. 18–20, note 8.
24. Thomas Sprat, *History of the Royal Society* (1667), ed. Jackson I. Cope and Harold Whitmore Jones, Routledge and Kegan Paul, 1959, pp. 40, 42.
25. 'Remarks on the *Empress of Morocco*', in *Works of John Dryden*, 1808, xv, p. 411.
26. *Letterbooks*, i, p. 271, 20 June 1665.
27. Sprat, *History of the Royal Society*, p. 113.
28. SP diary, vi, pp. 36–7, 15 February 1665.
29. Angelo Hornak cites St Benet Paul's Wharf, St Martin's Ludgate and St Edmund King and Martyr as three examples of Hooke's design. See his *After the Fire: London Churches in the Age of Wren, Hooke, Hawksmoor and Gibbs*, Pimpernel Press, 2016, pp. 40–1.
30. *The Posthumous Works of Robert Hooke*, Richard Waller, 1705, p. 131; Stephen Inwood, *The Man Who Knew Too Much: The Strange and Inventive Life of Robert Hooke, 1635–1703*, Macmillan, 2002.
31. Evelyn is credited with introducing the word 'avenue' into the English language.
32. Robert Hooke, *Micrographia*, 1665, Observation LIV, p. 211.
33. SP diary, vi, p. 2, January 1665; p. 17, 20 January 1665.
34. SP diary, v, pp. 240–1, 13 and 14 August 1664.
35. SP diary, vii, p. 226, 29 July 1666.
36. SP diary, v, pp. 32–3, 1 February 1664.
37. Montague Summers (ed.), *The Complete Works of Thomas Shadwell*, Fortune Press, 1927, i, p. 45.
38. *Complete Works of Thomas Shadwell*, ii, p. 126.
39. *Complete Works of Thomas Shadwell*, ii, pp. 130 and 132.
40. *Diary of Robert Hooke 1672–80*, p. 235, 2 June 1676.
41. *The Philosophical Works of the Honourable Robert Boyle*, London, 1725, iii, pp. 168–9.
42. *Complete Works of Thomas Shadwell*, ii, p. 128.
43. BL Add. Ms 78298, 18 July 1676.
44. *Diary of Robert Hooke*, p. 199, 10 December 1675; pp. 205–6, 1 January 1676.
45. Letter, 4 February 1672, Bodleian Library, Ms Aubrey 12, f. 66r. Pepys also harboured considerable animosity against Abigail Williams, see p. 232.
46. Thomas to William Molyneux, 9 June 1683, *Dublin University Magazine*, 18 (1841), p. 320.
47. *Diary of Robert Hooke*, p. 262, 15 December 1676.
48. John Evelyn, Preface to *Sylva*, 3rd edn, p. A/A1.
49. Adrian Johns, 'Science and the Book', in *The Cambridge History of the Book in Britain, Vol. IV, 1557–1695*, ed. John Barnard and D.F. MacKenzie, Cambridge University Press, 2002, p. 302.
50. JE diary, iv, p. 491, 15 December 1685.
51. JE diary, v, p. 39, 1 December 1690.
52. BL Add. Ms 78462, to Jack Evelyn, 12 June 1699; *Particular Friends*, p. 228, 8 October 1691.
53. *Particular Friends*, p. 285, 10 January 1701.
54. *Philosophical Transactions*, 23, 280 (July/August 1702). See R. Aspin, 'John Evelyn's Tables of Veins and Arteries: A Rediscovered Letter', *Medical History*, 39 (1995), pp. 493–9.

55. Dennis Duncan, 'Commentary', *Times Literary Supplement*, 15 January 2016.
56. Inwood, *The Man Who Knew Too Much*, p. 76.

6 Pleasure Above All Things

1. SP diary, vii, pp. 69–70, 9 March 1666.
2. JE diary, v, p. 538, 26 May 1703.
3. JE diary, ii, p. 22, 14 January 1639.
4. JE diary, ii, p. 287, 2 December 1644; p. 473, February 1646; p. 535, 3 March 1647.
5. John Wilson (ed.), *Roger North on Music*, Novello & Co., 1959, p. 294.
6. SP diary, iii, p. 80, 9 May 1662; ii, p. 115, 5 June 1661.
7. SP diary, i, p. 169, 5 June 1660.
8. SP diary, iv, p. 237, 22 July 1663.
9. SP diary, iv, p. 248, 27 June 1663.
10. SP diary, ii, p. 86, 23 April 1661.
11. SP diary, i, pp. 297–8, 20 November 1660.
12. SP diary, viii, p. 529, 15 November 1667.
13. Wilson (ed.), *Roger North on Music*, p. 299.
14. SP diary, iv, p. 394, 22 November 1663.
15. SP diary, vii, p. 414, 19 December 1666.
16. BL Add. Ms 78416C, 'Si linguis hominum'.
17. JE diary, iii, p. 144, 28 October 1654.
18. SP diary, p. 217, 22 July 1664.
19. Mathew Locke, Preface to *A Little Consort of Three Parts* published in 1656.
20. SP diary, viii, p. 458, 1 October 1667.
21. SP diary, viii, pp. 54–5, 12 February 1667: this was probably the composer Giovanni Battiste Draghi.
22. SP diary, v, p. 332, 27 November 1664.
23. SP diary, v, p. 258, 31 August 1664.
24. SP diary, vii, p. 228, 30 July 1666.
25. SP diary, iv, p. 140, 15 May 1663. The reference to a black man indicated that he was swarthy in complexion, like the King, who had been called a 'black boy' when he was a child by his mother, Henrietta Maria. Many inn signs still celebrate the Prince's dark looks.
26. SP diary, vi, p. 282, 29 October 1665.
27. *Letters and 2nd Diary*, p. 163, 2 March 1687.
28. JE diary, iv, p. 547, 19 April 1687.
29. Richard Luckett, 'Music', in SP diary, x, p. 206.
30. 'A Calendar of References to Music in Newspapers in London and the Provinces', *Royal Musical Association Research Chronicles*, i (1961), p. 13.
31. SP diary, i, p. 63, 21 February 1660.
32. JE diary, v, p. 289, 30 May 1698.
33. See Luckett's piece on music in SP diary, particularly p. 276. Pepys's reference to conning his gamut is to be found in the entry for 11 April 1668.
34. *Letters and 2nd Diary*, pp. 42–3, [4], 14 April 1673.
35. *Private Correspondence of Pepys*, ii, p. 105, letter to Dr Charlett, 5 November 1700.
36. JE diary, iii, p. 378, 5 October 1664; SP diary, v, p. 290, 5 October 1664.
37. JE diary, ii, p. 47, August 1641.
38. SP diary, ii, pp. 115–16, 6 June 1661.
39. R.T. Gunther, *Early Science in Oxford*, vi, Oxford University Press, 1926, p. 186; Hooke, *Micrographia*, pp. 172–4.
40. SP diary, vii, p. 239, 8 August 1666; ix, p. 147, 2 April 1668.
41. The translation is taken from M.E.J. Hughes, *The Pepys Library and the Historic Collections of Magdalene College, Cambridge*, Scala, 2015. The two volumes of the

Musurgia are PL 2467–8. Pepys's mention of buying them are in his diary, ix, p. 85, 22 February 1668.

42. John Birchensha's letter to the Royal Society, 26 April 1664, Royal Society letterbook copy, 1, 1666–73.

43. JE diary, iii, p. 377, 3 August 1664.

44. SP diary, ii, pp. 8–9, 13 January 1662.

45. SP diary, ii, pp. 36–7, 27 February 1662.

46. *Complete Works of Thomas Shadwell*, i, p. 221.

47. See Andrew Gurr and Farah Karim-Cooper (eds), *Moving Shakespeare Indoors: Performance and Repertoire in the Jacobean Playhouse*, Cambridge University Press, 2004, p. 15.

48. The National Archives, PRO, SP 18/128/198.

49. Bodleian Library, Rawlinson A.46, p. 293r.

50. SP diary, ii, p. 48, 2 March 1661; p. 52, 11 March 1661.

51. SP diary, v, p. 224, 28 July 1664.

52. SP diary, ii, p. 223, 29 November 1661.

53. BL Add. Ms 34,217, f. 31b.

54. SP diary, ix, p. 203, 18 May 1668. He was on his way to see Charles Sedley's *Mulberry Garden*.

55. François Misson, *Memoires et Observations Faites par un Voyageur en Angleterre*, originally published in French in The Hague, 1698, translated by John Ozell as *M. Misson's Memoirs and Observations in His Travels Over England*, London, 1719, pp. 217–20.

56. SP diary, ix, p. 2, 1 January 1668. The play was Dryden's *Sir Martin Mar-All*.

57. SP diary, viii, p. 55, 12 February 1667.

58. *The Virtuosi*, i, Dorset Garden, 1 May 1676.

59. Prologue by Mohun acting Abdelmelech, second part of *The Conquest of Granada*, Theatre Royal, 1670–1.

60. SP diary, iv, p. 181, 12 June 1663. The Lady Clapham doll (see Plate 53) in the Victoria and Albert Museum has a vizard, which would have been held in place by a bead that could be put in the mouth, rendering the wearer both mysterious and mute.

61. Quoted in Montague Summers, *The Restoration Theatre*, Routledge and Kegan Paul, 1934, pp. 82–3.

62. SP diary, viii, p. 517, 2 November 1667.

63. SP diary, viii, p. 406, 29 August 1667; Anthony Hamilton, *Memoirs of the Count de Gramont*, trans. Peter Quennell, Routledge and Kegan Paul, 1930, p. 262. Henry Brouncker was later impeached for his disastrous intervention in the Battle of Lowestoft (p. 30).

64. Nell told the story that the King was her Charles the third.

65. SP diary, ii, p. 203, 28 October 1661. The play was *Argalus and Parthenia*, a romantic pastoral written in the 1630s by Henry Glapthorne.

66. SP diary, ix, p. 189, 7 May 1668.

67. JE diary, iii, p. 309, 9 January 1662; ii, pp. 465–6, 18 October 1666.

68. SP diary, vi, p. 289, 5 December 1665; the play, BL Add. Ms 78358.

69. SP diary, ix, p. 203, 18 May 1668.

70. *Works of John Dryden*, xvii, p. 56.

71. SP diary, iv, p. 8, 8 January 1663.

72. JE diary, iii, p. 350, 8 January 1663.

73. SP diary, vi, p. 4, 4 January 1665; JE diary, iii, p. 371, 27 April 1664.

74. SP diary, p. 56, 23 February 1663.

75. JE diary, iii, p. 350, 5 February 1664; iii, pp. 510–11, 11 June 1668.

76. SP diary, ix, p. 183, 2 May 1668.

77. Quoted in JE diary, iv, p. 416, note 3.

78. JE diary, iii, p. 570, 9 February 1671.

79. SP diary, ix, p. 519, 14 April 1669.

80. SP diary, v, p. 230, 2 August 1664.
81. SP diary, ix, p. 94, 27 February 1668.
82. BL Add. Ms 78359, 19 March 1667.
83. Epilogue to *The Ordinary, A Collection of Poems*, 1673.
84. PL Mornamont Mss, ii, p. 1192.
85. SP diary, ix, p. 54, 6 February 1668.

7 Hortulan Affairs

1. *Letterbooks*, i, p. 104, letter 36, 2 December 1651. The letter was written to his wife's uncle, William Prettyman.
2. John Evelyn, *Elysium Britannicum or The Royal Garden*, ed. John E. Ingram, University of Pennsylvania Press, 2001 (hereafter *Elysium Britannicum*), p. 31.
3. SP diary, vii, p. 247, 4 September 1666.
4. The publication in question was *Plantarum Historia Universalis Oxoniensis. Letters and 2nd Diary*, p. 275, Pepys to Charlett, 17 April 1699.
5. JE diary, ii, pp. 109–10, 28 February 1644.
6. JE diary, ii, pp. 130–1, 1 April 1644.
7. JE diary, ii, pp. 132–3, 3 April 1644.
8. JE diary, ii, pp. 392–3, 5 May 1645.
9. The *hortus siccus*, or *hortus hyemalis*, is now in the British Library, Add. Ms 78334; SP diary, vi, p. 289, 5 November 1665.
10. *Letterbooks*, ii, p. 1049, letter 726, to James Chadwick, a potential tenant for Sayes Court, 8 February 1695.
11. *Diary and Correspondence of John Evelyn*, ed. William Bray and H.G. Bohn, 1859, vol. iii, p. 73, letter to Jeremy Taylor, 27 April 1656.
12. BL Add. Ms 78219, letter to Sir Richard Browne, 23 January 1654.
13. *Letterbooks*, i, p. 271, letter 165, to Thomas Browne, 28 January 1660.
14. *Elysium Britannicum*, p. 269.
15. Brian Vickers (ed.), *The Major Works of Francis Bacon*, Oxford University Press, 2002, pp. 54–5.
16. *Elysium Britannicum*, p. 140.
17. SP diary, vii, p. 213, 22 July 1666.
18. BL Add. Ms 78439 to Sir Samuel Tuke, late 1663.
19. *Sylva*, 1664 edn, in *Works of John Evelyn*, pp. 187, 190; *Sylva*, 1670 edn, p. 245.
20. Quoted in Darley, *John Evelyn*, p. 148.
21. *Elysium Britannicum*, Appendix 7 ('on tulips'), pp. 445–8; Appendix 9 ('on daffodils'), pp. 453–4.
22. JE diary, iii, p. 594, 17 October 1671.
23. University of Sheffield Library, Hartlib Papers, 51/23a, 27 September 1658.
24. *Letterbooks*, ii, letter 773, to William Wotton, 28 October 1696.
25. JE diary, iii, p. 225, 6 December 1658.
26. Translation by June Tabaroff in '"Wife unto thy Garden": The First Gardening Books for Women', *Garden History*, 11, 1 (1983), p. 4.
27. *Fumifugium*, pp. 5, 7, 24.
28. *Letterbooks*, i, p. 250, 6 July 1659.
29. *Elysium Britannicum*, p. 98.
30. See Peter H. Goodchild, '"No Phantasticall Utopia, but a reall place": John Evelyn, John Beale and Backbury Hill, Herefordshire', *Garden History*, 19, 2 (Autumn 1991), pp. 105–27; Michael Leslie, 'The Spiritual Husbandry of John Beale', in *Culture and Cultivation in Early Modern England: Writing and the Land*, ed. Michael Leslie and Timothy Raylor, Leicester University Press, 1992, pp. 151–72.
31. *Elysium Britannicum*, insertion on p. 55.
32. SP diary, vi, p. 289, 5 November 1665.

33. *Letterbooks*, ii, letter 409, 1 July 1679.

34. *Sylva*, 1664 edn, p. 25; 1670 edn, p. 44.

35. G. Thorn Drury (ed.), *The Poems of Edmund Waller*, Routledge, 1905, ii, p. 40.

36. *Sylva*, dedication in 2nd edn; JE diary, iii, p. 354, 30 April 1663.

37. BL Add. Ms 78219, 22 December 1665.

38. Keith Thomas, *Man and the Natural World: Changing Attitudes in England, 1500–1800*, Viking, 1983, p. 109.

39. John Pell to Theodore Haak, 30 March 1667, Bodleian Library, Ms Aubrey 13, ff. 93v–94r.

40. *The True Domestick Intelligence, or News both from City and Country, published to prevent False Reports*, no. 34, 31 October 1679, Burney Collection of Newspapers, 81:83. The full review is reproduced as an appendix (pp. 253–4).

41. *Directions for the Gardiner and other Horticultural Advice*, ed. Maggie Campbell-Culver, Oxford University Press, 2009, p. 121.

42. *Letterbooks*, ii, letter 629, 16 June 1690.

43. BL Add. Mss 78316 and 78298, 12 January 1659.

44. JE diary, iii, p. 496, 21 September 1667; iii, pp. 561–2, 23 September 1670.

45. BL Add. Ms 78306, f. 109, 28 September 1663; f. 111, 7 October 1663.

46. See Gillian Darley, 'John Evelyn's Norwich Garden', *Garden History*, 34, 2 (Winter 2006), pp. 249–53.

47. BL Ms Sloane 1906.

48. JE diary, iv, pp. 361–3, 25 January 1684; pp. 364–5, 4 February 1684.

49. *Philosophical Transactions*, 158 (1684), p. 559.

50. *Elysium Britannicum*, p. 47.

51. BL Add. Ms 78628B.

52. JE diary, iii, 9–19 June 1662, pp. 324–5. Pepys commissioned paintings from the Dutch topographical artist, Hendrick Danckerts, of the royal residences of Hampton Court, Greenwich, Whitehall and Windsor, as recorded in his diary for 22 January 1669, ix, p. 423.

53. JE diary, vii, p. 182, 25 June 1666.

54. SP diary, iii, p. 96, 8 May 1654; p. 169, 27 March 1656.

55. John Gibson, 'A short account of several gardens near London, with remarks on some particulars wherein they excel, or are deficient, upon a View of them in December 1691', *Archaeologia, or Miscellaneous Tracts relating to antiquity, 1770–1992* (January 1796), 12, British Periodicals, p. 181.

56. Anon, *The life of Henry Compton*, London, 1713, p. 42.

57. *Silva*, 1706 edn, see pp. 25, 26 and 39.

58. *Particular Friends*, p. 171, 1 September 1686.

59. Quoted in Alicia Amherst, *A History of Gardening in England*, John Murray, 1910, pp. 168–9.

60. JE diary, iv, p. 289, 1 August 1682.

61. *Memoires for my Grand-son*, p. 17.

62. BL Add. Ms 78291, 21 November 1692.

63. BL Add. Ms 78318, f. 64, 24 March 1694.

64. JE diary, iii, p. 549, 9 June 1670.

65. SP diary, vii, p. 246, 14 August 1666; vi, p. 295, 9 November 1665.

66. JE diary, iii, p. 498, 10 October 1667.

67. Mark Laird, 'Purity in the Parsley Bed: John Evelyn's Battles with Instability in his Garden Elysium at Sayes Court', in Laird, *A Natural History of English Gardening 1650–1800*, Yale, 2015, pp. 26–61.

68. John Evelyn, *Acetaria*, 1706 edn, pp. 132, 134, 138.

69. *Private Correspondence of Pepys*, ii, p. 1, 1 July 1700.

70. JE diary, v, pp. 427–8, 23 September 1700.

71. 'Bishop Nicolson's Diaries: Part II', ed. Henry Ware, *Transactions of the Cumberland and Westmorland Antiquarian and Archaeological Society*, 2 (1902), p. 164.

72. The training under Morison is noted by Blanche Henrey in *British Botanical and Horticultural Literature before 1800*, Oxford University Press, 1999, i, p. 121.
73. *Private Correspondence of Pepys*, i, p. 179. I am grateful to Professor Jonathan Dancy and Dr Gregory Farrelly for their help with this unconventional Latin.
74. *Letters and 2nd Diary*, p. 313, 8 October 1700, OS.
75. JE diary, v, p. 550, 26 November 1703.
76. *Silva*, 1706 edn, p. 350.
77. *Memoires for my Grand-son*, p. 34.
78. Stephen Switzer, *The Nobleman, Gentleman, and Gardener's Recreation*, London, 1715, pp. 44–5.

8 Exotic Extravagances

1. *Particular Friends*, p. 226, 13 November 1690.
2. His memoirs were first published in Germany in 1582. Nicholas Staphorst's English translation was included in the first volume of John Ray's *Collection of Curious Travels and Voyages*, London, 1693, p. 92.
3. JE diary, ii, p. 18, 29 May to 2 July 1637.
4. John Evelyn, *A Character of England*, 1659, p. 28.
5. SP diary, i, p. 253, 25 September 1660; viii, p. 302, 28 June 1667.
6. *The Closet of the Eminently Learned Sir Kenelm Digbie Opened*, London, 1669, p. 133.
7. Transcribed from a paper of Thomas Povey, 20 October 1686, BL Ms Sloane 1039, f. 139.
8. SP diary, ii, p. 88, 24 April 1661.
9. SP diary, v, p. 329, 23 November 1664.
10. *Letterbooks*, i, p. 500, 27 July 1670.
11. See Joyce Lorimer, 'The Failure of the English Guiana Ventures 1595–1667 and James I's Foreign Policy', *Journal of Imperial and Commonwealth History*, 21 (1993), p. 16.
12. Daniel Defoe, *A Plan of the English Commerce*, Charles Rivington, 1728, pp. 304–5.
13. SP diary, iii, pp. 190–1, 5 September 1662.
14. SP diary, vi, pp. 257–8, 8 October 1665.
15. London Metropolitan Archives, CLA/002/02/01/0500.
16. JE diary, ii, pp. 99–100, 3 February 1644.
17. *Letterbooks*, i, p. 93, 29 July 1651.
18. JE diary, iv, p. 99, 9 October 1676.
19. SP diary, ii, p. 130, 7 January 1661.
20. SP diary, vii, p. 378, 21 November 1666.
21. SP diary, iv, p. 391, 21 November 1663; p. 415, 12 December 1663.
22. London Metropolitan Archives, DL/AM/P1/01/1672, 033.
23. SP diary, v, p. 8, 8 January 1664.
24. SP diary, ii, p. 66, 6 April 1661.
25. SP diary, vii, p. 315, 8 October 1666.
26. JE diary, iii, pp. 464–5, 18 October 1666.
27. SP diary, iv, p. 299, 5 September 1663.
28. JE diary, iii, pp. 425–6, 30 December 1665.
29. See James Knowles, 'Jonson's Entertainment at Britain's Burse', in Martin Butler (ed.), *Re-Presenting Ben Jonson: Text, History, Performance*, Macmillan, 1999, pp. 50–9 and 116–22.
30. JE diary, iv, p. 343, 4 October 1683.
31. SP diary, ii, p. 17, 18 January 1661; p. 23, 25 January 1661.
32. Bodleian Library, Rawlinson A.191, f. 7r, 31 March 1674; reply, 28 September, in J.R. Tanner (ed.), *A Descriptive Catalogue of the Naval Manuscripts in the Pepysian Library*, Navy Records Society, 1903, ii, p. 362.
33. Bodleian Library, Rawlinson A.170, f. 256r, John Wyborne to Pepys, 14 January 1687; f. 254r, John Wyborne to Pepys, 20 January 1687; A.179, ff. 132–4v, John and Katherine

Wyborne to Pepys, 1 January 1688; f. 86r, Katherine Wyborne to Pepys, 8 June 1688; f. 134v, Katherine Wyborne to Pepys, 1 January 1688.

34. *Private Correspondence of Pepys*, i, p. 230; PL 2719.
35. The National Archives, PROB 11/548/345, 20 August 1714 with codicil 2 October 1715, proved 26 October 1715.
36. BL Add. Ms 78431, Evelyn papers, CCLXIV, f. 171v, 11 November 1695.
37. *Letterbooks*, ii, p. 1108, 6 October 1696.
38. BL Add. Ms 78403 (1702).
39. English translation in Harold J. Cook, *Matters of Exchange: Commerce, Medicine and Science in the Dutch Golden Age*, Yale University Press, 2007, p. 317.
40. BL Add. Ms 78300, f. 40, 14 August 1691.
41. Now in the National Portrait Gallery.
42. Mark Laird, 'Nursing Pretty Monsters', in Laird, *A Natural History of English Gardening*, pp. 64–123.
43. *Letterbooks*, i, p. 334, 30 March 1664.
44. *Directions for the Gardiner and other Horticultural Advice*, ed. Maggie Campbell-Culver, Oxford University Press, 2009, p. 99.
45. JE diary, iii, p. 293, 9 August 1661; p. 513, 19 August 1668.
46. Quoted in Sue Minter, *The Apothecaries' Garden: A History of Chelsea Physic Garden*, Sutton, 2000, p. 5.
47. JE diary, iv, p. 462, 6 August 1685.
48. John Evelyn, *Kalendarium Hortense*, 1691, p. 126.
49. Painted by Jan Weenix, before 1697, now in the Amsterdam Historisches Museum.
50. BL Egerton Ms 2395, ff. 270–5.
51. Thomas Birch, *The History of the Royal Society of London*, iv, A. Millar, 1757, p. 228.
52. Robert Hooke's diary, 26 October 1689, in Gunther, *Early Science in Oxford*, X, iv, p. 160.
53. W. Derham, *Philosophical Experiments and Observations of the Late Eminent Robert Hooke*, London, 1726, p. 210.
54. JE diary, ii, p. 49, August 1641.
55. JE diary, v, p. 295, 6 August 1698.
56. PL 1353.
57. George Villiers, 2nd Duke of Buckingham, *A Letter to Sir Thomas Osborn*, H. Brome, 1672, p. 11.
58. BL Ms Sloane 45.

9 The Affection Which We Have to Books

1. SP diary, vi, p. 252, 5 October 1665; PL 789.
2. John Evelyn, *Instructions Concerning Erecting of a Library*, London, 1661, pp. 57–8.
3. PL 520.
4. *Particular Friends*, p. 198, 26 August 1689.
5. BL Add. Ms 78632; Geoffrey Keynes, *John Evelyn: A Study in Bibliophily*, 2nd edn, Clarendon Press, 1968.
6. *Particular Friends*, p. 295, 20 January 1703.
7. Kate Loveman, *Samuel Pepys and his Books*, Oxford University Press, 2015, Chapter 8.
8. *Letters and 2nd Diary*, p. 244, 4 August 1694.
9. *Letters and 2nd Diary*, p. 247, 10 August 1694; p. 250, 2 September 1694.
10. See Antony Griffiths, 'John Evelyn and the Print', in Frances Harris and Michael Hunter (eds), *John Evelyn and his Milieu*, British Library, 2003, pp. 95–113.
11. *Letterbooks*, ii, p. 1045, to Dr William Lloyd, Bishop of Coventry and Lichfield, 5 February 1695.
12. BL Add. Ms 78274, f. 100, to Richard Evelyn, 25 October 1637.

13. The group included William Faithorne, Josiah English, Isaac de Caus, Francis Clein and Edward Pearce.
14. *Letterbooks*, ii, pp. 1046–7.
15. Griffiths, 'John Evelyn and the Print', p. 107.
16. SP diary, vi, p. 289, 5 November 1665.
17. *Particular Friends*, p. 73, 21 August 1669.
18. Now hanging in the Pepys Library, Magdalene College.
19. PL 2979, 'My Collection of Heads in Taille-Douce & Drawings', ii, p. 217.
20. SP diary, i, p. 266, 15 October 1660.
21. SP diary, i, p. 273, 24 October 1660.
22. SP diary, iv, p. 202, 28 June 1663.
23. SP diary, v, p. 307, 26 October 1665.
24. SP diary, viii, p. 213, 26 May 1668.
25. SP diary, iv, p. 218, 5 July 1663.
26. SP diary, vi, p. 340, 27 December 1665.
27. SP diary, v, p. 352, 22 December 1664.
28. SP diary, vi, p. 2, 2 January 1665.
29. SP diary, vii, p. 378, 1 November 1666.
30. SP diary, vii, p. 235, 5 August 1666.
31. SP diary, iii, p. 273, 2 December 1662.
32. SP diary, viii, p. 575, 11 December 1667.
33. SP diary, i, p. 325, 31 December 1660.
34. SP diary, iv, p. 326, 6 October 1663.
35. SP diary, i, p. 251, 22 October 1660.
36. SP diary, vii, p. 283, 9 October 1666.
37. SP diary, ix, p. 215, 27 May 1668; pp. 400–1, 25 December 1668. Lord Brouncker had written a translation of Descartes's *Musicae Compendium*.
38. SP diary, ix, p. 431, 29 January 1669.
39. JE diary, iii, pp. 386–7, 28 October 1664.
40. Giles Mandelbrote, 'John Evelyn and his Books', in Harris and Hunter (eds), *John Evelyn and his Milieu*, p. 77.
41. SP diary, vi, p. 217, 8 September 1665; vii, p. 76, 19 March 1666.
42. SP diary, vii, p. 237, 6 August 1666.
43. JE diary, iv, pp. 367–8, 13 February 1684.
44. SP diary, vi, p. 227, 17 September 1665.
45. SP diary, iv, pp. 410–11, 10 December 1663. Pepys later bought all of these books with the exception of Salomon Gesner's theological work. The following are in the Pepys Library: Chaucer's *Workes* (1602, PL 2365); Sir William Dugdale's *History of St Paul's* (1658, PL 2444); John Stow's *Survey of London* (1633, PL 2476); Jonson's *Works* (1692, PL 2645), Beaumont and Fletcher's *Fifty Comedies and Tragedies* (1679, PL 2623); Shakespeare's *Works* (The Fourth Folio, 1685, PL 2635); Thomas Fuller's *History of the Worthies of England* (1662, PL 2438); *Cabala* (1663, PL 2261); J.N. de Paravil's *Délices de la Hollande* (Amsterdam, 1678, PL 147); Butler's *Hudibras* (1689, PL 889).
46. Evelyn put the figure of £200,000 in a letter to Samuel Tuke, 27 September 1666; SP diary, viii, p. 526, 11 November 1667.
47. Pepys used the fact that he had a copy when defending before Parliament the charge that he had Catholic books in his household.
48. SP diary, vii, p. 377, 8 August 1667.
49. SP diary, ix, pp. 21–2, 13 January 1668; pp. 57–8, 8 February 1668.
50. SP diary, ix, p. 367, 18 November 1668.
51. SP diary, ix, pp. 160–1, 10 April 1668; p. 173, 24 April 1668; p. 335, 23 October 1668.
52. SP diary, vii, p. 48, 19 February 1666.
53. *Letterbooks*, i, p. 310, 5 May 1662. Evelyn also directed Digby to the Clerk of the Stationers' Company, John Burroughs, who was planning to update London's catalogue.

54. This quarrel, along with interventions from other booksellers, is detailed by Graham Pollard in Graham Pollard and Albert Ehrman (eds), *The Distribution of Books by Catalogue: From the Invention of Printing to AD 1800*, Roxburghe Club, 1965, pp. 129–31.
55. *Letters and 2nd Diary*, p. 189, 30 June 1688.
56. Quoted in J.E. Hodgson, 'Romance and Humour of the Auction Room', *Connoisseur*, June 1939.
57. *Particular Friends*, p. 226, 13 November 1690.
58. *Letters and 2nd Diary*, p. 266, letter 249, 16 March 1697.
59. Robert Hooke's diary, 21 March 1693, in Gunther, *Early Science in Oxford*, x, p. 223.
60. Ned Ward, *A Fair Step to Stir-Bitch-Fair* [Stourbridge Fair]: *with Remarks upon the University of Cambridge*, London, 1700.
61. *Particular Friends*, p. 201, 6 August 1689.
62. JE diary, iii, pp. 303–4, 3 November 1661.
63. *Letterbooks*, ii, p. 949, 15 May 1691.
64. SP diary, vii, p. 214, 23 July 1666.
65. The National Archives, PROB 11/548. The books were 'the Heathen Gods[,] the description of the Castle and Water Works of Versailles and a little French Book of Heraldry called Jeudarmoer all coloured by my Self'.
66. *Particular Friends*, p. 279, 25 August 1700.
67. *Particular Friends*, pp. 198ff., 26 August 1689.
68. *Memoires for my Grand-son*, p. 51.
69. 'Mr Pepys on the Conditions of a Private Library', in *Private Correspondence of Pepys*, ii, p. 247.
70. John Bagford, 'An account of several libraries in and about London, for the satisfaction of the curious, both natives and foreigners', in *The Monthly Miscellany; or, Memoirs for the Curious*, June 1708, pp. 178–9.

Epilogue

1. JE diary, v, p. 536, 14 May 1703.
2. *Particular Friends*, Appendix I, p. 315, 28 May 1703.
3. JE diary, v, pp. 537–8, 26 May 1703.
4. JE diary, v, p. 622, 27 January and 3 February 1706.
5. BL Add. Ms 78435, to Ralph Bohun, 8 March 1706.
6. *Memoires for my Grand-son*, p. 34.
7. Tomalin, *Samuel Pepys*, p. 375.
8. *Private Correspondence of Pepys*, ii, p. 248.
9. Quoted in Anthony Hobson, *Great Libraries*, Weidenfeld & Nicolson, 1972, p. 220.

SELECT BIBLIOGRAPHY

Primary Manuscript Sources

The British Library has over 600 volumes of Evelyn papers, 133 directly associated with John Evelyn. These include:
his letterbooks, Add. Ms 78298, Libers I, II, III and Add. Ms 78299, Liber IV (now in printed form, see Chambers and Galbraith (eds), *Letterbooks of John Evelyn*, below)
22 volumes of correspondence (Add. Mss 78300–22)
diary manuscripts (Add. Mss 78323–6)
commonplace books (Add. Mss 78327–33)
devotional manuscripts (Add. Mss 78360–92)
occasional verse (Add. Ms 78357)
records of his library (Add. Mss 78630–43) including the 1687 catalogue
Mary Evelyn's papers (Add. Mss 78430–9)
Sir Richard Browne's papers (Add. Ms 78614)

Samuel Pepys papers:
Bodleian Library, Rawlinson A.170 to A.195A and C.598
Pepys Library, Magdalene College, Cambridge, Mornamont Mss in two volumes
will of Samuel Pepys of Westminster 1703, The National Archives, PROB 1/9
will of Mary Skynner of Westminster 1715, The National Archives, PROB 11/548/345

Inventory of Edward Gunn, Indian gown maker, London Metropolitan Archives, DL/AM/P1/01/1672, 033
Inventory of Sir Martin Noell, London Metropolitan Archives, CLA/002/02/01/0500

Primary Printed Sources

Anon. [Mary Evelyn?], *Mundus Muliebris, or the Ladies Dressing-Room unlock'd*, London, 1690.
Chambers, Douglas C. and Galbraith, David (eds), *Letterbooks of John Evelyn*, 2 vols, University of Toronto Press, 2014 [*Letterbooks*].
de Beer, E.S., *The Diary of John Evelyn*, 6 vols, Clarendon Press, 1st edn, 1955, revised edn, 2000 [JE diary].

de la Bédoyère, Guy (ed.), *Particular Friends: The Correspondence of Pepys and Evelyn*, Boydell Press, 1997 [*Particular Friends*].

Dick, Oliver Lawson (ed.), *Aubrey's Brief Lives*, Nonpareil Books, 1999.

Evelyn, John, *The State of France*, 1652.

—— *An Essay on the First Book of T. Lucretius Carus, De Rerum Natura* (translation from the Latin), 1656.

—— *The French Gardiner* (translation from the French), 1658.

—— *A Character of England*, 1659.

—— *Fumifugium*, 1661.

—— *Instructions Concerning Erecting of a Library* (translation from the French), 1661.

—— *Sculptura*, 1662.

—— *Sylva*, 1664, 1670, 1697, 1706 (*Silva*).

—— *Kalendarium Hortense*, first published in *Sylva*, separately from 1666.

—— *The Compleat Gard'ner* (translation from the French), 1693.

—— *Acetaria*, 1699.

—— *London Revived: Considerations for its Rebuilding in 1661*, ed. E.S. de Beer, Clarendon Press, 1938.

Gibson, John, 'A short account of several gardens near London with remarks on some particulars wherein they excel, or are deficient, upon a view of them in December 1691', *Archaeologia, or Miscellaneous Tracts relating to antiquity, 1770–1992* (January 1796), 12, British Periodicals.

Gunther, R.T., 'The life and work of Robert Hooke, diary 1688 to 1693', in *Early Science in Oxford*, x, Oxford University Press, 1935.

Heath, Helen Truesdell (ed.), *The Letters of Samuel Pepys and his Family Circle*, Oxford University Press, 1955 [*Letters of Samuel Pepys and his Family Circle*].

Howarth, R.G. (ed.), *Letters and the Second Diary of Samuel Pepys*, J.M. Dent and Sons, 1932 [*Letters and 2nd Diary*].

Ingram, John E. (ed.), *Elysium Britannicum or The Royal Gardens by John Evelyn*, University of Pennsylvania Press, 2000.

Keynes, Geoffrey (ed.), *Memoires for my Grand-son by John Evelyn*, Nonesuch Press, 1926 [*Memoires for my Grand-son*].

Knighton, C.S. (ed.), *Samuel Pepys's Later Diaries*, Sutton Publishing, 2004.

Latham, Robert and Matthews, William (eds), *The Diary of Samuel Pepys*, 11 vols, Bell & Hyman, 1970–83 [SP diary].

Robinson, H.W. and Adams, W. (eds), *The Diary of Robert Hooke, 1672–1680*, Taylor and Francis, 1935 [*Diary of Robert Hooke*].

Sprat, Thomas, *History of the Royal Society* (1667), ed. Jackson I. Cope and Harold Whitmore Jones, Routledge and Kegan Paul, 1959.

Tanner, J.R. (ed.), *Private Correspondence and Miscellaneous Papers of Samuel Pepys, 1679–1703*, 2 vols, G. Bell & Sons, 1926 [*Private Correspondence of Pepys*].

—— (ed.), *The Further Correspondence of Samuel Pepys, 1662–1679*, G. Bell & Sons, 1929.

Secondary Sources

Aldersey-Williams, Hugh, *The Adventures of Sir Thomas Browne in the 21st Century*, Granta, 2005.

Barnard, John and McKenzie, D.F. (eds), *The Cambridge History of the Book in Britain, Vol. IV, 1557–1695*, Cambridge University Press, 2002.

Batey, Mavis (ed.), *A Celebration of John Evelyn: Proceedings of a Conference to Mark the Tercentenary of his Death*, Surrey Gardens Trust, 2007.

Boynton, Lindsay, 'Some Documented Pieces of English Furniture', *Antiques*, 99, 4 (1971), pp. 562–5.

Bryant, Arthur, *Samuel Pepys: The Years of Peril*, Cambridge University Press, 1935.

Burden, Michael (ed.), *The Purcell Companion*, Faber & Faber, 1995.

Cook, Harold J., *Matters of Exchange: Commerce, Medicine, and Science in the Dutch Golden Age*, Yale University Press, 2007.

Crill, Rosemary, *Indian Textiles for the West*, V&A Publishing, 2008.

Darley, Gillian, *John Evelyn: Living for Ingenuity*, Yale University Press, 2006.

—— 'John Evelyn's Norwich Garden', *Garden History*, 34, 2 (Winter 2006), pp. 249–53.

De Beer, E.S. (ed.), *London Revived: Consideration for its Rebuilding in 1661*, Clarendon Press, 1938.

Donaldson, Ian, *Ben Jonson: A Life*, Oxford University Press, 2011.

Earle, Peter, *The Life and Times of James II*, Weidenfeld & Nicolson, 1972.

Eyre, Hermione, *Viper Wine*, Jonathan Cape, 2014.

Forsyth, Hazel, *Butcher, Baker, Candlestick Maker: Surviving the Great Fire*, Museum of London and I.B. Tauris, 2016.

Fraser, Antonia, *The Weaker Vessel: Woman's Lot in Seventeenth-Century England*, Weidenfeld & Nicolson, 1984.

Gentle Author, The, *Cries of London*, Spitalfields Life Books, 2015.

Goodchild, Peter, '"No Phantasticall Utopia, but a Reall Place": John Evelyn, John Beale and Backbury Hill, Herefordshire', *Garden History*, 19, 2 (Autumn 1991), pp. 105–27.

Harris, Frances, *Transformations of Love: The Friendship of John Evelyn and Margaret Godolphin*, Oxford University Press, 2003.

Harris, Frances and Hunter, Michael (eds), *John Evelyn and his Milieu*, The British Library, 2003.

Hornak, Angelo, *After the Fire: London Churches in the Age of Wren, Hooke, Hawksmoor and Gibbs*, Pimpernel Press, 2016.

Hotson, Leslie, *The Commonwealth and Restoration Stage*, Cambridge University Press, 1928.

Hughes, M.E.J., *The Pepys Library and the Historic Collections of Magdalene College Cambridge*, Scala, 2015.

Hunter, Michael, *Science and Society*, Cambridge University Press, 1981.

—— *The Royal Society and its Fellows, 1660–1700: The Morphology of an Early Scientific Institution*, The British Society for the History of Science, 1982.

—— *Science and the Shape of Orthodoxy: Intellectual Change in Late Seventeenth-Century Britain*, Boydell Press, 1995.

—— *Boyle: Between God and Science*, Yale University Press, 2009.

Inwood, Stephen, *The Man Who Knew Too Much: The Strange and Inventive Life of Robert Hooke, 1635–1703*, Macmillan, 2002.

Jardine, Lisa, *The Curious Life of Robert Hooke: The Man Who Measured London*, Harper, 2003.

Jeffery, Sally and O'Reilly, Louise, *The Gardens at Ham House*, The National Trust, 2012.

Keynes, Geoffrey, *John Evelyn: A Study in Bibliophily*, Clarendon Press, 1968.

King, Melanie, *Tea, Coffee and Chocolate: How We Fell in Love with Caffeine*, Bodleian Library, 2015.

Laird, Mark, *A Natural History of English Gardening*, Yale University Press, 2015.

Lemire, Beverly, *Cotton*, Berg, 2011.

Leslie, Michael and Raylor, Timothy (eds), *Culture and Cultivation in Early Modern England: Writing and the Land*, Leicester University Press, 1992.

Lincoln, Margarette (ed.), *Samuel Pepys: Plague, Fire, Revolution*, National Maritime Museum/Thames & Hudson, 2016.

Loveman, Kate, *Samuel Pepys and his Books: Reading, Newsgathering, and Sociability, 1660–1703*, Oxford University Press, 2015.

Magdalene College, Cambridge, *Catalogue of the Pepys Library*, Brewer: ii, Ballads, 1992 and 1994; iii, Prints and Drawings, 1991; iv, Music, Maps and Calligraphy, 1989; v, Manuscripts, 1981 and 1992.

Miller, Elizabeth and Young, Hilary (eds), *The Arts of Living: Europe, 1600–1815*, V&A Publishing, 2016.

Myers, Robin, Harris, Michael and Mandelbrote, Giles (eds), *The London Book Trade: Topographies of Print*, The British Library, 2004.

Ollard, Richard, *Pepys: A Biography*, 1st edn, Hodder & Stoughton, 1974; 2nd (illustrated) edn, Sinclair-Stevenson, 1991.

Pollard, Graham and Ehrman, Albert (eds), *The Distribution of Books by Catalogue: From the Invention of Printing to AD 1800*, Roxburghe Club, 1965.

Prest, John, *The Garden of Eden: The Botanic Garden and the Re-creation of Paradise*, Yale University Press, 1981.

Scott, David, *Leviathan: The Rise of Britain as a World Power*, William Collins, 2013.

Scurr, Ruth, *John Aubrey: My Own Life*, Chatto & Windus, 2015.

Spufford, Margaret, *Small Books and Pleasant Histories*, Cambridge University Press, 1985.

Summers, Montague (ed.), *The Complete Works of Thomas Shadwell*, 5 vols, Fortune Press, 1927.

—— *The Restoration Theatre*, Routledge and Kegan Paul, 1934.

Taylor, Irene and Taylor, Alan (eds), *The Assassin's Cloak: An Anthology of the World's Greatest Diarists*, Canongate, 2000.

Thomas, Keith, *Man and the Natural World: Changing Attitudes in England, 1500–1800*, Allen Lane, 1983.

Tilmouth, Michael, 'A Calendar of References to Music in Newspapers published in London and the Provinces (1660–1719)', *Royal Musical Association Research Chronicles*, 1 (1961), pp. ii–vii, 1–107; 2 (1962), pp. 1–15.

Tinniswood, Adrian, *His Invention so Fertile: A Life of Christopher Wren*, Jonathan Cape, 2001.

Tomalin, Claire, *Samuel Pepys: The Unequalled Self*, Penguin Viking, 2002.

Uglow, Jenny, *A Gambling Man: Charles II and the Restoration*, Faber & Faber, 2009.

Willes, Margaret, *Reading Matters: Five Centuries of Discovering Books*, Yale University Press, 2008.

—— *The Making of the English Gardener: Plants, Books and Inspiration, 1560–1660*, Yale University Press, 2011.

INDEX